Making Money

Africa in World History

SERIES EDITORS: DAVID ROBINSON, JOSEPH C. MILLER, AND TODD CLEVELAND

James C. McCann
  Stirring the Pot: A History of African Cuisine

Peter Alegi
  African Soccerscapes: How a Continent Changed the World's Game

Todd Cleveland
  Stones of Contention: A History of Africa's Diamonds

Laura Lee P. Huttenbach
  The Boy Is Gone: Conversations with a Mau Mau General

John M. Mugane
  The Story of Swahili

Colleen E. Kriger
  Making Money: Life, Death, and Early Modern Trade on Africa's Guinea Coast

Making Money

Life, Death, and Early Modern Trade on Africa's Guinea Coast

Colleen E. Kriger

OHIO UNIVERSITY PRESS   ATHENS

Ohio University Press, Athens, Ohio 45701
ohioswallow.com
© 2017 by Ohio University Press

To obtain permission to quote, reprint, or otherwise reproduce or distribute material from
Ohio University Press publications, please contact our rights and permissions department
at (740) 593-1154 or (740) 593-4536 (fax).

Printed in the United States of America
Ohio University Press books are printed on acid-free paper ⊗ ™

27 26 25 24 23 22 21 20 19 18 17   5 4 3 2 1

COVER: King of Sestos Receives Jean Barbot.
The National Archives of the UK, Jean Barbot ms, ADM 7/830A.

Library of Congress Cataloging-in-Publication Data
Names: Kriger, Colleen E., author.
Title: Making money : life, death, and early modern trade on Africa's Guinea
  Coast / Colleen E. Kriger.
Other titles: Africa in world history.
Description: Athens, Ohio : Ohio University Press, 2017. | Series: Africa in
  world history
Identifiers: LCCN 2017036292| ISBN 9780896803152 (hc : alk. paper) | ISBN
  9780896802964 (pb : alk. paper) | ISBN 9780896805002 (pdf)
Subjects: LCSH: Guinea (Region)--Commerce--Great Britain--History--17th
  century. | Great Britain--Commerce--Guinea (Region)--History--17th
  century. | Royal African Company--History--17th century. | Slave
  trade--Guinea (Region) | Guinea (Region)--History--17th century.
Classification: LCC HF3920.Z7 G924 2017 | DDC 382.0966041--dc23
LC record available at https://lccn.loc.gov/2017036292

To My Students—Past, Present, and Future

CONTENTS

ILLUSTRATIONS

Figures

Maps

Tables

Transcriptions

SERIES EDITORS' PREFACE

The field of African history has developed considerably since it first emerged in the 1960s, coinciding with the independence that African nations were gaining from their European colonial overlords. An enormous literature has been generated over the ensuing decades, yet Africa's past remains largely unknown to nonspecialists. Consequently, myths and stereotypes persist unchallenged, continuing to help produce profound misunderstandings of the continent. In order to engage these misperceptions and bring knowledge about Africa to a wider audience, students and instructors need accessible points of entry into the continent's past.

To this end, Ohio University Press and the editors of this series seek to generate books for college and university instructors, and for undergraduate students, to bring the fruits of professional research on Africa to the attention of well-intentioned but often unaware readers in intriguing ways. The resulting books are intended to be both accessible and readily integrated into courses in world history, the history of the Americas, diasporic history, and the histories of other world regions.

In modern settings still rife with the residue of centuries of slaving and racial stereotyping, these books show Africans at work and at home, engaged in sport and a variety of other daily activities, and highlight the myriad ways that Africans have shaped the human experience throughout history. Although popular media focus on disease, political disorder, and destitution, the richness of the African experience, as showcased in the books in the series, suggests that the peoples of the continent, through their histories and cultures, bring great diversity to the human experience and enrich all of us. It is this enrichment that this series strives to offer.

The volumes in the series have displayed this diversity. Jim McCann's *Stirring the Pot*, Peter Alegi's *Soccerscapes*, and Todd Cleveland's *Stones of Contention* have each featured insights into Africa's past, plowing new ground on subjects seemingly familiar—cuisine, sport, and diamond mining—but largely misunderstood beyond the continent's borders. More recently, John Mugane's *Story of Swahili* traces the origins and myriad contributors to

Africa's best-known language, and Laura Lee Huttenbach's *The Boy Is Gone* uses extensive interviews to paint a compelling picture of a Kenyan freedom fighter who became a tea farmer in the last decades of his life.

This volume, authored by Colleen Kriger, extends these efforts by working a cache of recondite archival materials from the Royal African Company in London, bringing to life the Europeans, Africans, and Euro-Africans who together traded slaves—and so much else—on the Upper Guinea Coast of West Africa at the end of the seventeenth century.

Books currently in preparation will continue to provide readers with intriguing, relevant, and accessible points of entry into Africa's complex past and present. They will provide further opportunities for teachers and students to incorporate the continent into their courses and interests.

We invite readers of the series to call our attention to other topics they find promising for treatment along these lines, and we invite authors with themes that they are interested in developing to contact us about their projects.

ACKNOWLEDGMENTS

I will always be grateful to Gillian Berchowitz, Joseph Miller, and David Robinson for making it possible for me to embark on the adventure of writing this book and seeing it through to publication. Gillian shepherded me through the initial stages of the project with grace and aplomb, providing just the kind of responsiveness and patience that I needed. Her encouragement gave me the fortitude I needed to keep plowing on. When at last I entered the writing phase, Joe and Dave were stalwart readers and supporters, offering up all sorts of suggestions, options, and fruitful comments and questions. Together, these three editors and their commitment to the highest professional standards have energized and inspired me throughout.

Once again I must acknowledge York University's Department of History for supporting and training me in precolonial African history at the doctoral level. My isolation as their first Africanist PhD candidate turned out in my favor as Leslie Howsam, Lynn MacKay, and Susan Foote invited me into their British history circle. I remember fondly our many discussion meetings and meals together. Paul Lovejoy has been an important support and role model all these years and a continuing inspiration as he led the founding and development of The Harriet Tubman Institute for Research on Africa and Its Diasporas. Its international network of scholars stands now as a global treasure of historical inquiry.

In years leading up to this project, I was fortunate to participate in a number of conferences devoted to world history, which enabled me to see my work and interests from other angles and in much broader and longer-term frameworks. Thank you to the Global Economic History Network, London School of Economics, for organizing conferences on cotton textiles as a global industry in 2005. Many thanks as well to Beverly Lemire for including me on her panel for the XIV World Economic History Congress in 2006, and also to Joseph Inikori for inviting me to contribute to his panel at the XV World Economic History Congress in 2009. An especially stimulating conference held in Stirling, Scotland, in 2009, called "Rethinking Africa and the Atlantic World," was where I first began to think deliberately about writing a book along the lines of this one. Thank you to the Department of History at University of Stirling for bringing together scholars of African and American Atlantic history. Another inspiring conference, organized by Robin Law, Suzanne Schwarz, and Silke Strickrodt, addressed the complex interrelationships of commercial agriculture and slavery in Africa (sixteenth to twentieth c.). I am indebted to all the organizers of these conferences and fellow participants for their commitment to world history.

At a crucial time when I was designing this project and preparing a proposal to the press, four special colleagues generously offered comments and support. My most sincere thanks to Ralph Austen, Pat Manning, Peter Mark, and Don Wright.

I gratefully acknowledge assistance my university has given me by providing funds and release time for carrying out this research. I thank the provost of the University of North Carolina at Greensboro (UNCG) for a research assignment awarded to me in the fall of 2012, and to the Kohler Fund, the International Programs Center, and the dean of the College of Arts and Sciences for providing international travel support. Thank you also to the Lloyd International Honors College at UNCG for a Chancellor's Resident Fellowship and research stipend in 2013/14. A Faculty First grant from the provost at UNCG provided me with much-needed funding for travel and time spent in the United Kingdom in 2015 as I was completing my work in The National Archives and The London Metropolitan Archives.

A very deeply felt thank you goes to everyone involved with The National Humanities Center in Research Triangle Park, North Carolina, for awarding me the Hurford Family Fellowship during the academic year 2014/15. I could never have written this book while also teaching, as it entailed intensely focused concentration day after day in preparing to write and then shaping the writing itself. This gift of uninterrupted time brought with it the most rewarding intellectual experience in my career. Compounding that very personal internal pleasure was the amiable company of my fellow fellows of the NHC class of 2014/15. Knowing we were all experiencing similar struggles was a relief, and our lunchtime conversations were a balm. I will forever be in awe of all of you.

Many people have made it possible for me to bring this project to a close. I praise especially the consistently courteous and efficient staff at The National Archives, United Kingdom, whose expertise made my work enjoyable over these years of visits. For visual images and permissions to publish them, I thank the following: Rogier Bédaux for the digital image of the Sanga cotton tunic and Ingeborg Eggink of the Nationaal Museum van Wereld Culturen, the Netherlands, for permission to publish it; Karin Guggeis, Museum Fünf Kontinente, Munich, for her generosity and helpfulness with the image of their beautiful creole ivory horn; Tom Cohen and Joan Stahl of The Catholic University of America and Oliveira Lima Library for assistance with permission to publish images from Froger; staffs at The National Archives, United Kingdom, and The Massachusetts Historical Society for their efficient online permissions processes; Sally Welch, Ohio University Press, for her assistance with images in the public domain; Nancy Basmajian, managing editor of Ohio University Press, and copyeditor Brian Bowles, for their superb editing; and at UNCG, the incomparable Dan Smith, photography wizard, and Gaylor Callahan, interlibrary-loan librarian extraordinaire.

Long-standing colleagues and friends (with whom I now hope to spend more time!) have always been with me throughout this project. Apologies and affectionate thanks to Julia Fish, Françoise Grossen, Adrienne Middlebrooks, Ann O'Hear, Richard Rezac, Wendy Thomas, and Lisa Tolbert. Words are not sufficient to acknowledge Oded.

Finally, many years ago I had the great good fortune to spend a year as a Fulbright student at the University of Ife, Nigeria (now Obafemi Awolowo University), and one of the highlights was being inducted into the Palm-wine Drinkerds' Club. The many afternoons I spent with my fellow comrades drinking palm wine at the Uppermost Shrine were not just jovial occasions—I also got a taste of Nigerian Pidgin English and the creativity and wit it engenders. I thought of those times often as I wrote this book, remembering how wise it was for the club to flip the university's motto "For Learning and Culture" to "For Culture and Learning" as a deliberate turn toward singing and storytelling in the face of Western education. I might not have become so deeply interested in African history were it not for the club. I am honored to be a fellow, and so to all my comrades worldwide I say, You Are Carried!

Atlantic Lives

Anglo-African Trade in Northern Guinea

A EURO-AFRICAN widow named Hope Heath traveled the main car-
riage road leading from her residence in Leyton, Essex, to London in July
1697. There, on July 10, she married Samuel Meston at St. James Duke's
Place, the Anglican parish church of Aldgate Ward in the City of London.[1]
Her second marriage must have been a welcome new beginning for Hope
and her two-year-old daughter, Elizabeth, after enduring several years of
difficult family disputes and legal struggles in the wake of her husband's
death. What had set off seemingly endless rounds of acrimonious contro-
versy were the deaths of two important English men in Hope's life—John
Booker, her former master; and William Heath, her first husband. It was
because of them both that she had left the northern Guinea Coast, land of
her birthplace, to live the life of a free woman of color in London.

These three people were brought together by the Guinea trade and England's Royal African Company (RAC) at James Island fort on the lower
Gambia River. Booker had first arrived at James Island in 1680 and quickly
rose to serve as assistant to the company's principal agent there. William
Heath arrived in June 1683, serving as a soldier at the fort and then at Juffure, a company outpost on the mainland. In March 1686, Heath assumed
the important position of company factor, which put him in charge of keeping track of the trade goods stored in their warehouse and handling the
company's sales and purchases.[2] It was around this same time that Esperança (Hope) must have come to James Island, though involuntarily as a
child captive. Where she had come from and who named her Esperança

1

will probably never be known. She had been born into a community on the mainland in about 1675, but she then suffered some kind of horrible calamity that tore her from home and family and forced her into captivity. On James Island, she lived and worked as one of Booker's personal household slaves inside the fort, along with her so-called brother, Sanko. In assuming for himself the role of paterfamilias to his child slaves, Booker sent her away to a boarding school in England in the 1680s to learn to read and write in English. And young Esperança came to be known among English-speakers as Hope Booker.[3]

Her life changed dramatically upon the death of John Booker in early June 1693. Calling her "my girle Speranca," Booker gave Hope in a codicil to his will her unconditional freedom, title to her jewelry and other personal possessions, stewardship of his slaves, and an impressive lifetime annuity of £25 for her maintenance.[4] If Hope Booker and William Heath had not been acquainted earlier, they certainly did get to know each other very well as they collaborated to carry out Booker's funeral and burial arrangements and set about administering his personal estate at James Island. Heath began to court her, pleading that she agree to marry him there according to the local custom on the Guinea Coast and promising that at the first opportunity they would marry again in a formal Christian ceremony. Their marriage took place on the island in October 1693 at a public celebration in which they pledged before God and an audience of witnesses their lifelong love and devotion to each other.[5]

The following March, William Heath sent his wife to London, where he planned to join her after completing his work for the company and putting his own and what remained of Booker's affairs in order.[6] Delays kept him tied down at the fort for over a year, with the result that he was not able to be with Hope for the birth and christening of their daughter, Elizabeth. This failing he lamented publicly to his coworkers in the many toasts he drank to the health and safety of his wife and child.[7] When he finally did set out for England, he stopped over and spent several months in Lisbon, primarily to sell off some of Booker's estate and his own personal property and trade goods to contacts he had among English and Portuguese merchants who resided there. Sadly, when at last on the final leg of his homeward voyage, he died at sea in December 1695 without ever having made out a will.[8]

When the news of William's death reached them, Hope Heath was about twenty years old, well into her second year in England, and baby Elizabeth had just had her first birthday. A storm of wild accusations and outlandish charges was soon to erupt and further complicate Hope's already difficult circumstances. Her circle of English acquaintances centered on the contacts and associates of Booker and her husband, and they all had interests, as did she, in seeing to the administration of the estate Booker had amassed on the Guinea Coast. To that end, the merchant Humphrey Dyke, executor of Booker's original will, had already presented a copy of the codicil to it in the Prerogative Court of Canterbury (PCC) in August 1695. But when news of the death of William Heath arrived, William's brother, Samuel, filed a bill of complaint against Dyke and three others, including Hope. All of them, he claimed, were conspiring to defraud him of his right to inherit his brother's personal property. Referring to Hope as "Sparnissa, alias Hope Booker," he charged that she had lived with William Heath as his hired servant, not as his wife.[9] Dyke then appeared again before the PCC, this time to present evidence of the legality of Hope and William's marriage, the legitimacy of Elizabeth as their daughter, and thus the right of Elizabeth to inherit. The court ruled that the marriage and daughter were indeed legitimate and also granted Dyke the authority to administer the personal estate of William Heath.[10]

In records of the defendants' official answer to Samuel Heath's complaint, there appears a section that is of special interest, as it was framed by Hope Heath herself. In the section, she outlined her own specific concerns and objections. As written in the court documentation, she insisted on registering her proper English name, Hope Heath. And she understandably took great offense at the statement that she had been William's hired servant, which she firmly denied as an untrue and scandalous claim. Her most important point, however, centered on the nature of her relationship with William Heath and the evidence that Dyke had presented in court, which demonstrated the legality of her marriage and daughter.[11] That evidence, in fact, also provided stunning proof of Samuel Heath's mendacity. William's devotion to his wife and daughter was spelled out clearly and eloquently in letters written by William to Hope, to his family, and to Humphrey Dyke, and these were shown in court along with specimens of William's handwriting. More damning to Samuel, however, were four letters that had been written to Hope herself, addressed to her as Mrs. Heath, wife of William. Three of them were from William and Samuel's sister, Dorothy, and one was from Samuel's own wife, Elizabeth.[12] In other words, the Heath family was well aware of William's marriage to Hope and had formally acknowledged it in writing. Whatever thoughts and sentiments had moved Hope to preserve

these family letters, she could not have envisioned how sadly and annoy-
ingly useful they would turn out to be.

Hope Heath's story highlights several important themes in early modern African and Atlantic history that are central to this book. Here we see
the direct intervention in an English court of a seventeenth-century Euro-
African woman and recently freed slave who was actively pursuing her own
economic and legal interests.[13] She had managed to secure the annuity that
was bequeathed to her by Booker along with an untold amount in personal
property and bills of exchange through various of her merchant contacts.
Her literacy in English was a key to her success, but so too were aspects of
her character that had been noted by others, such as her respectability, well-
mannered bearing, and sharp intelligence.[14] And on July 12, 1696, almost
one year to the day before her second marriage, Hope was baptized at St.
Mary's, the parish church in Leyton. Describing her as "Hope Heath a Black
mayd about 21," the record suggests that she was a practicing Christian and
had some understanding about the importance of the Anglican Church and
its centrality to English law at the time.[15] Hope stands out as a particularly
poignant example of the various forms of mixed Euro-African identities
people created for themselves as they lived and worked within the multicultural social networks of Atlantic commerce.

Hope's childhood experiences of captivity and enslavement illustrate
some of the special particularities of early modern Atlantic history, a history that was marked by people's increasing geographical mobility as well
as their considerable social fluidity, even for some of the unfree. To sharpen
and bring home these features more fully, a recurring motif in this book
about individual people and their daily lives is the role played by contin-
gency or happenstance in shaping them. Lives as they are lived seem and
are in many ways highly unpredictable and even, at times, contradictory. A
focus on particular people's lives and careers also takes us inside the complex
social worlds of Euro-African trade, allowing us to see how it was organized
and carried out on the ground and how it worked on a day-to-day basis.
More specifically, the focus here is on global Anglo-African commerce at
a particular time and place on Africa's Guinea (western) coast. This book
presents one richly detailed example of what were many and varying local
histories in the early modern Atlantic basin.

My main sources for writing this history are archival primary sources—
records of the RAC, especially for the period 1672 to 1713, when the company held a monopoly on England's trade in Africa.[16] Many scholars have

tapped into this archive for writing histories of the company itself, British economic history, British trade and colonization, precolonial Africa, and Atlantic trade. Company correspondence, for example, provides useful details about matters of concern between its officials in London and their many far-flung employees. Three volumes of letters between London and the Guinea Coast between 1681 and 1699 have been transcribed, edited, and published by Robin Law, making these sources available to scholars around the world.[17] Less well known are all sorts of other business and accounting records kept by the RAC. They, too, have been used by some scholars, albeit infrequently and rather selectively. These are the records that have been especially important in my research for this book, both as a counterweight to the London-centered views that predominate in the company correspondence and as a vehicle for gaining access to the myriad roles, interests, and experiences of individual people on the West African coast, especially Africans, who took part in Atlantic commerce. This African side—Africans' involvement as captives and also as merchants, landlords, suppliers of exports and provisions, laborers, artisans, interpreters, seamen, porters, consumers, and providers of information and services—still needs to be spelled out for particular times and places all up and down the Guinea Coast.[18]

My geographical focus is Upper (or northern) Guinea, where the RAC took over and maintained a massive trading sphere around its three forts and many outstations. It was a huge, socially complex, dynamic zone of commerce, intercommunication, and cultural change as well as a supplier to the transatlantic slave trade and trade with Europe. Recognizing that the slave trade was part of a much larger multilateral and intercontinental commercial system utterly transformed and enriched my understanding of it, especially for this time and place. Seen from the vantage point and perspective of the Upper Guinea Coast, and situating it in the longer-term context of world history, the Guinea trade represents both a continuation of older historical patterns and the ushering in of totally new ones.

This West African coast, called Guinea by Europeans, was the final coastline of Africa to be opened up to international maritime commerce. The Guinea Coast was renowned among European sailors for its seemingly impossible navigational barriers. Its constant southwesterly winds and ocean currents appeared to preclude voyages of return, so no one dared sail south very far beyond the Canary Islands. It was not until the 1430s, after much investment and experimentation, that Portuguese mariners discovered how they could sail their ships down the Guinea Coast and make a return trip home via a different set of more favorable wind patterns they had found farther out into the Atlantic. This breakthrough opened up the Guinea Coast for the first time to European exploration and Euro-African Atlantic commerce.

Direct trade with Europe started out as comparable to Africa's ancient external trading networks along her Mediterranean, Red Sea, and Indian Ocean shores, by which goods such as gold, ivory, animal skins, rhinoceros horn, ostrich eggs and feathers, and captives were exported in exchange for precious stones such as agate and rock-crystal, beads made of coral or shell, plain and patterned textiles, and a variety of containers large and small, made of ceramic, glass, or copper alloy. What set the Euro-African Guinea trade apart from these earlier ones was its later timing and much greater intercontinental scale and—above all—the regularity and volume of the trade in captives, which grew enormously during the years described in this book and even more so during the eighteenth and early nineteenth centuries. The intensity of the trade in slaves between Africa and the Americas was a totally new, dramatically different, and tragic episode in world history. Ships were loaded and sent off across the Atlantic with cargoes made up entirely of hundreds of imprisoned and suffering human beings.

Looking back on the late seventeenth-century north Atlantic, one might see it simply as a time of gradual transition, as merely a backdrop to revolutionary events that came in the mid-eighteenth to nineteenth centuries.[19] For those people who experienced it, however, with no knowledge of where their strategies and decisions might take them, it must have seemed a particularly volatile and uncertain time, demanding much experimentation with very high risks. This comes across repeatedly in the RAC records as they show how important the nonslave African exports were to the company and how its officials in London entertained enthusiastic but ultimately unrealistic wishes to establish plantations of tropical products on the Guinea Coast.[20] Viewed especially from the vantage point of northern Guinea, and considering its convenient location relative to Europe, the transatlantic slave trade can be seen in its full global context as an important part of what was actually a much more complex and expansive economic picture. And it is this larger, multilateral global network, which linked the Guinea Coast directly with Europe as well as to the Americas, that I refer to generally as the Guinea trade. West Africa performed multiple roles in early modern Atlantic trade—as a supplier of slaves to the Americas, as a supplier of some slaves along with gold, ivory, dyewood, and other raw or processed materials to Europe, and as a market for European exports and reexports from Asia.[21]

There are two interrelated parts to this book. One part is global in scale, laying out the West African setting and the origin and production of Afro-Eurasian commodities that were traded. The other part shifts to a human scale—a social history of human activity and personal relations—focusing on individual people who were involved in RAC trading operations on the Upper Guinea Coast. Chapter 1 takes the reader through an overview of West Africa prior to the era of Atlantic trade, showing how centuries of Islamic commerce across the Sahara had shaped and reshaped its regional and interregional markets and trading networks. This was the social, economic, cultural, and material environment to which European merchants had to adapt. The overview continues in chapter 2 and expands the geographical scale to include the production and producers of the major global commodities—European, Asian, and African—that were central to the Guinea trade. Early modern Euro-African trade was built with the skills and labor of countless people worldwide.

The core of the book—chapters 3, 4, and 5—is a social history of RAC traders, support staff, suppliers, and captives in northern Guinea during the company's well-documented monopoly period. The chapters represent three main categories of people who were active participants in the trade, willingly or unwillingly. Chapter 3 tracks the careers of free Africans and Euro-Africans who supplied export goods, provisions, and services to the RAC. Chapter 4 shifts to the experiences, fates, and fortunes of people in successive stages of captivity or enslavement and instances when they actively refused unfree status. And chapter 5 surveys the surprisingly varied employees of the RAC on salary, some of whom were hired from nearby African communities. Taken together, these people's intertwined lives and careers present the reader with a vivid and memorable picture of the African side of early modern Atlantic trade, showing what it could mean to its participants—European, African, and Euro-African—and how those in this particular corner of the world carried it out.

In the writing of this book I have followed several guiding principles. One is that I hope to reach a wide audience, and to that end I aim for language that is clear and accessible. African history, especially precolonial African history, is not widely taught and may seem so distant and unfamiliar to readers that it comes across as an unappealing, intimidating, or even impenetrable topic. My years of teaching African history have shown me that describing the experiences of individual people in Africa's past offers to the uninitiated an effective and welcoming entryway. Readers may wonder about how and on what basis I selected the named individual people whose stories I tell in my chapters of social history. They are mainly a self-selected sample of people who chose to work for or with the company for a sufficiently significant amount of time such that they repeatedly entered the company's documentation, thereby giving me the opportunity to track their careers. I could have included more Luso-African individuals in the group, but I was aiming also to present a cross-section of people, showing complexities and variations in their identities. For each of them I gathered many fragmentary pieces of their lives and kept them in files until I began to write, and it was only then that I could fully see and appreciate both the individuality of people in the sample and the remarkable and sometimes surprising things they did over time.

Finally, my writing reflects my commitment to teaching historical thinking—showing students where history comes from and how historians examine, wonder about, grapple with, and interpret their primary sources.[22] I often refer directly to the evidence, the particular sources, what they may or may not mean, what they may indicate, and also what seems to be missing. These historical actors who turned up in my archival sources have intrigued and humbled me again and again, and in gratitude for the richly rewarding opportunity to do this work I aim to understand and respect their lives, not to judge them.

CHAPTER ONE

Buyers and Sellers in Cross-Cultural Trade

LONG BEFORE the beginning of Atlantic commerce, camel caravans linked tropical West Africa to the Mediterranean basin and western Asia through a complex system of interlocking trans-Saharan trading networks.[1] Referred to by early Muslim geographers as *Bilad al-Sudan,* The Lands of the Black People, West Africa became famous in Islamic communities after Mansa Musa, leader of the Mali Empire, which was the principal supplier of gold to the Mediterranean world, dispensed lavish gifts of gold in Cairo as he passed through on his pilgrimage to Mecca in 1324. Mali's renown spread even farther, into the courts of Christian medieval Europe, via the Catalan Atlas, a richly illustrated map drawn between 1375 and 1380 and given as a gift from the king of Aragon to Charles V. It depicts the "known world" at that time with Europe, the Near East, Asia, and North Africa shown in relation to one another and interconnected by travel and trade, including sub-Saharan African kingdoms and their major entrepôts such as Gao and Timbuktu. The visual imagery on the map ranges widely from detailed ren- derings of architecture and geographical features to local varieties of flora and fauna and items of commercial interest. Among the individual figures depicted is a profile of Mali's leader, shown seated on a throne, adorned with European-style crown and scepter and holding up a large nugget of gold as a sign of his empire's storied wealth. Facing him is an approaching merchant mounted on a camel, dressed in the characteristic turban and veil of Saharan Berbers. The map conveys the message that he is one of our allies—a generous and trustworthy trading partner and a major source of gold for the coinage system of Eurasian trade. Henceforth West Africa in the minds of Europeans became legendary as a "Land of Gold." And it was the hope of securing direct access to sub-Saharan African gold, as well as to the spice and silk trade of Asia, that propelled Portuguese mariners to explore Africa's western coastline in the fifteenth century, thus opening up the Guinea trade and a new Atlantic era in world history.[2]

This chapter lays out the trading networks and protocols Europeans encountered on the Upper Guinea Coast as direct Euro-African maritime commerce developed. The major regional and interregional commodity currencies of West Africa, originally tied to trans-Saharan trade, would be deployed in new directions and along new axes while Europeans added greater supplies of them, thus reshaping the structure and intensifying the dynamics of commercial operations between the coast and interior regions. At the same time, the business of trading and how it was carried out tended to follow well-established patterns and arrangements that had existed for hundreds of years. Added to familiar ways of calculating measures and values came new ones from the Atlantic. With the arrival of Europeans—first the Portuguese in the fifteenth and sixteenth centuries, then the Dutch, English, and French in the 1600s—this new Euro-African commercial zone expanded on local African practices while at the same time creating new networks and patterns of trade.

Money: Commodity Currencies

Much of the system that Portuguese caravels skirting Africa's north Atlantic coastline in the fifteenth century were entering was in the hands of specialist Muslim merchant groups known generally as Juula. Based mainly in regions along the southern shore of the Sahara, Juula merchants created extensive trade diasporas that linked major trans-Saharan routes with myriad local, regional, and interregional networks to the south.[3] Evidence from archaeological sites and from Arabic written sources provides a general indication of just how extensive these networks were, reaching overland and along rivers to connect towns and cities in the grasslands and forests there with the primary entrepôts of Saharan caravan traffic. Prominent among the surviving material remains of this commercial system are foreign manufactures that crossed the desert and found their way as far as the tropical rainforests, well before the arrival of the Portuguese. For example, two archaeological sites at Igbo-Ukwu (in modern southeast Nigeria) are especially significant on this score. Among the priestly burial, regalia, and treasure unearthed at those sites is a spectacular trove of over 165,000 trade beads from the Mediterranean and Asia. Dating to the ninth or tenth century, the sites provide

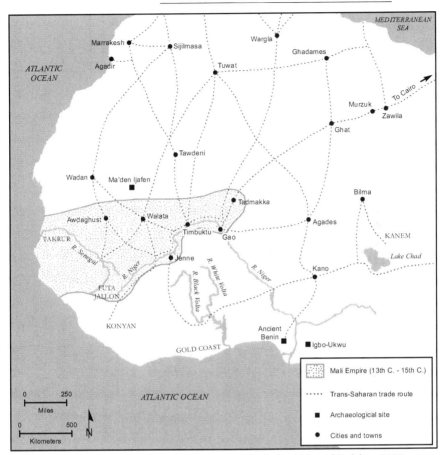

MAP 1.1 Places mentioned in chapter 1. *Map by Brian Edward Balsley, GISP.*

us with general temporal markers for the economic history of West Africa. They indicate that on the eve of the second millennium communities deep in the rainforest belt were indirectly linked with avenues of trans-Saharan trade, receiving beads that came from distant towns in Africa or beyond.[4]

This material evidence also presents visually dazzling corroboration of the rather cursory references to trade beads in the Arabic-language written sources. There is, however, an important caveat: the beads themselves are of only limited use in identifying specifically where they came from. Red beads made of carnelian, for example, which were found at both Igbo Ukwu and Gao, might have been from Gao itself or, alternatively, from other known supply centers as far away as Egypt or India. Monochrome glass beads found in those same sites and others could have been from Morocco, Egypt, or the

Near East, which were the major known suppliers of such beads between the twelfth and fifteenth centuries.[5] Whatever their precise origins, however, beads from these early archaeological sites are important historical sources for understanding West Africa as a socially diverse zone of bead connoisseurship that persisted into and during the era of Atlantic trade with Europeans.

Commercial exchanges depended on various forms of West African currencies—what they were, how they were valued, and specifically where and how they circulated. It is important to note that during the centuries of trans-Saharan trade, West African merchants did not adopt coinage from North Africa as a general form of currency south of the desert, although limited numbers of gold dinars and silver dirhams did at times circulate in some cities and towns. Instead, they continued to use commodity currencies, the major West African ones being gold dust, rock salt, cotton textiles, bar iron, and sea salt, along with cowry shells from the Indian Ocean. These items served as general-purpose currencies largely because demand for them was widespread, steady, and consistently high. They were important as trade goods and also functioned as money, being used as a medium of exchange, as a store of value, and as units of account in valuation and pricing. Each had its own history. Some were products rooted in local natural resource endowments, and some were the products of far-off contacts and cultural influences arising out of long-standing ties with the wider Islamic world. Sufficiently detailed histories of these currencies are not yet possible owing to the very limited written and archaeological sources for documenting them, but there is no doubt that they worked together over time as a flexible, fluctuating, and interlocking system of currency flows across West Africa's geographical and linguistically rich social landscape.

The largest regional currency zone, extending over much of the West African interior, owed its existence to the importance of the trans-Saharan caravan trade. In this zone people reckoned prices and exchanged goods based on units of African gold, imported cowry shells, and Saharan rock salt. The other three currencies—cotton textiles, bar iron, and sea salt—circulated in and between smaller subregions and also into and out of Muslim trading networks. Sea salt produced along the coast was regularly sought out by inland merchants, especially those who had ready access to the strips of woven cotton cloth that artisans in the savanna and Sahel zones produced for export. Salt producers on the coast, for their part, preferred to bargain for cotton textiles, which were also accepted in exchange for gold in gold-producing areas and for captive humans in other places. Blacksmiths with access to locally smelted iron, either directly or by trade, worked it out into standard-sized units that Europeans called "bar iron," which then circulated as local and regional currencies in markets across West Africa.[6]

Combining the known production centers and circulation zones of these commodity currencies and plotting them on a map of West Africa presents a useful summary overview of the complexity of trade and commerce there ca. 1500. Map 1.2 includes the richest goldfields and Saharan rock-salt deposits, the central zone of cowry circulation, and major production centers of bar iron and cotton textiles for export. Coastal sea salt–producing areas were many and changing and so are not individually shown. In addition, the map shows prominent supply areas of kola nuts, mainly because of their importance in linking the forest zones where they grew to consumer

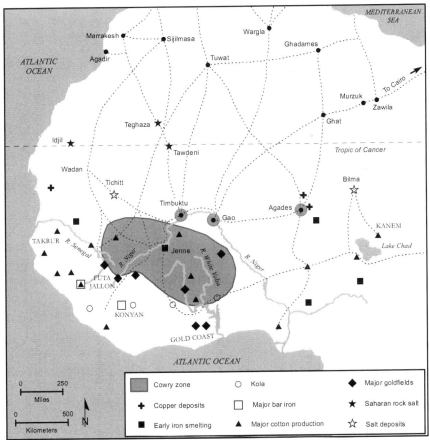

MAP 1.2 Production and circulation of commodity currencies in West Africa, ca. 1500. *Map by Brian Edward Balsley, GISP.*

markets for them in the savanna and Sahel regions. There they were of great cultural and social value—as well as being a source of caffeine—and served as a respectable welcoming gift among many peoples, Muslims and poly-theists alike. However, since they were perishable and therefore difficult to store for very long, they were a consumer product and not, strictly speak-ing, a major currency-like store of value. The map also includes areas of copper extraction, but the volume of production and circulation of local copper was relatively limited, thus setting up a significant opportunity for European importers of the metal and its alloys, brass and bronze. The basic spatial organization and material logic of West Africa's trading networks shown in the map allows for a sharper recognition and appreciation of Africa's participation in early modern Atlantic trade.

Of the six major commodity currencies, iron was probably the oldest. Early evidence for smelting iron ore comes from archaeological sites in what is now Senegal, Niger, Nigeria, and Cameroon, all of them roughly dating to the sixth century BCE. For the upper Niger River valley in what is now Mali, evidence of iron working dates from the earliest occupation of a major town in the region, Jenne-jeno, in the third century BCE. Especially intriguing is the fact that smelting iron ore and forging it into useful imple-ments and symbols of prestige were being carried out in locations that were some distance from both the ore deposits and the special hardwood trees necessary for making the charcoal that fueled the region's furnaces and forges. Such a complex spatial organization of the several components of iron production suggests a divided and specialized labor force that, for un-known reasons, had invested in these added costs of transport.[7] If and when a bar iron currency was adopted there is not presently known. Similarly, little is known specifically about the subsequent transfers of iron technol-ogy to other locales and workers, but it can be inferred that the knowledge and skills traveled local, regional, and interregional trade routes alongside iron products and other goods. As the southerly extension of trans-Saharan trade took on greater significance and intensity after the seventh century CE, it is likely that smelters and smiths would have become more produc-tive and diversified their iron wares with the increasing connections to new markets.

Then, in the second millennium, two gradual historical changes began that reshaped the human geography of West Africa and also the contours of its trading networks. One was a drier climate that prompted large scale southerly demographic movements and concentrations of people in new towns and settlements. The other was an expansion and intensification of Muslim trade across the Sahara, which increased the number of Muslims—both immigrants and local converts—among the populations of sub-Saharan Africa. These economic and cultural transformations led, in turn, to new sources and greater supplies of commodity currencies and more widespread circulation of them.

Climatic change brought transfers of iron technology into new geographical areas and communities. A dry period, lasting from ca. 1100 to ca. 1500, extended the reach of the Sahara's southern "shore," driving people southward in search of rainfall adequate for farming. Among them were iron smelters and smiths. By the end of the period, important new iron production centers had arisen in the Futa Jallon massif and the Konyan highlands, both of them mountainous areas that lay on the timber-rich forest edge in the hinterland of the Upper Guinea Coast.[8] Even though accessible surface deposits of iron ore were not unusual in West Africa and could be exploited in many locales on small scales, by the sixteenth century these two places in particular became major producers and exporters of bar iron.[9]

Standard units of bar iron currency usually took the form of semifinished tools or implements that were useful in land clearance, farming, hunting, or war, as well as being widely recognized units of value. Unfortunately, however, there is little to go by in knowing specifically what some of the earliest forms of bar iron were like. They remain obscure because metallic iron tends not to survive in the archaeological record, especially in tropical soils. Examples observed in later times can nonetheless suggest a range of possibilities. André Álvares de Almada, a Luso-African merchant from the Cape Verde Islands who traveled and lived at times on the Upper Guinea Coast in the second half of the sixteenth century, described a form of locally made bar iron being traded up the Gambia River at that time. He took care to note that it was the product of local mining and smelting operations, and he described the physical bars as measuring a hand-span long, three fingers wide at one end, and two fingers wide at the other. Among the dealers in this bar iron, Luso-African merchants were especially keen to have it for their trading voyages to the bays south of the Gambia River around Cacheu and Bissau.[10] High demand for bar iron in these latter two locales, together with the description of its form and dimensions, suggest that this particular bar iron unit was a semifinished quantity of the metal based either on agricultural tools, such as a hatchet or hoe blade, or on a personal weapon such as a knife blade.

A later example of bar iron, the famous so-called Kissi pennies of the nineteenth and twentieth centuries, was a much smaller currency form most likely based on a generic arrowhead. These particular units circulated among a number of different language groups in the forest and savanna areas of modern Sierra Leone, northern Liberia, and southern Guinea-Conakry.[11] That there were so many specific kinds of useful iron products meant that blacksmiths in different locales had the option of shaping particular bar iron currency units, from small ones to large, both "trade-marking" their own products and serving a complex consumer market made up of distinctive and various local needs and preferences.

However, several factors set limits on iron smelting that made it difficult to generate a sustained high-volume production of locally made iron. The hardwood trees preferred for making charcoal fuel became scarce at times through overexploitation, for example, especially in locales where smelters regularly operated large shaft furnaces in smelts that lasted several days or up to a week at a time. Other types of West African smelting furnaces were smaller and so required less charcoal, but they were able to produce only modest amounts of workable iron per smelt. Additional limitations came from the restriction of smelting to the dry season and from the control master smelters exerted over access to iron smelting technology and the specialized skills for carrying it out. Taking these limitations together, it is likely that blacksmiths' potential demand for supplies of smelted iron and consumers' demand for their finished iron products were not easily or consistently met. This general fluctuating scarcity helps explain in part why West Africans placed such a relatively high value on iron and why, in turn, European merchants in the era of Atlantic trade encountered such robust markets for their overseas bar iron, especially along the Upper Guinea Coast.

West Africa's other major historical change between the eleventh and fifteenth centuries—a steady growth in its population of Muslims—led to an increasing influence of Islam in its economies, cultures, and urban life. Al-Bakri, in a manuscript completed in Andalusia in 1068, provided general descriptions of what he called the kingdoms of Gao on the middle Niger River, Takrur in the valley of the Senegal, and Ghana between them on the edge of the desert. He drew his views of these kingdoms from knowledge and direct observations of Muslim travelers and traders as well as from the hearsay they had picked up south of the desert. Taking care to point out the towns in which there were mosques and resident Muslims, he also noted the persistence of polytheistic belief and customs in some locales, including among the leaders of important kingdoms such as Ghana. Other telling details—about the gold trade, the significant numbers of Muslim scholars and legal experts in Ghana, and the prominent positions of Muslims as advisors to its king—would have sent a welcome signal to his readers that their faith was on the rise south of the Sahara.[12] And this was indeed the case.

Eighty-six years later the Moroccan geographer al-Idrisi provided valuable additions to what was already known about The Land of the Black People, including news that Ghana's king was now a practicing Muslim. He also passed on general information about the alluvial goldfields adjacent to the kingdom and the vigorous and lucrative trade in gold northward to the Maghreb, where it was minted into dinar coins. Matters of dress were also of great interest, especially when they indicated that there were peoples south of the Sahara who displayed a Muslim sense of sartorial propriety. Respectable Islamic clothing consisted of waist-wrappers, mantles, tailored shirts, and loose-fitting trousers, made of either local cotton or imported wool or silk.[13]

Regular extraction of gold from deposits located south of the Sahara helped create an interregional currency zone and an early and important north–south axis of trade out of the goldfields and across the desert to North Africa. Muslim Berber merchants traveling southward from Morocco and Tunisia purchased rock salt that had been mined in Saharan deposits and then cut into standard-sized slabs by slaves from southern non-Muslim regions. They carried their units of rock salt onward to the edge of the desert, where they sold it to specialist long-distance Muslim Juula merchants for an agreed-upon measure of gold. Arabic was the language these merchants had in common, at least for trading purposes. Rock-salt slabs thus entered Juula networks and circulated widely in West Africa as a currency valued either by weight or by linear measure, especially in areas where sea salt was scarce.

The gold dust people exchanged in and around West Africa's towns and cities came from panning stream beds and surface soil in the resource areas around the headwaters of the Senegal and Gambia Rivers during the dry season, or, in some regions, nuggets were won by mining underground veins. The yields then circulated as a currency in units defined by weight. For measuring out units of gold dust currency, Juula merchants had adopted a special apparatus from the Muslim world via the trans-Saharan trade—a balance scale and a set of weights based on the Islamic ounce and pound. The *mithqal,* an Islamic unit of weight of about 4.25 grams, the standard weight of a dinar coin, thus became a shared currency value and a major vehicle that enabled and encouraged trade to take place between North and sub-Saharan African economies.[14]

The Cape Verdean Álvares de Almada recorded his own direct observations of Juula merchants buying gold in a town on the north bank of the upper Gambia River in the second half of the sixteenth century. Traveling overland in heavily guarded caravans, they carried their gold dust in small containers concealed in their clothing for safekeeping. Most of it was in the form of very fine flakes of metal, and Almada deemed it very high in quality, that is, it was not debased by the addition of brass filings or other impurities. He wrote admiringly of the Juulas' reliability and expertise in trading matters, especially the care they took in the skillfully precise handling of their weights and scales. He described the apparatus and equipment in some detail, noting in particular the accuracy of the balance scale, its elegant construction, and the fine quality of its materials. The weights were made of brass cast in a minutely calibrated range of sizes and shapes, which each merchant stored in the drawers of his leather-bound writing case. Almada's curiosity was piqued by the fact that when Juula traveled to the resource area, they acquired their gold mostly in exchange for copper bracelets, a transaction that from his perspective would not have been profitable to the suppliers of the gold since they acquired only a base metal in return. Making inquiries into the matter, he came to understand that the Juula were simply responding to the cultural values of peoples in the gold-fields who preferred copper ornaments to their gold. No doubt sensing a profitable opportunity, he inquired yet further into exactly how much copper would yield how much gold but found he had reached the limit of what the Juula—surely sensing his avarice—were willing to disclose about their commercial operations.[15] Secrecy was one of the ways people protected their trading networks, preferred markets, and most reliable suppliers.

Muslim merchants introduced another currency, cowry shells, from either the Near East or the Indian Ocean basin into West African networks via trans-Saharan trading routes at least as early as the eleventh century. Evidence of this traffic comes from travelers' accounts collected and written down by al-Bakri, which mentioned cowry imports observed at that time in the vicinity of Gao. Other written sources from the twelfth and thirteenth centuries make additional references to cowries being carried across the

Sahara along the western caravan route leading southward from Sijilmasa to Ghana. Archaeological remains of a portion of what was one such caravan offer material corroboration of these rather sparse and meager written sources. Whatever the reason for the demise of part of a caravan, whether it was attacked or wrecked by sandstorms and unstable dunes, several camels and their loads came to a halt en route, never reaching their destination. What survived of them is impressive. Along with approximately two thousand standard-sized rods of copper and copper alloy were several containers filled with cowry shells. The site, called Ma'den Ijafen, is believed to date to the twelfth century (see map 1.1).[16]

It is not known precisely when and where cowries first began to circulate south of the Sahara as a form of currency. The first mention of a cowry currency in the Arabic sources comes from al-Umari, who wrote in 1337/8 about the Mali Empire and what was remembered thirteen years after the pilgrimage to Mecca of its leader, Mansa Musa. Among his informants was one Ibn Amir Hajib, a governing official of Cairo, who had met and befriended Musa and claimed to have had many informative conversations with him. Hajib recounted to al-Umari some of what Mansa Musa had told him about Mali's history and culture. Gold was apparently collected as tribute but exported, and the main currency circulating in Mali at that time was imported cowry shells. He added that merchants who were specialists in the business of supplying cowry imports profited handsomely from it.[17] Ibn Battuta, a Moroccan traveler in West Africa from February 1352 to December 1353, provides a brief but very instructive eyewitness description of cowry currency in his written account of his travels. He noted that cowries were a currency there, specifying Mali and Gao in particular. Most precisely, he stated that in both places he had seen them changing hands at the same rate of 1,150 shells per gold dinar.[18] Cowries amounted to small change and were especially useful for making minor transactions. As fixed and durable units, they could circulate by count in single- or multiple-shell units or, if necessary, in larger quantities by weight. Creating standard gold-cowry conversion rates thus provided greater flexibility and social reach to West African commerce by enabling a Muslim gold-weight system to operate in regular and reliable contact with shell-counting systems of polytheistic and rural peoples.[19]

A growing trade in cotton textiles set off stunning cultural and economic changes in West Africa, first by way of the high prestige and popularity of imported cotton clothing, especially among Muslims, and then with widespread production of it locally. Cotton had been known and probably also produced and woven in the Nile valley in northeastern Africa very early on between the third century BCE and fourth century CE, but it is unclear whether cotton and spinning, weaving, and sewing technologies traveled into other parts of sub-Saharan Africa before the Muslim era in the later first millennium.[20] Cotton was a favored fiber for clothing in the Muslim world, and wearing high-quality cotton garments was a sign of elegance and modest good taste. Muslims promoted these values, thereby generating a "cotton culture" that extended beyond Islamic circles and over much of West Africa. Places in West Africa where cotton textile production became well-established—cultivating cotton fiber, spinning cotton yarn, weaving cotton cloth, and tailoring cotton garments—also became producers of cotton currencies that circulated widely.

Cotton technology spread into new areas of West Africa especially during the dry period of ca. 1100 to ca. 1500. Linguistic evidence in the form of words borrowed from Saharan Arabic for key aspects of this cotton culture demonstrates that the dissemination of cotton south of the Sahara owed much to these (presumably) Muslim merchants and their networks. Two separate groups of speakers of the language passed cotton goods and also the knowledge of cotton technology on to peoples living along the desert's southern shore and lent them also their word for cotton fiber, *kútan* and *gótun,* dialectal variants of the Arabic *qutn.* The general geographical locations of these two groups of Arabic speakers and the geographical locations of sub-Saharan speech communities who borrowed these Arabic words for cotton both match well with the known geographical locations of the main western and central trans-Saharan trade routes. A very general time frame for when this transfer of knowledge could have occurred can be estimated based on the growing prominence of Muslims in the towns, cities, and courts of tropical West Africa early in the second millennium. Hence these events could have been set in motion in the tenth or eleventh century. Convincing evidence in support of this time frame comes from archaeology. Material remains in the form of spinning tools and locally made cotton textiles and tailored garments together corroborate the linguistic evidence by dating from a broad period spanning the tenth to seventeenth centuries.[21] A superb example is this remarkably well-preserved cotton tunic, illustrated in figure 1.1, which comes from one of the cave burials at Sanga, an archaeological site located in the Bandiagara escarpment in what is now Mali. It is made of narrow cotton strips sewn together and tailored, and like many of

FIGURE 1.1 Cotton tunic, eleventh or twelfth c. CE, Cave C, Sanga, Bandiagara escarpment, Mali. Nationaal Museum van Wereldculturen, The Netherlands, RV-B237–755.

the roughly five hundred other garment fragments discovered at the site, it displays a repeat pattern woven with white and indigo-dyed thread. Skeletal remains associated with this tunic date to the eleventh or twelfth century.[22]

However, precisely when and where major cotton production centers arose is very incompletely known, especially for the period before 1500. The earliest written information about cotton and cotton textile manufacture in sub-Saharan West Africa comes from al-Bakri's eleventh-century compilation in which he states that the currencies of Sila (in the lower Senegal River valley) consisted of sorghum, salt, copper rings, and lengths of finely woven cotton. Weavers produced the cloth in a neighboring town where many households grew cotton on a small scale, apparently as a perennial. Al-Umari noted in the fourteenth century that one of the currencies in Kanem, in the vicinity of Lake Chad well to the east, was a locally woven cotton strip cloth, and that Mali, far to the west, was reportedly cultivating much cotton and producing high-quality cotton textiles.[23] By the time of the Guinea trade, European explorers and merchants took note of places such as Senegambia on the Upper Guinea Coast and the Bight of Benin in the Gulf of Guinea where cotton textiles were available for export to other coastal markets. As Euro-African trade expanded, locally made cotton currencies remained necessary for purchasing provisions and paying for labor. They thus continued to be produced in competition with the higher-priced cotton imports from overseas.[24]

West African cotton currencies circulated as narrow strips or breadths of various widths—woven on local handlooms and calculated as standard units based on the number of lengths that would make a finished cloth or item of clothing. Al-Bakri's report about the currencies in the lower Senegal River valley noted the cotton currency there circulated in lengths he referred to as *izar,* the Arabic word for mantle, the most basic and versatile of garments. Kanem's cotton currency as described by al-Umari circulated in lengths of ten cubits (the forearm length from the middle finger tip to the elbow bottom), and purchases could be made using fractions from one cubit upwards. Imported cowries, beads, copper pieces, and silver coins also circulated there as currency, but their values were calculated in terms of the local cotton cloth units. Al-Umari also noted that the excellent white woven cotton of Mali was called *kamisiya,* from the Arabic *qamis,* a generic term for shirt.[25]

These cotton currency units, based on linear measures of cloth or sometimes in reference to a garment, continued to be standard into and throughout the era of Atlantic trade. Álvares de Almada described a former time on the Upper Guinea Coast, probably when he lived there in the mid-sixteenth century, when Luso-African merchants could safely lodge with local nobles and purchase slaves very cheaply. They paid for them in cows and cloths called *sigas,* which he described as a fixed length of the cotton currency called *teada.* Major cotton currencies along the Guinea Coast were known in many West African languages by the vernacular names for wrapper-size cloths.[26]

The passage of more goods and commodity currencies through the Sahara, the Sahel, and the savannas, rainforests, and coastal regions depended on the variations of seasonal working patterns, the frequencies and locations of trans-Saharan caravan arrivals, and the fluctuating intensities of local mining, processing, and workshop production. The West Africa that European merchants encountered was much more than the "Land of Gold" they dreamed of. Though not a fully integrated economic system or single market, it was a dynamic multicentric zone of trade and currency flows as well as other exchanges and transfers of all sorts. Trade languages reached widely across the landscape, and more people became polylingual. West African merchants and traders became increasingly flexible and adept at working with various methods of measuring and counting goods; farmers and artisans familiarized themselves with and mastered new skills, tools, and technological knowledge; and cultural values were subject to change as consumers acquired new tastes for alternative modes of dress and social behavior. The economies of West Africa together formed a large-scale inter-communicating zone supporting a long-standing history of trading ties to North Africa, the Mediterranean basin, and other distant lands.

Atlantic Trading and the "Language of Goods"

Early Euro-African trade on the Upper Guinea Coast relied heavily on two of the major regional commodity currencies—bar iron and narrow strips of cotton cloth—that skilled artisans produced locally in standard units of linear measurement. Whether or not exchanged in their material forms, they served multiple functions as currencies of account and in reckoning market values and prices. In contrast to European currency systems, there was no government minting of coinage. But similar to coins, which historically have often been altered or melted down and turned into jewelry or luxury goods, these currencies had their own use values as well, which worked against debasement. Doubling as important basic commodities, bar iron and cotton strips could easily be taken out of circulation to be used for practical purposes if the need or desire arose. Each was also an intermediate good, that is, a semifinished material that skilled hands might turn into a well-known and valuable finished product. In the hands of blacksmiths, bar iron was fashioned into all sorts of useful tools, blade weapons, and productive agricultural implements. Cotton strips could be sewn by hand to become a wide wrapper called "country cloth" that a man or woman would wear draped around the body. Taken to skilled tailors, cotton strips were also made into sewn shirts and trousers worn by men. Iron and cotton thus moved into and out of currency flows, presenting another set of opportunities for their artisan producers.

European trading on the Guinea Coast has often been characterized simplistically as ad hoc "barter" for curiosities of little value, but what actually took place was much more complex than this stereotype allows. West African coastal trade was based on exchanges of two carefully calculated assortments, or bundles, of goods that were subject to differing valuations by the two parties. Each assortment consisted of a variety of goods that were negotiated and composed during the transaction. Assortments thus changed according to local negotiators and their circumstances. And over time, as supplies of and demands for specific commodities fluctuated, values of them in relation to one another changed as well. Furthermore, descriptions of particular commercial transactions illustrate that certain goods could serve as a measure of value for pricing and bargaining only, whereas corresponding quantities of other goods actually changed hands in payment. Parties who engaged in these transactions therefore had to make numerous and ongoing mental calculations, employing a special "language" of goods, specifying their names, their presumed unit values, and their equivalent valuations in relation to other goods. Each party could calculate by considering his or her own costs, values, and estimated profits and translating these into the language of goods shared with their counterparts. Though assortment bargaining on the Guinea Coast thus presented significant social, linguistic, and cultural challenges to parties on both sides, its flexibility offered a range of possible outcomes—deals could be sealed relatively smoothly and quickly, or difficult and protracted negotiations could be pursued with varying degrees of success, leading in some instances even to agreements to disagree.

Reliable commercial intelligence about the availability and origin of certain goods was key to successful trading on both sides, as were calculations of the current relative market values of goods. In some cases, parties would negotiate specific prices in good-for-good equivalences for major components of the bundles. But for the most part bargaining was primarily about the compositions of the assortments—which particular goods to include, their specific qualities, and how many of each. Instead of haggling over unit prices for each commodity, which would have been an overly cumbersome and time-consuming process, parties resolved variabilities of supply, quality, and demand by coming to agreement on the "mix" of the goods on hand at the moment. Crucial to the strategies of both parties was the inclusion of a wide range of goods—some cheap, others much more expensive. When they finally agreed on the two assortments—including, for example, undersized captives as well as strong adult males from the Africans, cheap beads as well as coral and long iron bars from the Europeans—and considered them as equivalent in value, the goods changed hands. And every completed assortment made a social statement about the buyer. An assortment selected by an African buyer represented his or her human geography and the cultural norms and preferences of specific consumers or customers he or she had in mind.[27] A European's assortment represented long supply chains and specific labor settings that determined the various destinations of their captives and other exports.

Some specialized West African merchants employed "arbitrage trading" to substantially increase their profit margins. "Arbitrage" is an economist's term for taking advantage of differing prices for a given good in distant and distinct markets by moving the good from one to the other. In the case of Upper Guinea's Atlantic trade specifically, new patterns of arbitrage trading developed between Europeans on the coast and suppliers and consumers in the interior. Detailed accounts of arbitrage demonstrate that a canny and intrepid trader who was armed with up-to-date commercial intelligence and willing to invest the necessary travel time could leverage his exchanges advantageously. Arbitrage was the practice of Juula long-distance merchants in the West African interior and also of some Luso-African traders on the coast in the early seventeenth century who linked the mainland to the offshore Cape Verde Islands and to Portugal (fig. 1.2). In this form of trade, rooted in the earlier, western African commercial system, a merchant would structure multiple trading routes in strategically selected segments going from one location to another and based on current pricing differences, which could be skillfully exploited to produce greater profit margins. A well-known account shows how merchants from the Cape Verde Islands leveraged a local salt resource through several steps into the final goal, which was a considerable sum of Spanish silver or its equivalent.

> The trade we called "coastal" is mostly undertaken, in small ships . . . by Portuguese who live on Santiago Island [in the Cape Verde archipelago]. First they load these with salt, which they conveniently obtain for nothing on the islands of Maio and Sal in the Cape Verde Islands, and they sail to Serra-Lioa with the salt and trade it for gold, ivory, and kola. Then from Serra-Lioa they sail again to Joala and Porto d'Ale in Senegal, where they trade a portion of the kola for cotton cloths. They also sometimes trade ivory obtained in Serra-Lioa for Cape Verde cloths. From there they sail again east to Cacheo, where they trade the rest of their kola and their remaining goods for slaves. They acquire fifty to sixty slaves in exchange for the goods they have obtained by trade along the coast, and each slave is worth to them 150 *reals,* or pieces-of-eight. So they make 9,000–10,000 *reals* out of nothing, in a manner of speaking. For they are willing to put

FIGURE 1.2 Map of the Upper Guinea Coast and the Cape Verde Islands. The National Archives of the UK, Nicolas Sanson, *L'Afrique en plusieurs cartes nouvelles* (Paris, 1656).

up with any discomfort, to an astonishing extent; and when they occasionally catch fish or come to a place like Serra-Lioa where everything is cheap, they eat like wolves.[28]

Arbitrage trading overland as practiced by the Juula Jahaanke of the upper Senegal River involved the intersection of a north–south axis of trade in gold and captives across the Sahara with an east–west trade in captives and overseas imports between the interior and the coast. A late seventeenth-century account of it featured exchanges for European goods on the coast, but Jahaanke merchants could just as easily have followed this same trading pattern before the Atlantic era by offering cotton textiles from inland in exchange for coastal sea salt. It began with Jahaanke merchants taking loads of locally woven cloth from Bundu on the upper Senegal River to the neighboring Bambuk goldfields, where they sold the cloth for gold. Traveling north to a desert-side entrepôt called "Tarra," they were then in a strong position to negotiate with merchants specializing in the gold trade to North Africa. The Jahaanke, for their part, could profitably use their gold also to purchase whatever male captives there were on hand who remained unsold, for it was usually the case that Muslim slave markets in and across the Sahara preferred women and children. From Tarra, Jahaanke caravans forced their captive men to march overland to the upper Gambia River. There they met up with merchants from downriver who were supplying the Atlantic and American markets, which preferred male slaves, and quickly sold them away in exchange for European imports. Some of these Atlantic goods could then be used to purchase gold in the Bambuk goldfields, thus beginning new circuits of arbitrage trading.[29]

Specialized merchants such as the Jahaanke were known to Europeans as being particularly adept at initiating, negotiating, and closing deals. And deals were complicated. They involved making a series of offers and refusals, some real and others feigned, on the composition of specific trade goods in each assortment to be exchanged and on the relative values of the assortments as expressed in an agreed currency of account. Francisco de Lemos Coelho, a Portuguese merchant based in the Cape Verde Islands who lived for twenty-three years in the mid-seventeenth century on the Upper Guinea Coast, recorded what he had seen of Jahaanke merchants conducting their business. Jahaanke-led caravans of merchants and their loads of goods and provisions were among the largest in the hinterlands of the Upper Guinea Coast. They regularly set out from their homelands in November as the dry season opened roads. By the time they reached the entrepôt of Barrakunda up the Gambia River in July, their caravans had swelled to several thousand people, including large numbers of captives, over two thousand donkeys, and quantities of ivory, cotton textiles, and gold. Some of the merchants continued on down to the coast, where they purchased salt with a portion of their cotton cloth. Others remained on the spot to do business with Europeans who came upriver to purchase captives, ivory, gold, and cotton cloth. It appears that the privileged and highly respected and powerful Muslim clerics who led them possessed the authority to negotiate market prices and deal directly with European agents. Several caravan leaders would meet with agents to agree on a fair equivalency in the commodities they carried for a fixed, often fictional, length of cloth, for example, and on how a purchase price was to be paid in practice, such as in units of writing paper (reams or quires), in beads, or in a combination of the two. Once these equivalents were established, the rest of the individual merchant sellers converged on the scene and, according to this witness, engaged in nonstop intense trading for up to twenty-four hours. As with

Álvares de Almada in the previous century, Coelho remarked admiringly that he saw no evidence of cheating or theft.[30]

Other merchant groups handled their commercial exchanges through whatever different procedures they found acceptable, but again, prices would be expressed in a currency of account while the actual payments would be made in other goods and currencies of exchange. Coelho witnessed smaller caravans of a hundred men or fewer arriving at Barrakunda from nearby areas and gave a description of how these merchants operated. What they hoped for was to sell their captives and ivory tusks and to be paid as much as possible in salt, but in this case they did not have a hand in deciding and setting prices. Trading was allowed to commence only after local officials in charge of the venue determined what the relative prices of goods and values of currency units would be in their domains. The example given by Coelho was for the largest and best-quality ivory tusk, which was priced at a notional ten cotton cloths. That price was to be paid partly in salt, whose value had been set per single dry unit of measure, in this case, a bowl of a certain standard size. Prices for other possible "payment goods" were then set in relation to the units of cloth and salt. What is most interesting is what Coelho had to say about the trade at Barrakunda in gold. Valuation of the precious metal in relation to other currencies and goods was such that European merchants who bought it discovered that it was not as profitable as buying other commodities and selling them later for gold-equivalent paper or favors of the powerful in European economies. In speaking of Atlantic commerce, Coelho claimed that European merchants could realize much greater eventual profits in this part of the Guinea Coast by dealing in ivory or captives rather than gold.[31] Whether or not he was deliberately trying to avoid royal interference in a profitable transaction by downplaying gold as a trade item there, it was indeed the case that Africa's gold exports in Atlantic trade came not so much from Upper Guinea as they did from the Gold Coast.

Bar iron was the essential commodity currency for Europeans trading on the Upper Guinea Coast. We see indications of concentration on this highly useful metal from the start with the establishment of Portuguese settlements on the Cape Verde Islands in the 1460s and then, increasingly in the 1500s, among the communities that *lançados* (men of Portuguese descent operating independently along the coast) were establishing on the mainland. Attempts by the Portuguese crown to regulate the commerce of these settler-traders and their Luso-African descendants were chronically unsuccessful as they evaded royal decrees and continued to work privately and independently, in direct competition with the official trade of Portuguese monarchs. Among the decrees issued in the late fifteenth and early sixteenth centuries to control these outlaws were regulations that specifically prohibited the sale of iron on the Guinea Coast, a convincing indication of its strategic importance. Local Portuguese interests, *lançados* and Cape Verde Islanders, were reportedly using it especially in transactions for the purchase of captives and ivory.[32] Where this iron was from, whether it was locally produced bar iron acquired in arbitrage trade or European bar iron either transshipped from Lisbon through the islands or acquired illicitly from other European traders in the vicinity, or a combination of all of the above, is not clear.

In the second half of the sixteenth century, small numbers of French and English merchants began to intrude on the Upper Guinea Coast. But they did so only in fits and starts since they were initially ill-equipped and hesitant to challenge Portugal's long-standing claims to trade with Africa. What trading they did was centered mainly on the Senegal River, along the Petite Côte, the coast between the Gambia River and south to the vicinity of Sherbro Island, and much farther south and east on the Gold Coast. These merchants were in search of captives, intermediate goods for European markets such as hides and ivory, and, above all, gold. Armed clashes with vessels manned by local *lançados* and Portuguese alike kept any serious expansion of the foreigners' trade there in check.

It is therefore of interest to consider the vituperative remarks of Álvares de Almada, who described commerce on the Upper Guinea Coast in the late sixteenth century as being in ruin because of the French and the English. His account exaggerates the influence of these newcomers prior to the seventeenth century so as to portray his compatriots as victims in dire need of royal favors. In the past, he complains, many vessels from the Cape Verde Islands had sailed to the mainland to purchase captives, cloth, wax, and ivory in abundance. However, rising competition with agents of French and English merchants had supposedly forced them to abandon the trade. They had bid up prices for African commodities and captives, he claimed, and the former peace and security they had enjoyed with their coastal trading partners no longer existed. In describing so dramatically the decline of Portuguese trade on the Upper Guinea Coast at this time, it is likely that Almada was deliberately using them to bolster his case for a stronger official Portuguese presence there as well as protecting the hidden activities of his fellow islander and *lançado* merchants.[33]

It was the seventeenth century that saw an increasing presence of Dutch, English, and French merchants on the Upper Guinea Coast—predecessors of the RAC—and with them came a flood of European-made bar iron and other overseas commodities. Since much of the larger-scale iron smelting in West Africa was done in regions of the interior, blacksmiths near the coast would have had very limited and uncertain supplies of the metal besides what little they got from recycling. Thus these new Atlantic sources of iron must have significantly enabled the work of these smiths. The Englishman Richard Jobson's account of his travels on the Gambia River in 1620–21 provides a valuable description of local blacksmiths, their workshops and products, and how much these new supplies of European bar iron were already becoming such a boon to them. He commented that among all of the artisanal occupations he had observed, the most important one was blacksmithing. He described how blacksmiths specialized in working bars of iron metal into finished goods such as swords, javelin blades, arrows, and especially agricultural tools. They themselves were not smelters and so depended on others for their supplies of iron. Therefore, the regular arrival of European bar iron on the coast meant that they and their workshops could flourish as never before. Initially, in Jobson's time, overseas iron was adapted to the preexisting norms for measuring and circulating locally made bar iron. The long and cumbersome imported European bars had to be cut down into the shorter lengths of their own standard bar iron currency units, which ranged between eight and twelve inches. This important conversion of imported commodity to local currency became a new task for smiths, many of whom traveled from town to town, setting up their workshops and supplying their own anvils, hand tools, charcoal fuel, and skills to work the iron possessed by local residents. Jobson noted that careful monitoring of the work was necessary because smiths were known to help themselves to extra portions of bar iron in the process.[34]

Demand for iron on this part of the Guinea Coast was particularly strong and continued to be so as the RAC established its presence there. And European bar iron was required especially for purchasing the captives sought by the company. Already in 1615, Cape Verde Islanders were noticing a marked increase in the market prices for captives, complaining that what they used to pay for two prime males was now being charged for a single unhealthy man. One likely reason for this rise in the price for slaves, or for the decrease in the value of imported metal, was the increasing flows of metal coming in mainly on northern European vessels. Luso-African traders, having no direct supplies of iron from Portugal, therefore had to rely on others—first the Spaniards, and then the English.[35] Jobson, too, noted the inflation of prices on the coast for slaves. The accepted length of bar iron currency there was twelve inches, but English traders up the Gambia River found that they could get away with using the shorter eight-inch bar iron currency units in calculating and making their purchases.[36] In the second half of the seventeenth century, overseas ("voyage") iron, in one-bar units, became the currency of account for trading by England's Royal African Company in this region of the Guinea Coast, though at differing valuations, and as such it was integrated into both the English and the West African trading systems.

Gifts and Protocols

European traders had to adapt also to local norms for receiving and hosting strangers and for establishing and maintaining the commercial relationships they offered. Salutations in local languages and offerings of food, drink, and gifts were essential social lubricants that enabled goods to move smoothly along the international channels of exchange. Some of these were regular and institutionalized, whereas others could be personal and idiosyncratic requests of the moment. During Coelho's twenty-three years of residence on the Upper Guinea Coast, he came to appreciate the local variants of these protocols and how they operated. Referring to the "Jolof coast" (the northern part between the Senegal River and Cape Verde), he advised that European merchants visiting there should not hesitate to be generous to local officials and the nobility and that they should host them regularly, serving them spirits and any other kind of refreshment they might request. He hastened to add a cryptic warning that holding back on such hospitality would not turn to their advantage. Paying proper respects began when first entering the vicinity of a coastal or riverine town with the sending of a respectful message of greeting accompanied by a gift to the local king. The business of buying and selling could not begin until the king's chosen day when he would arrive to officially exchange gifts, inspect the merchandise, and declare that trading negotiations could then commence.[37] Describing a purchase of captives at Ponta in the Bissagos Islands off Bissau, Coelho specified what kind of gifts were required. There, wine was the preferred social drink, whereas elsewhere it was brandy. Small beads were necessary both as a gift and also for purchasing food and other provisions. High-quality textiles were welcome favors to local hosts, who were also entitled to a tip from the seller for each captive sold.[38] Gifts operated thusly as a form of customs fee.

Such well-established proprieties assured visitors of good and regular business prospects. Regarding Europeans' purchases of kola in the environs of Sierra Leone, Coelho alluded to a time before the mid-seventeenth century when Portuguese ship masters were so suspicious and mistrustful of local merchants that they insisted that human pawns or hostages be placed on board as pledges of trust. He went on to say that in his time such wariness was no longer the case and that relations with kola suppliers were consistently productive. What he then described as typical of the kola trade presents another local variant of gift-giving protocols. Arriving ships would send an envoy to the king, who then sent envoys in return to deliver the message of when the king would come to formally greet them. Upon his arrival, accompanied by lesser kings, officials, and nobles, an extended period of feasting and socializing commenced. Ship masters together ceremonially rewarded the king with a gift, whereupon the king then gave permission for their traders to come ashore. Each trader then met up with one or another of the lesser kings and was escorted along with his merchandise to a village inland where he would purchase kola.[39] Once there, further rounds of feasting, gift giving, and socializing undoubtedly took place.

A rather less enthusiastic description comes from the French Huguenot (Calvinist) Jean Barbot, who wrote of his two brief voyages to the Guinea Coast in 1678–79 and 1681–82. His account of his time ashore in Senegal drew on conversations he had with employees of the French Compagnie du Sénégal and included a listing of the numerous dues and tolls that agents of the company had to pay when trading inland. These charges, which he attributed to the "black kings," were a determining factor, in his view, of how profitable the trade would be. He or his informants estimated them to be about ten percent of the total value of the trade and specified that they were paid in goods. He also listed other payments to individuals such as local officials and suppliers of wood and water. Still other gifts or payments were due to individuals in each town or village. In the example he gave of the village of Camalingue, there were gifts to minor officials, to the king's wife, to the valet and son of the town's governor, to the chief interpreter and his valet, and to others. These charges, while individually small, added up to a significant amount and were considered by Barbot to be too time consuming and troublesome to dispense.[40]

But even Barbot could warm to local kings on the Guinea Coast who, according to his judgment, behaved with good manners and propriety. Such was his impression of the elderly king of Sestos on the "Pepper Coast" (well to the south, in modern Liberia), where he visited for over a week during his second voyage.[41] He provides a detailed description of his meeting and exchange of gifts with the king, an event that took place in a special circular building where Sestos officials met to discuss and settle trade agreements with foreign merchants and other strangers (see fig. 1.3). Among its interior

FIGURE 1.3 King of Sestos receives Jean Barbot. John Barbot, "A Description of the Coasts of North and South-Guinea," in A. and J. Churchill, *A Collection of Voyages and Travels* (London, 1732). Collection of the Massachusetts Historical Society.

furnishings was a small shrine where ritual offerings were made and where oaths were declared and witnessed. Barbot's illustration of the meeting shows the king and his senior courtiers, all dressed in embroidered and flowing white cotton robes and seated on patterned mats. Barbot was careful to note the "grisgris," or charms, gracing the king's elaborate cap and necklaces.

After a formal welcoming of the visitors came a ceremonial exchange of gifts. Barbot's gift consisted of two long bars of "voyage iron," a selection of glass beads, several iron knives, and two flasks of brandy. The king offered his guests provisions—two hens and a container of clean (hulled) rice—which Barbot's men immediately prepared for the assembled to share.

What Barbot was seeking from the king was not only an arrangement to buy ivory but also permission to cut wood and to replenish their water supplies. At the conclusion of their meeting, the king's interpreter informed Barbot that he could expect a visit from the king very shortly. Over the course of his stay, Barbot managed to purchase a small amount of ivory along with stores of rice and about two hundred chickens. And his men, in addition to provisioning the ship with wood and water, took advantage of the fine fishing the river had to offer. Lacking Coelho's extensive and decades-long experience on the Guinea Coast and perhaps revealing something of his own puritanical values, Barbot characterized Sestos in idyllic terms as a community that lived in peace, quiet, and modest abundance.[42] A more experienced observer, however, would have been more circumspect. Considering the advanced age of the king, itself a portent of the approaching end to his reign, that peaceful time was likely to be soon interrupted by an unpredictable and possibly fractious interregnum period and in its wake any number of disruptive arguments or conflicts.

This chapter's general overview reveals West Africa up to the eve of the Atlantic era as having been far from socially homogeneous or economically unified. West Africa was instead a land characterized by great social variety and dramatic differences in local economies and subsistence production. A long-standing history of trade with the equally foreign wider Islamic world had left its mark in a host of commercial institutions, relations, and practices that Africans adapted and Europeans accepted in the subsequent era of Euro-African maritime trade. Islam and the Arabic language bequeathed a core commonality of values and trust among Muslim merchants, enabling their commercial networks and markets to reach into many locales beyond the Islamic sphere. West Africa's interlocking zones of trade, communication, and currency circulation cut across her many geographical, ecological, social, linguistic, and religious divides, thus forming a richly complex yet demonstrably viable commercial setting in which Europeans and Africans could develop their Guinea trade.

Europeans engaging in early modern trade on the Upper Guinea Coast had to navigate this complexity and adapt to a wide range of localized trading practices, markets, and values. They traded their goods in assortments that African traders wanted, and the process of coming to agreement on them was riddled with potential disagreements over specific matters of taste, quality, value, and price, all of which might change unpredictably over time and from place to place. Hence the social aspects of commerce—protocols, courtesies, favors, and gifts—carried great weight. To keep the flows of goods and currencies moving, European visitors had to show the proper deference and respect for their various West African trading partners and do so consistently and in the right ways. Merchants from Europe who wished to be successful learned that they had to prove themselves to be both well-informed and well-behaved—and therefore trustworthy—in Africans' terms.

_____

CHAPTER TWO

"Artificers" and Merchants

Making and Moving Goods

MISSING FROM historical maps showing trade routes and networks of the past are the complex and crucially important human dimensions of commerce. Much of what went into trade was essential work, though unnoticed and therefore unrecorded, for it was labor folded into the daily and seasonal routines of people's lives. Countless numbers and varieties of people—compatriots and foreigners in towns and countryside and on rivers and seas—became intricately interconnected through increasingly distant exchanges of what they made, often without their even knowing. In this respect, the early modern Atlantic trading system in Africa was no different from any other. Many disparate people played a role in creating it, and it took a far-flung host of other individuals with the complementing knowledge, skills, labor, and experiences to keep the circuits replenished. Merchants, often considered to be the primary actors in commerce, spent their lives and careers developing, revising, and exercising valuable intelligence about these makers of the goods they moved—the news and knowledge that enabled them to connect manufacturers with far-off markets of consumers.

These groups they connected—consumers as well as manufacturers—are equally important actors in commerce, although they can all too easily be overlooked. This chapter focuses on both groups, especially the producers of trade goods, in order to place Euro-African trade on the Upper Guinea Coast into the wider intercontinental contexts of the people who created and maintained it. They represent a wide range of ongoing human investments in training and skills that powered the preindustrial toolkits and labor-intensive workshops of artisans or "artificers." Workers of all kinds—men, women, children, unskilled, semiskilled, skilled, free, and unfree—generated and processed raw materials and turned them into semifinished goods, transportable commodities, or finished products of one kind or another. Tracking the supply chains that Atlantic trade commodities followed thus provides a more complete view of the geographical scale and social complexity of early modern commerce on the Guinea Coast. And taking into account the varied ways artificers' work was organized, how their working conditions changed over time, and how well or how poorly workers profited is a necessary part of the story.

European and Asian Makers of Western Africans' Imports

The general classes of overseas commodities that England's Royal African Company (RAC) brought to the Guinea Coast in the second half of the seventeenth century centered on textiles and metalwares. These remained the two most important categories of trade goods into and throughout the eighteenth century.[1] Looking more closely at the most important major products in each category sharpens the picture. By identifying them and tracking where and by whom they were made, it becomes possible to better understand both the full extent of Anglo-Atlantic trading networks in this early period and the reasons behind their reach. For in striking contrast with the eighteenth century, England did not herself produce many of the goods the RAC shipped to the Guinea Coast. Following on the Dutch example, whose supremacy in seventeenth-century commerce depended heavily on reexporting products that others made, the company instead tapped into established supply centers in the Baltic region and in South Asia to build the range of goods they had on offer. The opening of Atlantic trade had brought European mariners into direct contact with the tropics—tropical climates and seasonal patterns, tropical products such as cotton and dyewoods, and communities of people who lived and worked there. Thus, in this early period England relied on producers and suppliers in locations spread widely across the temperate and tropical zones of Afro-Eurasia (see map 2.1). Only very gradually and aided by their customers in Africa and the deliberate management of their Court of Assistants and Committee of Goods, the RAC was able to encourage and support English manufacturers (some of whom were shareholders in the company) in producing some of these reexport goods at home. And in doing so the RAC contributed in part

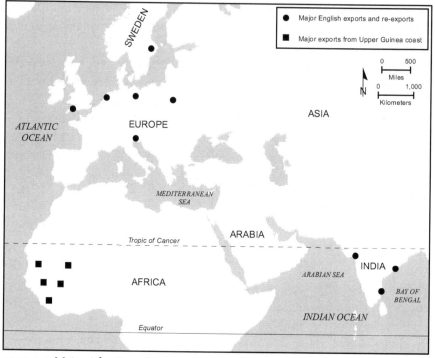

MAP 2.1 Major Afro-Eurasian exports in Anglo-African North Atlantic trade, seventeenth c. *Map by Brian Edward Balsley, GISP.*

to launching Britain's later and well-known successes in manufacturing in the eighteenth century.[2]

Someone reading today the loading lists and invoices of RAC cargoes would find the export trade to the Guinea Coast utterly incomprehensible. Products were known by a seemingly endless number of particular and sometimes peculiar names with strange and varying phonetic spellings that have long since lost whatever familiar meanings they once had. But setting aside these obscure names and focusing instead on precisely what the goods were like makes it possible to see a relatively coherent pattern of what the RAC had learned about which goods they needed to trade successfully on the Guinea Coast and from whom they could get them. An example is cotton textiles from India, which West African merchants and consumers consistently favored for purchase alongside the lower-priced cotton textiles made in West Africa. Among their different weaves and patterns, the most important were known as *allejaes, baftes, brawles,* Guinea stuffs, long cloths, *longees, nicconees, pautkes,* and *tapseels.*[3] If taken at face value, the specificity of these names might suggest that each of these textiles was markedly different from the others. That was not at all the case. These nine Indian textiles can be broken down into just two main types of cotton cloths produced in three distinct regions of the subcontinent. Long cloths were, as the name suggests, long lengths of plain white cotton, while *allejaes* were loom-patterned cottons, that is, with woven stripes or checks. Both were made on South Asia's east coast in Bengal and on the Coromandel (southeast) Coast. *Baftes* and *pautkes* were also plain white cottons (or sometimes dyed a solid color), whereas *nicconees, tapseels, brawles,* and Guinea stuffs were loom-patterned cottons, all produced in Gujarat (now northwest India) (see map 2.1).

The human dimension of these Atlantic trade textiles extended deep into the hinterlands of ports where more and more people came to experience the stimulus of this expanding market. Individual merchants and textile wholesalers who supplied export cottons to England's East India Company agents in Madras (Coromandel Coast) and Surat (Gujarat) were among the most obvious beneficiaries of this trade as long as prices were in their favor and weavers worked productively at their looms. The latter, who were male and usually worked as full-time professionals, were not rich by any means, but they were able to earn modest and relatively secure incomes by negotiating cash advances directly from local merchants to buy cotton fiber or thread and other supplies. In return they would agree to produce a specified quantity of one or another type of cotton textile. And as long as the prices they paid for raw cotton were not too high, these weavers might do reasonably well. Independent suppliers in the rural areas of Gujarat, Bengal, and south India could also profit from Atlantic trade, albeit in smaller ways. Men in agrarian households grew their own cotton, and their wives and daughters cleaned it, spun it into thread, and sometimes prepared the warps, or lengthwise threads, that weavers dressed onto their looms to make the cloth. Cleaning and spinning cotton was extremely labor-intensive, which meant that cotton manufacture relied on an enormous number of spinners. Estimates are that women accounted for more than half of the labor force in the production of Indian export cottons.[4] Modest cash payments for all of these essential preparatory tasks must have made noticeable differences in income for small farmers and their families in towns and in the countryside.

Another major textile product that the RAC sold in Upper Guinea was a linen known by them as *sletias*, after Silesia, the central European region of the Habsburg Empire where these cloths were made (see map 2.1).[5] Linen manufacture for export to world markets had been organized in rural areas there since the sixteenth century. But in this case, and in contrast to Indian cotton manufacturers, the producers hardly benefitted at all from their basic contributions to this labor-intensive process. Production of linen cloth began with the families harvesting home-grown flax, a fibrous grass that they then steeped, crushed, beat, and brushed to break down the stalks and soften the fiber for spinning.[6] Both men and women worked at preparing flax fibers and spinning them into thread, but the bleaching of thread was done by women of the household.

Deprivations these workers experienced under increasing pressures to produce more linens for export were dramatically more onerous than the experiences of their counterparts who produced cotton textiles in India. Silesian workers were serfs and peasants under the control of their feudal landlords and bound by a set of harshly extractive obligations and taxes. Male weavers, for example, had to pay fees to their lord just to be able to continue working at their trade, and they owed other fees for their marriages, for having children, and even for death. It was the lords, not the weavers, who entered into direct commercial agreements with English and Dutch merchants, and it was they who set the conditions of production. Yet despite the servile status and low incomes of workers, the volume of Silesian linen output and sales rose steadily over the seventeenth century. Workers resisted these miserable and worsening conditions by refusing to meet their obligations. At times, they even resorted to violent uprisings. One such instance in the late seventeenth century had to be put down by military force. Meanwhile, landlords were able to keep up production by settling even more desperate landless immigrant spinners and weavers onto their estates. However, the severe constraints of this feudal arrangement led to a contraction and stagnation of Silesian linen manufacture in the eighteenth century—at the time when British textile manufacture was embarking on fundamental technological changes.[7]

Of the RAC exports to Africa that were made domestically in England, woolen textiles were the most steady and significant. Broadcloth, a mainstay of English weaving, was inappropriate for far-off tropical markets because it was too heavy and too high in price. Lighter, cheaper woolens, however, served better in the Guinea trade, among them the simple plain weave textiles known as Welsh plains and bays, which the company bought in modest quantities on advance contracts (see figure 2.1). It was, above all, the development of a product line called "new draperies,"

FIGURE 2.1 European floor loom and weaver. Denis Diderot, et al., *Encyclopédie* (Paris, 1762). Martha Blakeney Hodges Special Collections and University Archives, The University of North Carolina at Greensboro, NC.

copying a major export of the Low Countries already in the sixteenth century, that allowed English woolens to become a successful commodity in warmer climates, including on the West African coast. These textiles, known generically as serges, had a sturdy, combed-wool warp and a soft, carded-wool weft. Their particular names varied widely based on the specifications and locality of their production. The two that were most important to the RAC were the *perpetuana* and the *say*, both of them recognized and highly valued on the Guinea Coast for being hard wearing, lightweight, and relatively cheap woolens.[8]

Supplies of these new draperies came to the RAC in London mostly from the towns and countryside of Devonshire in southwestern England, where they were made by smallholders or landless artisans, many of whom worked seasonally—either independently or under putting-out arrangements with merchants in Exeter (see map 2.1). In the putting-out system, a merchant would sell or lend raw wool to a male weaver who then arranged for it to be cleaned, prepared, and spun into yarn. Shipments of Irish wool with the long fibers requisite for spinning strong worsted thread for weaving serges came in on the northern coast of the peninsula to be carried overland to Exeter. The Irish sources of the weavers' basic raw material thus put merchants in control of weavers' fortunes. Wool with shorter fibers for the weft thread arrived via the coasting trade from the southeast, mainly Kent and Sussex, as well as from around the local countryside. Women and children were the ones who engaged in the primary work of preparing wool and spinning it, and skill levels, as well as wages, varied widely. Then, once a weaver wove the cloth, he sold his yardage either in the serge market or directly back to the merchant who had supplied the wool. It would then be the merchant who had the cloth finished and dyed.[9]

The RAC entered the process at this point. Serges came to them undyed and unfinished, and the company arranged with either an agent in Exeter or a representative in London to manage the transport of their woolen goods to London, where they contracted with specialists in the city to dye, set, press, and pack them for export. Perpetuanas were hard wearing and relatively cheap, and according to over twenty-seven years of reported figures, the company exported more than 170,000 pieces of them to the Guinea Coast. RAC officials, determined to maintain quality controls necessary to prevent spinners and weavers from pilfering wool or thread, instituted standards specifying a certain weight per measured length of woven yardage. The company exported says as well, especially during their first twenty years, when records show they shipped two thousand to three thousand pieces annually. RAC agents on the Gold Coast complained when lack of perpetuanas and says resulted in a falloff in their trade. They also faced keen competition there from the Dutch, who were adept at maintaining their own supplies of serges even into the first years of the 1700s.[10]

Among the RAC exports in the general category of metalwares, its second-most important category of goods, bar iron was the most significant, especially in the second half of the seventeenth century. For example, company records show that of the thirty-five vessels the company sent to Africa in 1685, twenty-nine of them carried the iron bars that supplemented the output of African smelting furnaces. During this period, at least, they did not export any English-made iron. Instead, regular supplies of bar iron came to them from importers in London who specialized in the Baltic trade and who also were shareholders in the company. Export iron circulated in trading networks as intermediate or semifinished goods, which meant that producers worked it into hammered iron bars that could later be turned into tools or other implements elsewhere, sometimes an ocean away. The RAC's main source of iron in the seventeenth century was Sweden (see map 2.1), where ironworkers produced bar iron for export in the form of bars of standardized dimensions and weight. In the mid-1680s, the company's contract with their supplier stipulated that the bars had to be stamped with a trade mark and weigh in at seventy-five to eighty bars per ton, or twenty-eight to thirty pounds per bar. Between 1673 and 1704, the RAC reexported well over five thousand tons of Swedish bar iron (around four hundred thousand bars) to the Guinea Coast.[11]

Sweden had only recently shifted production of iron toward the export trade. Previously, between the twelfth and seventeenth centuries, iron ore had been mined and smelted into iron metal in communally held blast furnaces and then processed yet further into units of workable iron for local and regional users. Agrarian households living in the ore resource areas carried out this work seasonally and on a relatively small scale. In the early seventeenth century, however, larger-scale specialized ironworks began to be set up by individuals who acted on new economic policies that were put into place by the Swedish Crown. Outside the areas of ore deposits, merchants and noblemen set about establishing privately owned estates designed to combine agricultural production with the production of bar iron for export. These new ironworking estates generated more refined and standardized iron in greater quantities than ever before. And as iron exports rose steadily during the seventeenth century, the Crown also set up a Board of Mines to monitor and regulate them.[12]

Although some independent peasant ironworkers continued to produce bar iron on a small scale, a majority of agrarian households produced iron for export and found themselves working under a much more rigid and restrictive division of labor. Crown regulations divided the stages of mining, smelting, and forging more sharply from one another by geography and by workforce. This scheme restricted peasant ironworkers to just the primary stages of mining and smelting the ore. Secondary manufacture, that is, refining smelted iron and forging it into bars, was far more profitable. Under the new regulations, it was carried out separately in workshops on the private estates. These were strategically located in provinces adjacent to where the ore deposits were and where the mining and smelting went on. Some of the larger estates also began to operate their forges year round.

In this new arrangement, the peasant workers came under much closer scrutiny and direct control. Royal decrees restricted access to iron ore only to those farmers who were engaged in pig-iron production for the estates, and each mining district was put on a work schedule. Labor in mining—the extracting of ore from the pit mines, sorting it and loading it into horse-drawn carts, and transporting it to the blast furnace—was shared by the farmer's household. So, too, was the work of making the charcoal fuel used in smelting the ore. But since most of this work, including the actual smelting process, was carried out in winter, peasant households could potentially realize noticeable economic benefits in the form of either subsistence or cash by entering into contracts to supply the ironworks estates with pig iron. Over time, however, as ironmasters running the estates sought to increase production and lower costs, peasant workers came under harsher conditions and constraints. More of them found that the terms of their contracts that laid out the amount and price of the pig iron they were to produce ended up leaving them bound to an ironmaster by debt. And if they were able instead to contract with merchants who sold pig iron to the estates, indebtedness would more often be the result in that case as well. Thus, for most Swedish ironworkers, intensification of iron production for Atlantic trade was clearly not a boon, and so those who could do so retaliated by embezzling raw materials or working on their own accounts.[13]

Second in significance among RAC exports of metalwares was a wide variety of drinking vessels, plates, and containers made of copper, brass, or pewter. Copper- and brasswares of English manufacture were not exported at this time, and so, as with iron bars, the company relied on re-exports from elsewhere, in this case mainly northern Germany via the Baltic trade (see map 2.1). Cast copper bars, an intermediate good, were one important category of these wares, as were finished copper basins that the company acquired from suppliers in Amsterdam. Containers made of brass required several stages of manufacture, beginning with the alloying of the metal, then the pressing of it into sheets, next the skilled battery work of hammering the sheets out over specially designed anvils and molds, and finally turning out the finished trade good (see figure 2.2). The RAC brasswares were mainly basins, pans, and kettles made in a variety of shapes and sizes especially for the Guinea trade and known by particular names such as tackings, neptunes, diglings, wire-bound kettles, and driven kettles. Pewter, an alloy of tin, had been made in England since the eleventh century, and by the mid-fourteenth century pewter craftsmen had formed a guild in London. They, too, hammered out their pewter

FIGURE 2.2 A coppersmith at work. Image after Jost Amman, 1568, H. Hamilton, *The English Brass and Copper Industries to 1800* (London, 1926).

sheets into a variety of wares such as basins, jugs, plates, tankards, and porringers. It is unclear how much of England's domestic pewter actually contributed to the Guinea trade, as there were ongoing problems with foreign competitors who sold at much lower prices but did so by cutting back the alloy's tin content. Another problem faced by English pewterers was a custom fee that was added to discourage exports. It is therefore likely that the RAC at this time had to rely on reexports of pewter as well.[14] All of these metal goods were significant in the seventeenth-century RAC trade on the Upper Guinea Coast, where local people put them to many uses ranging from important social and ceremonial presentations to the productive work of processing beeswax and intensifying the making of sea salt.

Firearms were a third significant component of RAC exports of metal-wares, supplied in the early years of their trade mostly by the Dutch. English guns were difficult to sell as exports, and even when London gunsmiths produced copies of the popular Dutch models, their asking price was not competitive. Undeterred, they petitioned against the company for import-ing cheap trade guns and in 1685 succeeded in getting the practice prohib-ited by an act of Parliament. The RAC managed to avoid the prohibition by sending ships to Amsterdam, where they were laden with guns and powder and then sent directly on to the Guinea Coast. But in just over a decade a variety of firearms, including muskets, were being produced for the export trade in England—due in large part to Europe's wars in the 1690s and early 1700s, which brought expansions in arms production. Between 1701 and 1704, the RAC was able to send over thirty-two thousand muskets, carbines, pistols, fowling pieces, and fusees (light muskets) to the Guinea Coast, many of them purchased on contract.[15]

Trade guns, however, as well as gunpowder, were notoriously inconsis-tent in quality, and buyers on the Guinea Coast were quick to notice. They deemed guns and powder offered by Dutch and Danish traders to be the best. Moreover, the parts of firearms that were made of iron, even those that were polished steel, corroded quickly in the high humidity of the trop-ics. Thus, buyers came to prefer special mountings made of brass.[16] It was therefore not uncommon for RAC factors at the trading forts to find them-selves with old or damaged firearms on hand and in some cases choosing to send them back to the company in London. Attempts to have repairs done were not entirely successful. In one instance in 1704 the company asked a group of ten London gunsmiths to evaluate the condition of five hundred fusees they had contracted to be repaired in Plymouth. The gunsmiths de-clared in a deposition that the weapons in question had not been cleaned and repaired in a workmanlike manner and were therefore not suitable for market.[17] This incident demonstrates how troublesome it was for the RAC to monitor the condition of and repair its goods, adding yet another set of costs the company had to absorb.

The third major category of goods that the RAC sent to Upper Guinea, after textiles and metalwares, was beads, arguably one of the most misunderstood items in world trade, frequently characterized disparagingly as "trinkets." Eric Williams, famous historian of Britain's African trade, presented a particularly contemptuous version of this stereotype: "The slave cargoes were incomplete without the "pacotille," the sundry items and gewgaws which appealed to the Africans' love of bright colors and for which, after having sold their fellows, they would, late in the nineteenth century, part with their land and grant mining concessions."[18]

So goes the "gewgaw myth" that ignorant primitives could be hoodwinked into giving up valuable goods, property, and even people with the offer of worthless trinkets.[19] Of course the myth makes no sense economically and is an artifact of cultural chauvinism. A more appropriate approach would be to consider instead why people desired and chose certain trade goods over human labor and access to land. In this case, why was it that so many people in Africa valued beads so highly?

Beads were a form of money. The long history and prominent role of beads in ancient and Islamic trade made strong cultural imprints throughout the world, including in Africa. Whether made of stone, organic material, or glass, beads were acquired, circulated, hoarded as a store of wealth, worn as jewelry, buried as treasure, then perhaps unearthed by scavengers and polished to be exchanged anew. As was noted in chapter 1, imported beads were prominent among trade and burial goods found in some of the earliest archaeological sites in West Africa, which show evidence of the Islamic caravan trade across the Sahara. With the rise of the Atlantic era, Europeans built on and adapted to this long-standing commercial and cultural foundation.

In their dealings on the Guinea Coast, the RAC noted the well-established markets there for particular kinds of beads. On the Upper Guinea Coast, people used coral (a red organic material), crystal, and glass beads as well as cowry shells as cash to purchase food or drink or to pay a person for labor or services. People also hoarded these small currency units for making larger purchases or for major family investments. Crystal beads were desired up the Gambia River, where they were necessary in the trade assortments for captives and export goods. Coral and amber also served as jewelry on the Upper Guinea Coast, worn by prominent titled women and valued by them as highly as gold and silver. Beads of coral were also in great demand farther down the coast in the Benin Kingdom, where they were displayed ceremonially as part of the royal regalia. And cowries were an essential item in Euro-African trade all along the Bight of Benin.

The Dutch East India Company brought cowries—a shell currency originally from the Maldive Islands in the Indian Ocean that circulated in and around Islamic trading zones—in quantity as ballast for its ships on their voyages homeward. In the early years of the RAC monopoly, they purchased their cowries in Amsterdam, but it did not take long for London dealers who specialized in other Indian Ocean goods to become the company's main suppliers. For their early supplies of clear crystal and colored glass beads, the company relied on Holland until London dealers developed reliable contacts to get them direct from producers in Venice. The RAC managed to acquire a direct supplier of German amber, a fossilized yellowish resin that is hard as stone, when one of their dealers in Baltic goods put them in contact with an associate in Danzig (see map 2.1). Beads made of coral also came from various sources via London dealers.[20] Together, these efforts demonstrate that the RAC had clearly learned the high value and importance of beads in their trading even though they were far from easy to store and transport. There was always a potential for losses when loose beads were packed in barrels for shipment, an expense which had to be considered alongside the labor costs of having them strung.[21]

RAC: Shipping and Coasting in Northern Guinea

Atlantic trade along the Upper Guinea Coast in the second half of the seventeenth century followed a complex and shifting set of overland, riverine, and coastal traffic patterns. In the interior of western Africa, the thriving trans-Saharan systems continued to move captives and goods such as salt, gold, and kola interregionally, primarily on routes running along north–south axes. Meanwhile, the newly developing Atlantic system intensified a regional east–west commerce that previously had been relatively small in scale. Formerly the riverways attracted inland merchants to the coast, eager to exchange their locally made cotton textiles with producers of sea salt. Now the maritime traffic from Europe was turning these networks into major corridors of overseas global trade.[22] Employees of the RAC stationed on the Upper Guinea Coast thus encountered and worked within an increasingly complicated network of multilateral trade in western Africa and, no matter what their employers in London might have wished, had no choice but to adapt.

Company employees conducted their operations from three island trading forts: James Island at the mouth of the Gambia River; Bence Island in the Sierra Leone estuary to the south; and York Island a bit beyond at Sherbro.[23] The RAC presence, however, was not simply confined to these forts.

Staff at each main station established additional satellite out-factories in various locales and also developed contacts at regular ports of call. When combined, these extended their influence all along the coast from Cape Verde in the north to Cape Mount in the south, a stretch of over seven hundred miles (map 2.2). This vast trading network made waterborne traffic in, out of, and around the forts and factories an ongoing logistical

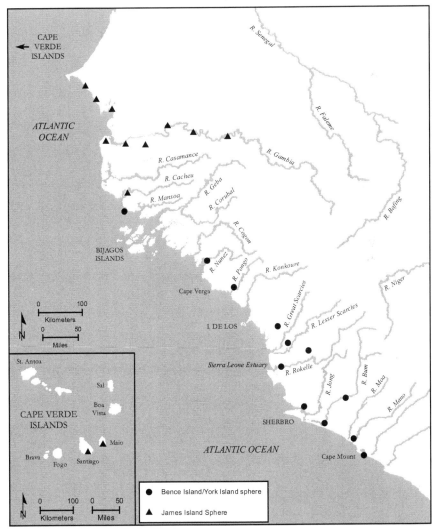

MAP 2.2 Royal African Company forts, outstations, and coasting destinations, Upper Guinea Coast, seventeenth c. *Map by Brian Edward Balsley, GISP.*

challenge. It involved not only the heavily fitted and armed ocean-going sailing vessels coming in from London and departing for London or the Americas but also all sorts of smaller sloops and smacks engaged in shorter voyages to and from offshore islands or along coastal waters. Still smaller work boats and canoes propelled manually by oarsmen were essential for transporting people and small cargoes along rivers and between ship and shore. Thus, the trading forts served as hubs for a much broader sphere of commercial traffic and activity.

The forts operated both independently and in cooperation with one another at various times. Ocean vessels from London would periodically arrive on the Guinea Coast loaded with provisions, supplies, and trade goods along with company instructions on where to put in and unload, what return cargoes to seek, and where to take them. Agents at the forts had their own plans and pressing needs, oftentimes in their own interests, which could delay a vessel in port or divert it into local affairs or business. As the northernmost fort, James Island was usually the first stop for supply ships arriving from London on the Upper Guinea Coast. This priority caused resentments at times among the agents downwind at Bence and York Islands to the point where they sent letters of complaint when they felt they were not getting their fair share of goods or when vessels were being delayed in continuing southward. In one instance in 1679, the agent at Bence Island reported that he had received letters and invoices from the company for the last three ships they had sent down but that most of the trade goods they covered had been unloaded at James Island. He claimed that as a result he had not been able to take an active part in that year's trade in captives and ivory.[24]

Ship captains followed their instructions when it was possible or when it best suited them, but unpredictable events and changing conditions had a way of intervening and altering their courses. One voyage of the *Benjamin* serves to illustrate these kinds of complications. This particular vessel was recorded arriving from London at James Island, Gambia, in early November 1685. Its incoming cargo was relatively small, having been selected and organized specifically for the Cape Verde Island market where the overseas goods were to be exchanged for "high cloths," the elaborately patterned cotton textiles produced at Santiago. They presumably were to be sent to Cape Coast Castle on the Gold Coast. However, for unknown reasons the captain decided to go instead to Gambia. Captain, crew, and vessel apparently remained there for the next nine months. A company scribe at James Island recorded in late January that a funeral had taken place for John Samuel, a crew member of the *Benjamin,* and his unsold personal effects (including one boy captive) were entered into the James Island stores.[25] In June the *Benjamin* joined with one of the company yachts in a coasting voyage north to Joal on the Petite Côte, returning with forty-eight captives, ivory, several thousand hides, and a cake of wax. While there they lost a "company slave" on salary by drowning—whether by accident or in attempting to escape is not known. Then in August 1686 the *Benjamin* was loaded up with a cargo of captives and provisions for the middle passage to the West Indies. Half of the captives were branded to identify them as coming from the fort at Sierra Leone, having been brought to James Island in July on the *Charles,* with the other half branded to identify them as "Gambia negroes." The *Benjamin* then set sail for Antigua, even though the company had consigned the *Charles's* captives to Barbados.[26] RAC officials in London frequently complained about such drastic changes in their orders and questioned why they occurred.

The Atlantic export trade at the forts was variable and also multilateral. Although Atlantic trade is conventionally described as *trans-*Atlantic, emphasizing crossings between the Americas and Afro-Eurasia, vessels leaving the Upper Guinea Coast in the late seventeenth century did not always follow that pattern. Neither was it the case that they specialized in one particular route. An example to illustrate the variety of voyages and shipping destinations is the vessel *Delight,* under the command of Captain William Barton, which delivered captives to Barbados in March 1683. Later that year he brought the *Delight* into port at James Island, although the exact date was not recorded. In late January and early February 1684, Barton took her up the Gambia River in search of exports, bringing back to the fort six captives and a load of ivory tusks, beeswax, and hides. Made ready for her return trip and laden with this substantial cargo of ivory, wax, and hides (the fate of the captives is not known), the *Delight* set off soon thereafter in the middle of March for London. By October, after a six-month turnaround, Captain Barton had brought the ship back to James Island with another cargo of overseas goods. Loaded up again with ivory, wax, hides, damaged guns and muskets, as well as some samples of local indigo, the *Delight* left in mid-December for London. This time, however, her captain was James Bardwell. What had happened to Barton is unclear, but Cleeve, the company agent at Gambia, wrote to them that aboard the ship were two of Barton's "negroes."[27] If these captives managed to survive the voyage, they would have joined the small but growing number of people of color who in one way or another landed in England, not the Americas, after having been torn from their families and homelands.

RAC officials in London designed their cargoes of overseas goods specifically for certain markets on the Guinea Coast and sent their ships with instructions to load up and deliver equally specific types of cargoes. Depending on what these cargoes were, a ship would either return to England or sail across the Atlantic. Exports varied from place to place and over time. Records of voyages in the late seventeenth century show that all of the forts on the Upper Guinea Coast were exporting to both European and American markets, and each had a clear profile of available exports. James Island sent captives and provisions to the Caribbean and to Virginia and also had a strong trade in ivory, beeswax, and hides back to England. Fewer records exist for Bence Island, but there, too, captives and provisions were exported, mainly to Barbados, while ivory, beeswax, camwood (a red dyewood), and gum went to England. York Island in Sherbro was primarily an exporter of camwood and also sent ivory and occasionally gum to England. Fewer and smaller cargoes of captives crossed over from Sherbro to either Jamaica or the Leeward Islands in the Caribbean.[28]

A significant feature of this time period was the company's interest in expanding this range of export commodities. Its most energetic and costly effort was an attempt to organize large scale export-oriented indigo production on the Upper Guinea Coast in the 1680s and '90s, but they also requested samples of Senegal gum, cleaned raw cotton, and lime, among other things, which agents from time to time sent to London for their inspection.[29] Thus a view of Atlantic trade from the perspective of the Upper Guinea Coast at this particular time reveals it as an export trade in captives, mostly to the Americas, and in intermediate goods, commodities, and occasionally captives directly to Europe. It was not simply and only an Atlantic slave trade.

Logistically on the coast, export-oriented commerce from Upper Guinea was both a fort-based trade and a ship-based trade. Local African merchants and all sorts of other individuals regularly traveled from the interior to the forts to trade on a small scale or sometimes in bulk. This fort trade was limited and subject to fluctuations, especially in the face of serious competition from "interlopers," that is, independent European or Euro-African merchants who were an alternative source of overseas imports. Company agents who were most effective in serving their London employers' interests had to work hard to stay well-informed about interlopers and their where-abouts, for they were often believed to be offering local sellers superior goods and better export prices. Some were even known to be direct threats to the security of the company's employees and property and were willing at times to risk seizing or even destroying ships and their cargoes. For all of these reasons it made sense to RAC employees on the Upper Guinea Coast to supplement the fort trade with ship trading. Agents at each island station organized visits to their out-factories and also periodically sent their small craft on coasting voyages or up rivers to known bulking centers on their banks where goods could be had at prices that were lower than on the coast. Carrying overseas goods out to these inland points and then bringing ex-port goods back to the fort required having a variety of small craft on hand and in good repair as well as having sufficiently loyal and armed manpower to ward off thieves and interlopers and, in the case of the transport of cap-tives, to prevent escapes or insurrections.

The locations of out-factories and coasting destinations for each fort were chosen strategically (see map 2.2). At any given time, James Island had eight to ten or more out-factories, some staffed with just a soldier or two and others with as many as four or five company men. In most cases they were located nearby, that is, in and around the mouth of the Gambia River at sites where Portuguese traders and missionaries had been based earlier and where their Luso-African descendants remained. Major Luso-African communities were the factories at Vintang on the south bank of the Gambia River and Geregia, which was located about fifteen miles up Vintang Creek.[30] The latter factory was known to the RAC agents and em-ployees as Sangrigoe, a toponym probably derived from the Portuguese *São Gregório*. On the north bank of the river directly across from James Island was Juffure, not far from a former Portuguese settlement named San Do-mingo. Juffure served not only as an important RAC factory but also as the fort's main source of fresh water.[31] Tankular, known in the RAC sources as Anchorwall, located about twenty miles upriver, was yet another site where earlier Portuguese traders had been based. Farther up the Gambia River were major stations such as Mangegar, approximately fifty miles from the fort, and Barrakunda, some two hundred miles up, both of them located on the north bank at entrepôts where long-distance trade routes intersected with riverine commerce.

River traffic to and from the out-factories supplied the fort with addi-tional captives, ivory tusks, processed hides for export, and locally made cotton textiles, among other goods and provisions. But agents in charge at James Island, never knowing exactly if, when, or how many vessels would arrive from England, had to further augment their stores of exports by sending their sloops on coasting voyages. In the 1680s, vessels went northward twice a year to the Petite Côte, where they had contacts who supplied them with captives, ivory tusks, and hides. Voyages southward to Cacheu were even more worth the risk as that trading center of the Portuguese became one of the RAC's most important sources of processed beeswax during the late seventeenth century.[32] All of this local and regional commercial activity made James Island, at least in peacetime, a bustling center of the Upper Guinea Coast's Atlantic trade.

Similar networks of out-factories, as well as established destinations for coasting voyages, centered on Bence Island and York Island. Agents at Bence Island were able to supplement local fort trading in and around the Sierra Leone estuary by maintaining an out-factory about fifteen or twenty miles up Port Loko Creek, a small stream flowing westward just north of and parallel to the Rokelle River. Both waterways emptied into the estuary about five miles east of the fort (see figure 2.3). From Loko factory the fort received ivory tusks, some captives and camwood, and rice provisions. Another station known as Samo was much farther away beyond the estuary and up the coast, more than sixty miles from Bence Island. Agents enlisted the company longboat, equipped with mast, sails, and oars, to travel northward along the coast past the Great Scarcies River to the next waterway, the Melakori, and up that river to the Samo station. There it unloaded overseas goods and loaded up captives and ivory to take back to the fort.

Another important out-factory was known to English speakers as Tassily. Maintaining contact with Tassily was exceptionally challenging because it was located at some distance north on an island just south of Cacheu, over three hundred miles up the coast from Bence Island. It supplied the fort with ivory, wax, some captives, and locally made cotton cloths. And Bence Island agents also organized northward coasting voyages to the mouths of the Nunez, Pongo, and Scarcies Rivers to acquire captives and ivory tusks. In the case of York Island, two of its out-factories were not far from the fort: one called Boome was located just up the Bum River; and the other was at Kittam, a waterway running parallel to the coast just south of the inlet leading into the Sherbro estuary. A third factory was an additional fifty miles or so to the south at Gallinas. All three of these stations supplied exports of camwood, along with some ivory. To maintain inventories

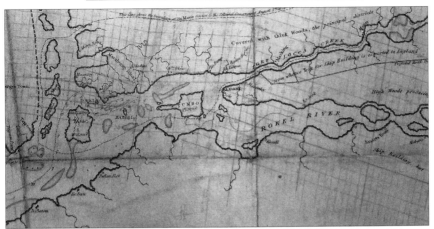

FIGURE 2.3 Map showing Port Loko Creek and the Rokelle River emptying into the Sierra Leone Estuary. The National Archives of the UK, CO 700/SierraLeone3.

for unpredictable arrivals of company ships, agents at Bence and York sent coasting voyages north to the Pongo and Nunez Rivers for captives and additional stores of ivory tusks. They also made southward voyages to Cape Mount, just beyond Gallinas, to bring back the locally made cotton cloths and tailored cotton shirts and trousers that were necessary for exchange in the camwood trade.[33]

Taken together, the locations of RAC forts, stations, and coasting destinations map out where and how Anglo-African commerce operated at this time. And over the passing years and decades the many and varied people living and working within this trading and intercommunicating zone selectively adopted shared habits, languages, tastes, and fashions, thereby creating a new and dynamic "creole" culture borne of African, Asian, Euro-African, and European elements.[34] Developing quite differently from the ways creole languages were created, creole material cultures were yet another notable result of trade and intensive social interaction on an intercontinental scale. A number of the people who appear in the following chapters decidedly embraced a new "mixed" Afro-Eurasian culture as their own. They continually renewed it in the way they dressed, carried out ceremonies, and hosted social occasions as representations of their widening multicultural world.

Western African Merchants and Atlantic Exports

Acquiring captives to labor in their American colonies was one of the main motives behind the formation of the RAC in 1672, and the company's shareholders must have looked forward to what they believed would be very good prospects for their investment. Adding to their confidence were the potential profits to be made in Europe on such African commodities as gold, ivory, camwood, and hides, as well as the American tropical products such as cane sugar, which was then starting to reach England regularly from the West Indies.[35] They could not have foreseen how badly the RAC would fail financially. Many factors contributed to this failure, among them the unprecedented management challenges brought on by the enormous scale of the company's commercial organization; the attempts to control its many employees and their diverse and distant activities; the high risks inherent in maritime trade, especially the trade in slaves; and the economic risks of any commodity market, such as the relatively low price for sugar during the time of their monopoly. In the end, they never realized their ultimate goal, which was to make substantial returns on the investments made by their shareholders.[36]

But even though the company shareholders in England were not seeing the net profits they had hoped to see in Atlantic trade, other individuals did see some success, including specialized merchants engaged in long-distance trade in the interior regions of West Africa. Captives and export goods came to the Upper Guinea Coast from places inland and sometimes over very long distances. A majority of those merchants were Muslims, in some cases Muslim clerics literate in Arabic. And their commonly held religious beliefs, cultural values, and legal institutions gave them a sense of shared identity and trust and recourse to courts when disputes arose. Adding to their success was the efficacious use they made of an important West African social and economic strategy often termed the "landlord-stranger" relationship.[37] In it, traders in widespread merchant communities, such as the Juula described in the preceding chapter, were "strangers" traveling to visit and exchange commodities in resident "landlord" communities. A Mandinka version of this widespread practice in Senegambia recognized two different sets of obligations for properly hosting visiting traders, based on the degree to which the trader-stranger was able to get along on his own or not. If he was almost entirely dependent on his host-landlord, he might end up marrying into the landlord's family and settling permanently. Such stable relationships enabled groups of merchants to create widespread networks of strategically located individuals and households for conducting their regional and interregional trade on a regular basis.[38]

Inland "stranger" merchants organized caravans of porters and donkeys laden with trade goods and conducted them across the savanna and Sahel regions of West Africa. Along the way, they gathered commercial intelligence about markets and bulking centers and guarded this valuable intelligence fiercely. By the early seventeenth century, Juula had extended their trading spheres into the Gambia watershed and the advancing frontiers of Atlantic trade. So, too, had the Jahaanke (also described in chapter 1), who specialized in the overland trade routes between the entrepôt of Barrakunda on the Gambia River and the upper Niger region over four hundred miles to the east.[39] Such merchants were able to achieve their commercial success by linking the centuries-old trade in West Africa's interior regions with the more recent and growing trade in the Atlantic basin. Caravans led by other "stranger" merchant groups varied in size from smaller ones that might have forty to one hundred men to others made up of more than a thousand armed men and hundreds of captive porters.[40]

Captives who in the past might have found themselves forced to cross the Sahara were sometimes directed instead toward the Atlantic in the late seventeenth century. Figure 2.4 shows a misleadingly sanitized and sche-

matic drawing of two captives being purchased on the coast of Senegambia at that time. Much larger numbers of captives traveled in caravans. How many arrived at the RAC forts is not precisely known, nor is it known exactly how many were put on company vessels bound for the Americas or for England. Even less is known about them as individuals, such as their names, their origins, how they became captives, or how many died on

FIGURE 2.4 Schematic drawing of the trade in captives, Senegambia Region. François Froger, *Relation d'un voyage fait en 1695, 1696, et 1697* (Paris, 1700). John Carter Brown Library, Providence, RI. *Internet Archive*. Web. 16 Nov. 2016.

the way to the coast.[41] In an early estimate for the number of slaves sold by the company in the English West Indies, Davies put the total at 90,768, which is low even as an American import figure reduced by mortality at sea from the total captives boarded in Africa.[42] A more recent rough estimate for the number of slaves disembarked in the British West Indies by British carriers between 1672 and 1711 puts the total at 327,700, more than three times as many, but this figure is not limited to RAC vessels.[43] An illegal and largely unrecorded private trade, especially between the Upper Guinea Coast and the Caribbean, would have added significantly to this total.[44] But whatever the precise numbers, shipping human cargoes was without doubt important company business even in this early period and despite recurring losses from high rates of mortality in addition to shipwrecks, warfare, and plunder at sea.

Of the three English forts on the Upper Guinea Coast, the one on James Island was the main contributor to the company's export trade in captives. Local traders intermittently brought in small numbers of them for sale, but most came from up the Gambia River, either delivered by the company's out-factories there or purchased on voyages upriver in company vessels. It is likely that even before the eighteenth century some of these captives would have come from regions far in the interior via overland caravans organized by either Juula or Jahaanke merchants. Descriptions by observers of slave trading on the Upper Guinea Coast in the second half of the seventeenth century refer to particular groups of captives from the interior such as the Tanda and Bambara, whose communities lived beyond the headwaters of the Gambia River (see map 2.1). Their origins give some indication of how far the Atlantic trade frontier had reached by then, even if they do not fully resolve the question of who the captives were.[45] RAC exports from Bence Island show similarly diverse sources, with some captives brought in from nearby coastal areas while others came from interior regions either by canoe or overland along the rivers' banks. It is very likely that among the latter were captives from in and around the highlands of Futa Jallon, where many of the river systems south of the Gambia originated. Voyages from the Bence Island fort to its out-factory at Samo, as well as coasting trips to the Nunez, Pongo, and Scarcies Rivers, returned with captives who also may have been forced to travel great distances overland as well as by river.[46]

Captives who survived the long journey to the coast, the dreadful time there in pens and sheds waiting for company ships to arrive, and the treacherous middle passage across the Atlantic were more often than not disembarked by RAC agents in England's American colonies. Voyage data for the second half of the seventeenth century suggest that at this time a great majority of slave exports on English vessels went to Barbados and Jamaica, where sugar estates were multiplying in number. The Leeward Islands received smaller and fewer cargoes of captives, as did Maryland and Virginia.[47] There was also a considerable further trade in slaves within and around the Caribbean and mainland America once they arrived from across the Atlantic. Also, although recorded only sporadically and therefore incompletely and not included in the online database of transatlantic voyages, there are the small but not insignificant numbers of captives the RAC exported to England. Between 1679 and 1704, there appears to have been a slow stream of "negroes," mostly men and boys, aboard vessels headed from the Guinea Coast to London. Many of these were deemed prerogatives of ship captains to send home as part of their commission on sales of slaves and the goods they shipped to Upper Guinea. Company agents also sought permission to send home captives as their own servants or as "gifts" to family members or colleagues. Dalby Thomas, the RAC's chief agent on the Gold Coast, could hardly contain himself as he wrote to London in 1704 that he was sending a gift of "Black Boys" to four members of the RAC Court of Assistants and that he intended to send a "Boy" to all of his friends.[48] It is debatable precisely what these boys' legal status would have been once they arrived in England, where slavery was not recognized in English law, and so the topic continues to generate a wide range of viewpoints.[49]

The major commodities the RAC exported from West Africa to England were gold, ivory, beeswax, and camwood (known as redwood at Bence and York Islands), assembled from outstations at the company's forts. Practically all the gold came from the Gold Coast and went to the Royal Mint, where it was made into special gold coins called guineas. They bore on one side a miniature image of an elephant, the RAC symbol, and between 1673 and 1713 over five hundred thousand guineas were struck. But the company's contribution to England's monetary system was, on balance, a relatively minor one. The other three commodities were ultimately destined for England's manufacturing workshops. The RAC's ivory, which came mainly from Upper Guinea and the Ivory Coast, went to makers of swords, cutlery, combs, furniture, and specialty items such as inlaid or carved ivory boxes. Company records show a total of about 856 tons of ivory brought in, or somewhere between twenty thousand and thirty-eight thousand tusks, depending on their size. Not all of these would have been of suitable quality, however, as is evident in the wide range in prices paid for ivory at company sales. Beeswax, evidently more consistent in processed quality, garnered more standard prices. The company shipped a total of just over three hundred tons of it to England, mainly from the Upper Guinea Coast, and most of it was used for the manufacture of candles. Cargoes of camwood were far more profitable for the company than either ivory or wax, especially during the late seventeenth century when prices for it on the Upper Guinea Coast were still quite low. Company ships conveyed a total of over two thousand tons to England, where it underwent processing to be used as a dye for woolen textiles. Before the turn of the century most of the company's camwood came via their York Island fort.[50]

Ivory passed through all three of the company forts on the Upper Guinea Coast, with James Island as the main supplier. By the late seventeenth century, herds of elephants near the coast had already been mostly killed off, which meant that the frontier for supplies of ivory was moving steadily inland. In this respect exports of ivory paralleled exports of captives since in both cases new source areas in the hinterlands of the coast grew in importance over time (see map 2.1). The hunting of elephants was carried out only by the most skilled and experienced hunters and only rarely with guns until the late eighteenth century. Hunters also customarily owed a share or fee to masters of the lands in which the kill took place, which might be assessed as one of the two tusks. These constraints placed limits on the amount of ivory that would be available for export, leading unskilled ordinary people to scavenge for elephant carcasses and tusks in the countryside. Merchants then transported gathered or hunted ivory in caravans overland, carried either by donkey or by captives forced to serve as porters, to bulking centers. Elephant ivory from the remote interior was supplemented by the ivory of hippopotamuses living closer to the Atlantic shore. Rivers along the Upper Guinea Coast hosted large populations of these "water horses," which were hunted as a source of food and also to reduce a destructive nuisance to rice-growing farmers. Their tusks were smaller than those of elephants, and the ivory was of inferior quality. Nevertheless, RAC agents included hippo tusks from time to time in their purchases. Company employees sorted the tusks of both species by size, and judging by the wide price spreads for ivory sold at auction in London, there was a very great range in quality.[51]

Beeswax was a byproduct of honey production, which was practiced in many areas of the Upper Guinea Coast and its hinterlands. Major specialists were Mandinka beekeepers living in communities around the Gambia watershed. They intensified and managed the production of honey by constructing portable hives that they hung conveniently in nearby trees. Although honey was important as the region's major source of sugar, even as imported cane sugar was becoming more available, the wax of the drained honeycombs had apparently not previously been exploited. Discovering there was a market for beeswax among Europeans, beekeepers seized it early on in the trade, although it required important additional labor. After harvesting the honeycomb and squeezing the honey from it, the wax had to be processed and consolidated for transport and sale. Basic processing was done by melting the wax in cauldrons of boiling water and molding it into cakes. Processing it even further, however, was well worth the effort. Straining and filtering the wax through cloth resulted in a much cleaner and better quality of wax that sold at higher prices. Juula and other merchant groups took to buying up semiprocessed wax from others and reprocessing and molding it into large cakes that could weigh anywhere between 20 and 130 pounds.[52] Luso-African merchants also were among some of the most prominent wax exporters. Their entrepôt of Cacheu became a major source of processed beeswax cakes for the RAC at Gambia and also at Bence Island via the company agents stationed at Tassily. It is very likely that much of Cacheu's large-scale processing of wax for export was done by slaves.[53]

Camwood was a highly profitable tropical commodity for the RAC, especially during the seventeenth century.[54] It had been important to England already in the years between 1623 and 1648 when a Sherbro king granted rights to a London firm, appropriately known as John Wood and Company, to purchase it for export. Camwood trees could be found growing throughout the coastal forests of the Upper Guinea Coast and had to be felled and trimmed into billets, then transported to vessels waiting at the nearest riverside. The RAC focused their energies on the Bum River near York Island and the Rokelle River in the Sierra Leone estuary. Men from farming communities in these watersheds did the work of cutting and moving logs during the dry season before preparing fields for planting. Hauling and transporting shiploads of timber down to the coast had to be carefully calculated to take advantage of times during the rainy season when water levels were high enough for floating such heavy loads. In 1681 there was an unusually heavy rainfall that enabled an RAC agent to ship an impressive 195 tons of camwood that year. Once it reached the coast, agents sorted the camwood into lots by stacking it in a stockade that measured out one quintal, or hundredweight, of the wood.[55]

In Senegambia, hides were yet another important commodity sent to England in the late seventeenth century, but there are no aggregate figures for the numbers shipped during this period. Supplies of hides came in to James Island regularly, especially in the dry season, and live cattle were also purchased and kept at Juffure as future provisions. Cattle-raising areas were located mainly in the interior regions of the Upper Guinea Coast in particular zones that were free of the tsetse fly species most lethal to cattle. Relatively open, cleared areas of savanna north of the Gambia River best met these criteria. Cattle production on a large scale was an intensive and specialized activity that required careful management of the herds. Specialists among the Moorish herders north of the Senegal River had developed effective strategies that took advantage of seasonal changes in rainfall and markets, moving their herds southward with the onset of the dry season to maintain access to good grazing and also gaining potential for better meat prices. There were other specialist cattle herders among Fulbe-speakers, who not only kept their own large herds but were hired by others to care for their cattle during the rainy season when they drove the animals north and away from planted fields. Areas south of the Gambia River were generally not suitable for raising cattle except for the fly-free Futa Jallon highlands. There it was Fulbe herders who were the great cattle producers. It is very likely that most of Gambia's cowhide exports came from the cattle of these groups of specialized Moorish and Fulbe herders. The hides the RAC acquired on the Petite Côte, said to be the best in the seventeenth century, could have been from either group or both, whereas Fulbe herds would have been the main source of cowhides they purchased along the upper Gambia River. Moreover, a variety of other hides from game animals such as antelope, hunted in the wild, were also available on the Gambia.[56]

The leather workers who transformed cattle skins into cowhides are far less identifiable than the herders who produced and managed the cattle. Much has been written about specialist artisans in Mande communities and whether or not they belonged to so-called castes, among them the leatherworkers known as *garankéw*.[57] However, these male artisans specialized in secondary manufacture, that is, the making of finished and sometimes elaborately patterned and ornamented leather goods. Meanwhile, primary manufacture—the technological processes of turning skins into hides and tanned leather—has been given relatively little attention by historians. What few descriptions we have from historical sources are not very informative. One of them, a listing of trade goods available on the

Gambia River in the middle of the seventeenth century, mentions five different types of hides and skins: raw hides; calf-skins; goat-skins; antelope-skins; and "salted" hides. It notes also that large numbers of the last were exported from the Petite Côte and that they were considered to be of very good quality. Raw hides were apparently available in some locales, and the account goes on to briefly describe only that process, with no mention of tanning. A much later description written during the early 1930s in Senegal lays out the different stages of processing hides but presents them in a very general and cursory manner, suggesting that the observer was not very well-informed about the basic technologies and their possible variants. Moreover, there is no mention of exactly who it was who did this kind of work or the degree to which it was specialized at that time.[58]

These points are especially important because the numbers of hides exported in the seventeenth century were, at times, impressive. Figures from the Dutch trade on the Petite Côte in the 1620s and '30s show that for eight of the nine years of records over twenty thousand hides were shipped out annually. Their hide exports appear to have reached a peak in the 1670s when in one year the number was between forty and fifty thousand. RAC export figures for hides were comparable to those of the Dutch, with about thirteen thousand shipped from Gambia to England between November 1679 and April 1680. However, by the end of the seventeenth century the prices for hides had fallen so low that this sector of the export trade collapsed and did not revive until the early nineteenth century.[59]

The overwhelming geographical scale and human complexity of commodity manufacture and overseas trade in the Atlantic basin in the late seventeenth century is evident in this survey of the import-export trading system between England and the Upper Guinea Coast. Its many currents framed Anglo-African trade on the coast and inland, as the following chapters trace in greater detail, emphasizing above all the human labor, energy, and expertise that propelled it. On both sides of these exchanges, specialized merchants were building on much older, established trading zones, networks, and relationships even as they opened up new ones. The RAC's contacts in the Baltic sent them Swedish bar iron that might find its way into towns and hamlets far in the interior of West Africa, carried there by Juula and then Jahaanke caravans. There, a local master blacksmith might then turn the raw metal into special axe or hoe blades for local farmers or perhaps into an elegant sword for a special customer among the nobility. Similarly, a

Tanda captive, struggling to carry a large ivory tusk from beyond the head-waters of the Gambia, would never imagine that his own journey and that of the tusk had just barely begun. If he was fortunate he might remain on the Guinea Coast and eventually achieve some measure of social belonging in his new West African creole culture. If he was not he could very well end up living a tragically short and terrible life on a sugar plantation in Barbados or Jamaica. As for the tusk, it possibly got sold into the workshop of a London artificer whose skills then transformed it into the luminous and delicately carved ivory combs that graced the tresses of wealthy and stylish London women.

CHAPTER THREE
_____

West Africans Profiting in Atlantic Trade

THOSE LIVING on the Guinea Coast might choose for all sorts of self-interested reasons to take part in the Atlantic trade as the main economic game in their homeland—assuming they were not brought unwillingly into that trade as captives. And the participation of the coastal inhabitants was essential to its operations. This new and unprecedented intercontinental trade could not have been developed without the labor, commercial knowledge and expertise, specialized services, and well-established consumer tastes of the men and women who lived in the vicinity of ports along the Guinea Coast and on the overland routes from there to hinterland towns and communities. The land was their turf, and they had the upper hand. European merchants and ship captains could never have carried out the Guinea trade all on their own.

Revealing the geographical and temporal specifics of the African side of Atlantic trade—its "hidden half"—takes us more fully and deeply into Atlantic history.[1] This chapter focuses on West Africans on the Upper Guinea Coast who dealt with the RAC on a regular basis between the 1670s and early 1700s over multiple years or even decades. Some of them are mentioned intermittently in company letters between officials in London and their employees in northern Guinea, but local RAC agents, all too aware of how much they depended on them, kept track of their visits and transactions in the accounting records now found in the company books. Those agents' social relationships with a variety of people living in their environs, evident in these records, were key to commerce. To achieve any measure of commercial success, such relationships had to be affirmed continually. And at least for that time and place, RAC accounting records provide invaluable details about who some of these people were, Africans and Euro-Africans, revealing also the longevity of their relationships and some of their twists and turns.

Foremost among these important relationships were those that RAC agents were required to establish and maintain with local kings and masters of towns, along with minor officials and occasionally their wives and clients. As temporary residents from far away, trade agents received permission to remain on the Upper Guinea Coast only as long as they showed the necessary respect and upheld the terms of agreements they had to negotiate regularly with their hosts. In addition to managing these ongoing relations with kings and their courtiers, RAC employees had to rely on a wide range of suppliers and wholesalers across the social and economic spectrum who provided them with essential goods, services, and vital information. Many of them—men and women—were members of the well-established and numerous Luso-African communities that lined the coast and had long-standing experience in the coastal Atlantic trade. Others were independent traders of various nationalities who made themselves useful to the company for their own advantage. Even the occasional Muslim man found reasons to trade with these Christian strangers, if only for a limited time. Offsetting the company's vulnerable position, at least in part, was its main attraction—the potential profits one could gain from the inflows of overseas goods the RAC had on offer.

Landlords and "Customs"

European merchant-ship captains putting in at ports on the Guinea Coast had to receive permission to engage in any trading and negotiated the current "customs" charges owed to local authorities. These requirements they met anew with each visit, presenting more gifts to officials and paying again the requisite fees. Fort-based trading involved far more complex and ongoing logistical arrangements and relationships with a variety of individuals, all of whom had to be carefully cultivated over time. Even so, standing agreements and terms changed without notice and on occasion could cause major holdups for agents in charge of the forts. These geopolitical subtleties of fort trading thus created multiple and dynamic cross-cultural settings, each one presenting its own mix of opportunities and obstacles. Some RAC agents reacted negatively to these realities of fort and factory trading in Africans' terrain, even suggesting that their dependence on local officials was a nuisance that should be evaded. One such agent at the James Island fort wrote to the company directors in London that he thought it preferable to have several vessels continually trading from port to port rather than stationing factors at permanent outposts where they were at the mercy of their landlords.[2] Other agents seem to have understood and accepted these ongoing landlord-stranger social relations as a necessary cost of doing business.

RAC officials in London were late in realizing the strategic importance of these local customs negotiations and expenses. As their monopoly era began to wane after 1698, they urged agents at their forts to keep better and more regular accounts, including payments of the endless fees necessary for keeping up good relations with "kings" and "great men." Everything had to be itemized and its value entered, they insisted, from the rates of rents and the customs charges paid to kings to the presents, food, and drink in "palavras" with local officials.[3] Expectations in London were chronically unrealistic. Even if company directors had understood the importance of these costs much earlier, keeping such detailed accounts was simply not possible alongside all the other managerial and labor requirements their employees on the Guinea Coast faced as they tried to find a footing in the shifting sands of trading there.

During the 1680s and '90s the company's three forts in northern Guinea each had its own particular geopolitical context. James Island sat isolated and exposed in a five-mile-wide section of the lower Gambia, potentially vulnerable to maritime attack and plunder. Froger's schematic map (see figure 3.1) shows it inaccurately as closer to the southern shore but does convey how very small it is in relation to the river's widening mouth. It was important strategically as a gateway into the lucrative upriver markets where waterborne traders met up with overland caravans bringing goods and captives from far-off entrepôts in the vast interior regions of West Africa. That location, and the fabled gold trade it attracted, made this fort the most important of the RAC's stations in northern Guinea, and company directors struggled to keep it as well-defended and well-supplied for commerce as they could. They were mostly unaware, however, of the complex set of institutionalized African landlord-stranger relations their agents had to manage. Their African hosts would have recognized RAC agents as *samalan*, strangers or visitors, who were not necessarily in need of economic support from their designated landlords but who were unquestionably dependent on them for social and cultural guidance, advice, and sometimes direct assistance. For providing these invaluable services, a landlord would

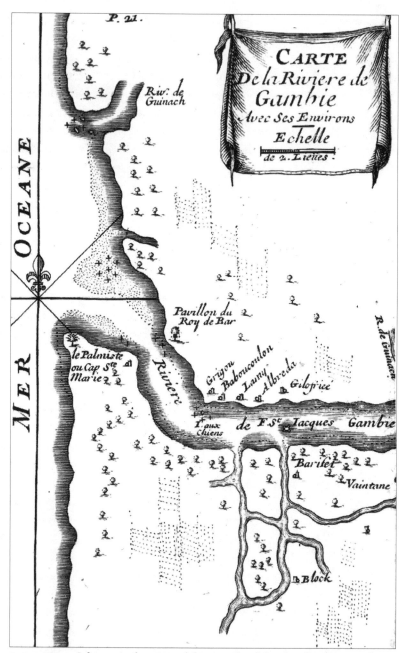

FIGURE 3.1 Schematic drawing of the mouth of the Gambia River and James Island (F. St. Jacques). François Froger, *Relation d'un voyage* (Paris, 1700). John Carter Brown Library, Providence, RI. *Internet Archive*. Web. 16 Nov. 2016.

expect proper cordiality expressed in increasingly novel or valuable gifts and regular payments of rent.[4]

The kings of Barra and Fogny were the most crucially important of the company's landlords for James Island. Their lands, on the northern and southern shores of the lower Gambia, made up the fort's immediate neighborhood. Permissions to occupy the island, construct and repair the fort, and conduct business in the Gambia estuary had to be regularly renewed with each of these rulers. Signaling a recognition of their reciprocal responsibilities, both of the kings, upon learning of a change in the company's governance in 1678, presented the RAC with the gift of a "Negro boy."[5]

Although clearly meant to mark the importance of the occasion, such "gifts" present several major problems of interpretation. Being designated in the RAC records as "Negro boys" and not simply "negroes" or "slaves" identified them, in English terms, as a fashionable gift among London gentry at the time or possibly as a ship captain's assistant or personal servant. But one wonders whose children they may have been and how they had come into the kings' hands. Questions arise about just what the boys' social status was and what the kings themselves might have envisioned or intended as to how the company would receive them and what their futures would hold. A visit to or residence in London would certainly be very different from a career at sea, not to mention the alternative of a hard and short life of forced labor on a Barbados sugar plantation. To whom they were sent and what happened to them apparently did not concern the company and so is not known. As for the kings, RAC records indicate that they were not particularly important as suppliers of commercialized captives to the company at this time, selling only some few irregularly, one or two at a time.[6]

Customs payments to these rulers and their successors and to others in their domains, though not recorded systematically, show varying patterns in their timing and values. Over the 1680s, for example, customs payments to the king of Barra were sent monthly until 1685, when they changed to a single yearly payment. This new schedule suggests that a new king had been installed and demanded the change and timing, but the yearly rate, listed only by value as 40B (40 bars of iron, the RAC's standard currency of account), does not indicate the components and value of the assortment of overseas goods he selected, which came to 385B in value—almost ten times the nominal fee. It might well be that agents agreed to such generous overpayments as part of a deliberate strategy of appeasement, for one never knew when or for what reason a landlord's assistance might be necessary.

More than a year later, for example, an English sea captain, accused of violent crimes against some of the townspeople at Juffure, was taken prisoner there along with several RAC employees, including the agent for James Island. They were held hostage for a number of days by yet another newly installed Barra king, who finally agreed to accept a ransom payment for their freedom. In this case, his intervention on their behalf may well have saved their lives. Meeting even the most extravagant demands of the kings of Barra was thus a wise investment that paid off in the long run. Company payments to the king of Fogny, in contrast, appear to have been lower and more regular, their values only rarely exceeding 40B per assortment. Other payments went out from time to time to masters of the nearby towns of Brefet and Vintang, whose traders sometimes supplied ivory and wax for export and where RAC vessels were allowed to be hauled ashore for major repair work.[7]

Agents also had to manage a constellation of other relations in the Gambia River trading sphere. An itemized account of the company's expenses in marking a special event, namely, the ending of Alexander Cleeve's term as agent for James Island, effectively lays out the wide range of social and commercial relationships he had developed and maintained and their full geographical extent. Entered into the books in February 1689, these expenses included a feast held on the island for the king of Barra, his wives, and some of his courtiers, as well as gifts they received on the occasion, among them an exotic and fashionable "morning gown" made of vividly colored silk and probably intended for the king himself. Listed also were gifts sent by messenger to many others: lesser officials in Barra; the king and alcade of Geregia; the king and alcade of Combo; the kings of Fogny and Bojanna; the king of Jurunku; the Bur Saalum; and masters of the towns of Brefet, Vintang, Juffure, Sika, and Banyon Point (map 3.1).[8] Most of these places were within twenty or twenty-five miles of the fort. According to company accounts, not all of them were owed customs on a regular basis. Even so, this strategically orchestrated event suggests that agents like Cleeve recognized elaborate social niceties as important parts of doing business, whatever the cost. In this case, the total expense was quite high, coming to 239B, or roughly one and a half times the yearly salary of an RAC agent.[9]

The James Island trading sphere reached into other markets and supply areas beyond the lower Gambia. Among them were several upriver locations where James Island agents sent sloops on trading voyages, which could last a month or longer. At times, they settled permanent factors in

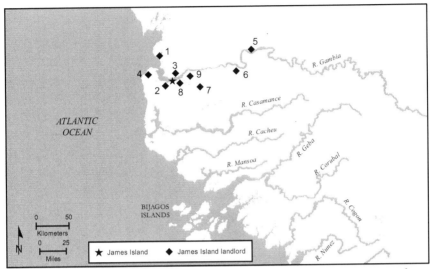

MAP 3.1 Landlords in the Lower Gambia River: (1) King of Barra; (2) King of Fogny; (3) Master of Juffure; (4) Master of Combo; (5) King of Saalum; (6) King of Jogery; (7) King and Masters in Geregia; (8) Master of Brefet; (9) Master of Vintang. *Map by Brian Edward Balsley, GISP.*

some of these upstream ports, but even in those cases they still had to send ships up to provision them and to bring cargoes of commodities for export down to the coast. One of the most important and enduring of the upriver destinations was the Sereer kingdom of Saalum, about one hundred miles upstream from the fort on the river's north bank. Called "Barsally" in the company records, kings of Saalum had held an open account with English merchants since at least 1666, owing to the regularity of trading voyages they sent there, which were usually once or twice a year. In this case, as with other major upriver ports such as Barrakunda, customs charges and other payments and agreements would have been negotiated per visit. The same was true for their coasting destinations of Joal and Portudale to the north, on the Petite Côte.[10]

Agents at the fort on Bence Island, well to the south in the Sierra Leone estuary, had an equally particular set of local landlord relations to manage (map 3.2). Among them was a regular ground rent and customs charge owed to the Bai ("king") of the Bullom communities on the north side of the entrance to the estuary. Referred to in the RAC records as "Bysama," he and his closest advisers were the most important of the local landlords to the company in this location. And here too, the permission to inhabit and

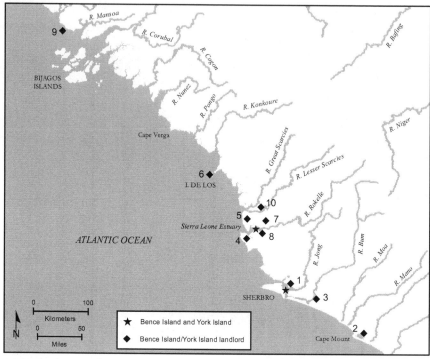

MAP 3.2 Bence Island and York Island landlords: (1) King of Sherbro; (2) King of Cape Mount; (3) King and Nobles at Kittam; (4) John Thomas; (5) King of Bullom; (6) King and Nobles of Îles de Los; (7) King and Nobles of Loko; (8) King of Baga; (9) King and Nobles at Trois-îles (Tassily); (10) King of Scarcies. *Map by Brian Edward Balsley, GISP.*

maintain their island fort was conditional and had to be renewed regularly in order for the company to continue its operations in the estuary. Still other negotiations had to be carried out to establish and maintain their smaller, strategically located out-factories, which provided vital supplements to Bence Island's relatively modest export trade in ivory, captives, and beeswax. The most important of these over time were Tassily (Trois-îles), which was far to the north near Cacheu; Samo, up the Melakori River; Loko, up Port Loko Creek; and a post up the Scarcies River. Coasting voyages sent once or twice a year to supply areas such as the mouths of the Nunez and Pongo Rivers and the offshore Iles de Los negotiated their customs charges per visit.[11]

When records of these payments were kept regularly, they can reveal some of the ways local people profited from rents in the Guinea trade and also something of the impact of overseas goods on local consumer tastes and cultural practices. RAC agents paid monthly fees to the Bullom king and also at times to John Thomas, a Temne official living on the south side of the estuary who administered permissions for ships to anchor near his settlement and replenish their stores of water and firewood.[12] In the early 1680s, individual payments like these tended to be small in value, and the assortments of overseas goods almost always included liquor, usually brandy. European varieties of liquor had quickly become essential items in the business culture of the Guinea trade, offered to guests and others as proper signs of welcome and enjoyed as a central feature in the carefully orchestrated social settings of Euro-African trading talks. Textiles in payment assortments indicate both continuities and changes in styles of dress. They included an Afro-Eurasian array of fabrics from both near and far, with locally made cottons and indigo-dyed cloths such as *barafulas* changing hands alongside vividly dyed and patterned *pintados* from India and tailored cloth coats from Europe. One dozen brass chains in a large assortment paid out at Iles de Los in 1680 sounds an ominous note of reminder of the captives held prisoner at transit points along the Guinea Coast, awaiting their forced removals to America.[13]

In addition to making the obligatory payments owed by the company to their landlords and hosts, agents at Bence Island also recognized the potential benefits of inviting them to special feasts and celebrations. These, too, were occasionally recorded in the company's books. One such case was a December celebration in 1680 that brought together several of the local kings and their closest advisors, turning the occasion of the company's payments for customs, port charges, and factory rents into a major diplomatic event. The amount of gunpowder expended in firing off salutes from the great guns of the fort publicly signaled the thundering degree to which the RAC was indeed giving special recognition to them all. As the brandy and Madeira wine flowed, the honored guests must have eyed their particular favored items from among the rich assortment of goods on display—iron bars, swords, knives, kettles, brass basins, and pewterware from Europe, plain and elaborately patterned West African cloths, brightly colored *pintados* from India, European linens, coats, hats, and lastly, shiny brass trumpets—a European addition to their own choruses of luminous and elegantly carved ivory horns. A creole-style example of the latter, exhibiting Euro-African features, was acquired in the vicinity of the Sierra Leone estuary and brought to Europe, where it joined the other exotic "curiosities" of a Bavarian priest whose collection achieved renown in the eighteenth century (see figure 3.2).[14] Another RAC event, smaller but no less important, was celebrated in March 1683 when the company entered into a new treaty of peace with Bai Samma and members of his court. In addition to the usual brandy, they were given the very special honor of booming salutes set off from the great guns. After the festivities, they departed for the Bullom shore with a long bar of iron for smiths to divide among them, along with individual knives, personal swords, a coat, men's thread stockings, and slippers.[15]

RAC agents and factors at York Island in Sherbro, the other main RAC fort on the Upper Guinea Coast, were involved in a set of local relationships that were even more complex, demanding, and precarious than that of their counterparts at James Island and Bence Island. The reason for these challenges was camwood, Sherbro's main export. Supplies of it came from forested areas on the mainland, especially those located up the many small rivers and creeks that cut into and across the marshy sunken coastline. Camwood had long been used locally for a variety of purposes—from building materials and hand tools to medicines and ceremonial displays—but it was not normally available in quantities sufficient for export.[16] Recruiting labor to cut it and carry it to the water therefore became a major and recurring burden for the company. Men living in nearby villages had to be hired and organized as laborers to fell the camwood trees, strip off the bark, and trim the wood into smaller-sized billets for transport down to the coast later on. After this came the equally strenuous work of hauling the billets of wood to the nearest waterway and loading them onto barges or other river craft. Only in the rainy season were water levels in the rivers high enough to make a safe and sure passage downstream with such heavy cargoes. Still more men were called on to work when the time came to transfer the bulked billets onto company vessels preparing to sail back to London. Holdups were possible at every stage. Moreover, since local cottons or tailored men's garments from Cape Mount served as the usual payments for this work, agents also had to send periodic coasting voyages southward to replenish supplies of them.

The example of Zachary Rogers, who was RAC agent at York Island from 1678 to early 1681, illustrates how much the company had to depend on cooperation from the local ruler in Sherbro and what could happen if they fell out of favor with him. Rogers was a well-informed trader, having worked for the RAC's predecessor, the Company of Royal Adventurers, from the

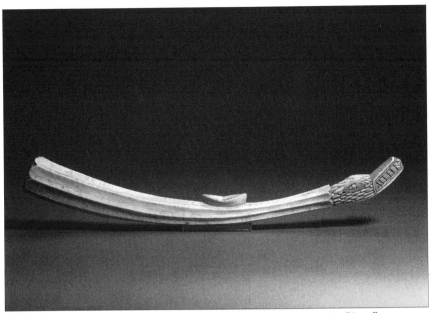

FIGURE 3.2 A Creole ivory horn, seventeenth c. Sierra Leone. Its "Sape" carver retained the African placement of the mouthpiece on the horn's side and terminated its smaller end with an alligator head. On the body of the horn he carved European/Muslim-style fluting. Orb.20, Museum Fünf Kontinente, Munich. Photograph: Swantje Autrum-Mulzer.

mid-1660s and having married a highly respected woman from a nearby community.[17] Rogers's wife was well-connected politically, and it was this important social advantage and his fluency in one or more of the languages in the area that enabled him regularly to enlist the cooperation of local rulers in the organization of labor for cutting and moving the camwood. His early letters to London display his long experience and deep geographical knowledge of the coast from Sherbro southward and the logistics of maneuvering in and among its varied and shifting waterways. Even with his skills, however, he recognized how unpredictable the camwood trade could be and warned the company that he was never sure how long he could rely on contracts he made with his wood suppliers.[18] Keen to protect his hard-won expertise, he did not share it freely with others and declined to keep written accounts for the company, a precaution that aroused suspicions and ill-feelings among some of his fellow employees.[19] Nevertheless, during his time of service with the RAC, he managed Sherbro's export trade in camwood and ivory relatively well.

His sudden death in February 1681 triggered a major camwood holdup, one that was not resolved until eight months later. The chronically under-staffed fort at York Island had been left with only one man, Joshua Platt, to take over as chief agent, an individual described as "unfit" because of his lack of experience and his having no language other than his mother tongue.[20] Platt was wise enough, however, to solicit the invaluable advice and assistance of a local multilingual interpreter, Thomas Skinner, when the crisis hit, and it was Skinner's insight that enabled Platt to convey so vividly the details of the holdup and the major issues underlying it in his explanatory letter to London. Thomas was one of three Sherbro traders named Skinner—Matthew and James were the other two—who were probably brothers and among the considerable numbers of residents of Anglo-African ancestry on the coast.[21] All three supplied exports to the RAC, but Matthew was the one who worked more regularly for the company on salary, serving for a time as camwood factor at their outpost at the Gallinas River. In the 1680s and '90s, the Skinners earned them-selves widely recognized reputations as successful independent exporters of camwood, ivory, rice, and captives.[22]

Initially, it would not have seemed that Zachary Rogers's death would develop into a serious business crisis. On February 16, Platt set about taking an inventory of the overseas goods and local exports on hand at York Island fort, as well as all the other supplies, buildings, and equipment. He noted that deliveries of over fourteen tons of camwood were expected. However, it being February, the middle of the dry season cutting time, the fact that the billets had not yet arrived would not have been a cause for concern. In late February Platt paid the usual customs assortment to the Sherbro king, including some kettles, pewterwares, ten great knives, two yards *pintados*, one piece of linen, and small beads, all to the value of 8B. Entered into the books on the same day was another payment to the king, an unusual one, presented to him on the occasion of Rogers's death. It was a much larger and complex assortment that included very special items, such as four yards of red woolen cloth, two *barafula* cloths, and ten gallons of brandy, the entire array of goods having the value of 49B, or eight times the normal customs charges. Also in the company books, among several loose and undated pages, is a record of the expenses they paid for items chosen for Zachary Rogers's funeral and burial, transcribed and illustrated in transcription 3.1. Coming to a total of 71B in value, the expenses included European hard-wares, metal utensils, lengths of plain and patterned cotton cloth from

India, beads, three dozen mats, four goats, rice, and a brass trumpet, all the makings of a public "cry," or funeral feast, held in honor of the deceased.[23] It would seem that the social respect and obligations fit for a former stranger, now assimilated into his landlord's society as husband, father, and import-export merchant, were being carefully paid and met.

TRANSCRIPTION 3.1

DEATH OF ZACHARY ROGERS: "CRY" AND BURIAL EXPENSES

Source: T 70/361, loose pages at end of volume. TNA.

	Barrs
6 yds. of Broad Kalico	2
1 yd. of ditto	⅓
7½ cwt. of Iron Hoop	½
3 cwt. of Small Beads	2
4 cwt. Pewter Basons	3½
1 Trumpett	3⅓
4 Goats	8
500 cwt. of Rice	16
1 faddom of Broad Kalico	⅔
1 Blew Pott	½
20 Knives	2
2 Wyrebound Kettles wt. 19 cwt.	8½
2 strings of Christoll	⅔
2 Ironbound Kettles wt. 24 cwt.	9⅔
2 faddom of narrow Kalico	1
2 old Hatts	1½
3 faddom of Pintadoes	3
6 cwt. of Small Beads	4
3 Dozn of Matts	4½
	—
	71

A shipment of camwood and ivory departed Sherbro for London shortly after, in March 1681. With the coming of the rains in July, the fort must have received some new supplies of camwood since they were able to ship out another forty-one tons of it on the *Margaret*.[24] In August or September, another parcel of camwood was delivered down to the coast, but by late September or early November, the Sherbro king and Rogers's powerful widow were holding it back from being loaded onto the company's ship. Their demands were that they should be given the wages owed to Rogers at the time of this death and that the prices of overseas goods should be lowered. If their demands were not met, they threatened to sell the wood instead to Flemish private traders they knew of in the vicinity. Platt and Skinner quickly arranged to pay a visit to the "great woman," as Rogers's widow was known, to try to reach a settlement with her. She spoke vigorously and at great length before finally demanding a substantial and itemized assortment of overseas goods.[25]

What she received consisted mainly of a variety of metalwares and textiles, and the total amount of 48B was not an unreasonable equivalent of what her late husband's wages would have been due him for the last three and a half months of his life.[26] Platt paid it out and took the widow along with Skinner to a visit with the king. But the king was not ready to settle. His demands were that he would not agree to anything until Platt entertained him and his closest courtiers, surely with suitable honors. He also insisted that Platt promise to write to the RAC in London to inform them that the prices of their goods were too high. Platt agreed to all that the king demanded and paid out the feast expenses in the form of various European metalwares, textiles from India and England, two hats, ten gallons of brandy, a chair, a trumpet, a goat, and rice, to the total value of 45B, transcribed and illustrated in transcription 3.2. With that the king at last allowed the wood to be laden on their ship, the *William*. However, he continued to insist that he wanted a pledge from the RAC to lower the prices of their goods, especially the brasswares, adding that he hoped they would sell them as they had been "in Mr. Woods time."[27] This last detail is remarkable for its accuracy, as the king was remembering and comparing pricing from the time of the London firm of Wood and Co., which had indeed had redwood merchants operating at Sherbro between 1625 and 1648, that is, roughly thirty years earlier. The king had good reason to be concerned about the price for brasswares since metal basins were used to boil sea water down to its saline mineral residue as a way of making sea salt more intensively, and therefore more costly and profitable, than by solar evaporation. Hence the prevailing high prices for brasswares meant an increase in the cost of local salt-makers' capital equipment, adding difficulties to the working lives of his subjects.[28]

TRANSCRIPTION 3.2

GOODS EXPENDED AT SHERBRO TO BRING OF THE REDWOOD

P THE WM BY THE MEANS OF MR. ROGERS WOMAN

Source: T 70/361, loose pages at end of volume. TNA.

	Barrs
14 cwt. Iron bound Kettles	5¾
12 cwt. Wyre bound ditto	5⅓
8 cwt. Tatchetts	4½
2 Annabasses	3⅓
4 cwt. Brass Basons	2
4 yds. Welch Plaines	2
2 Old Hatts	1½
6 yds. Baftes	2¼
10 gal. Brandy	10
1 Chaire	2
1 Trumpett	3⅓
1 Goatt	1½
112 cwt. Rice	1½
	—
	45

This entire episode shows that incomes from hosting Atlantic traders were especially high in the Sherbro area. The total value in goods that went to Rogers's widow (for funeral expenses and her late husband's wages) and to the Sherbro king (for king's charges related to Rogers's death and for the wood palaver) were 119B and 94B, respectively. For this sequence of events alone, the king's share represents over half of what Zachary Rogers probably earned yearly. A tally of customs and other charges that went to Sherbro kings over each of five years in the 1680s and each of four years in the 1690s shows that the annual payments were substantial and that they increased over time. The average for the 1680s was 155B, just under the usual yearly salary of a RAC agent, and by the mid-1690s the average had risen to 251B. RAC salaries had risen as well, some being as high by the late 1690s as £65 (217B) per year, but the king's charges by this time were still greater than an agent's salary.[29]

The profitability of charging customs fees and rents to foreign traders could have marked effects on local politics, sometimes generating conflicts among rival factions that could interfere with trade relations. In such cases of competing claimants to their duties, company agents had to decide what course of action, if any, to take. In one instance, recorded in July 1693, agents at York Island decided to honor the wish of the Sherbro king that he and his courtiers should be entertained at the fort. He had apparently been deposed and forced to retreat to his former town and so was delivering a request to the company that they settle a factor in his new location. Five months later he and some of his men were invited again to the fort for a special Christmas feast, a sign that they were still on good terms.[30]

There were other times, though, when customs payments could become a volatile issue. Questions, rumors, and outright accusations circulated about private traders dealing with local people without paying customs, setting off disturbances that threatened to disrupt the trade. In one such case in early 1692, the RAC sent word out that an English trader named Wilkinson was operating in the vicinity of Sherbro and was not a company employee, and so they urged that he be required to pay customs to local authorities.[31] The issue was apparently never resolved. Six years later the old king of Sherbro was dead, and some of his subjects rose up and attacked at least two Anglo-African traders living in their vicinity. Storming the home of Richard Bridgman, a former RAC employee, they robbed him and burned down his property and plantations. The same was done to Matthew Skinner.[32] It is not clear what exactly had provoked these violent acts or why these particular men were among the targets. Seeking to calm public passions, the company wrote an official letter to the new king, but the available abstract of it provides only a very general description of what had taken place. The directors expressed disapproval of the injuries that some "ill-designing" persons had done to him, his subjects, and also to his predecessor, and referred also to false information that had been spread about the company. Primarily they were hoping for a restoration of their longstanding alliance and resumption of business as usual. Appearing rather desperate, they closed their letter by offering the king peace and a fruitful friendship, along with the gift of a robe and cap.[33]

Suppliers and Short Supplies

The RAC and their employees had a great deal to learn about how to manage the trade itself when they began staffing and supplying their three forts on the northern Guinea Coast. For one thing, the commercial environments they were trying to enter were extremely varied. In some locales, such as the predominantly Luso-African entrepôts of Cacheu and Bissau, import-export commerce was well-established and thriving, while in other places trading opportunities were limited, sporadic, and unpredictable. Bringing sufficient supplies of export goods in to the forts to load onto outbound company ships thus required having current and reliable commercial intelligence in addition to knowing the right kinds of overseas goods to offer in exchange. Competition for a viable share in the export markets was fierce. Not only were other European-based companies operating on the Upper Guinea Coast, but all sorts of private traders were at work as well, some of them brazenly hostile. Forts as well as ships were vulnerable to attack and plunder.

Employees hired in London to staff and run the company's forts and outstations arrived desperately ill-equipped. They were, for the most part, unfamiliar with the geography and unaccustomed to the tropical climate and seasonal patterns of the Guinea Coast, which hampered their ability to meet the challenges of engaging in commerce there. They also had to learn on the spot, and as quickly as possible, how to understand and speak the coastal lingua franca, a Portuguese-based Crioulo, and, if possible, other local languages as well.[34] Then a new regulation imposed by London in 1680 put them at an even greater disadvantage: every employee was sworn under oath not to trade on his own account. This RAC prohibition was strikingly different from the liberality of England's East India Company, which allowed its employees to engage in trade on their own and thus augment their salaries. Not so for the company men on the Guinea Coast, however, and over the following two decades this prohibition created chronic problems involving embezzlement and fraud and at times sparking intense and violent personal conflicts.[35] Some men left the company to become private traders, while those who stayed on had to be ever watchful, resourceful, and clever.

One recurring concern of agents posted at James Island was how to deal with the commercial acumen of Luso-African merchants based to the south in and around Cacheu, shown schematically in figure 3.3. They were, on the one hand, reliable suppliers of commodities for export, but on the other hand they were extremely shrewd bargainers who knew well how to leverage their strong market positions. Agreements with them could fall apart with little notice, leading to vexing delays and losses. RAC agents often

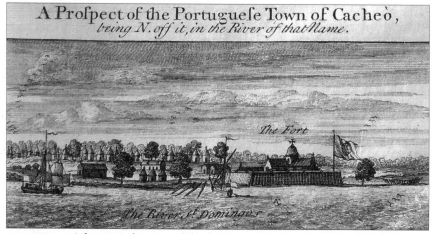

A Profpect of the Portuguefe Town of Cacheò, being N. off it, in the River of that Name.

FIGURE 3.3 Schematic drawing of the fort and harbor at Cacheu. John Barbot, "A Description of the Coasts of North and South-Guinea," in A. and J. Churchill, *A Collection of Voyages and Travels* (London, 1732). Collection of the Massachusetts Historical Society.

registered strong feelings of ambivalence toward Cacheu's merchant community in their letters to London. Writing in March 1678, agent Thurloe declared that the very best of their trade overall was with Cacheu for ivory and beeswax. Continuing on in a seemingly positive vein he explained that the commander of Cacheu's local military post had recently offered him a trading contract guaranteeing exclusive rights to the RAC if they could come to an agreement on pricing. But prices in Cacheu were a chronic problem. Thurloe admitted as much when he noted that Cacheu captives were too costly, attributing the high prices to vigorous competition from merchants serving the Spanish-American market.[36]

Writing in a more optimistic tone later in the month, he announced that he had made a specific investment in their future trade with Cacheu. It was a 90-ton ship purchased from the French, which he justified by explaining that the enormous amounts of bar iron Cacheu merchants demanded in their payment assortments were too heavy for RAC ships.[37] The news of this unauthorized expenditure could not have pleased London. Then, just two months later, Thurloe wrote despairingly that he had been failing in trade on all fronts—on the Gambia and Casamance Rivers, at Cacheu, and on the Petite Côte. Whatever the reasons were, he blamed it on competition from private traders, two French and one Irish, and the threat posed by a 450-ton Dutch ship coming into the Gambia estuary in search of ivory, wax, and hides.[38] Such were the unpredictable turns of events in the Guinea trade.

Records for James Island fort in the 1680s offer enough trading data to develop a sense of just how difficult it was for company agents to bring in consistently high volumes of their main exports of captives, ivory, hides, and beeswax. Above all, success in trade required deployment of an array of coasting and river vessels to supplement the small streams of exports arriving periodically from individual wholesalers. As long as agents had the right ships available and in good repair, the men on James Island might have had the wherewithal to fulfil the RAC's orders and specifications for cargoes intended for London or the Caribbean. But optimal conditions did not often present themselves, as correspondence from agents detailed. Their pleadings for coasting vessels, for more manpower, and for replenishing their stores of tools and supplies expose in sharp relief just how insufficiently equipped and supported the forts were.

Estimated quantities of exports delivered to James Island during two periods—1680–82 and 1683–87—give some indication of the efforts and investments it would have taken to increase the volume of the company's export trade. Records for the earlier period exhibit two main strategies devised by agent Cleeve for meeting directors' expectations. One was centered on their factory at Geregia, with the hopes that stocking it with ample overseas goods would allow the station to redirect exports from the supply areas of Cacheu overland toward the lower Gambia.[39] The other was to regularly dispatch the company's coasting and river vessels laden with trade assortments appropriate for their particular destinations. But neither strategy realized its potential in 1680–82. Geregia sent down to the fort only small numbers of hides and cakes of beeswax, while voyages to Cacheu, to the Petite Côte, and up the Gambia River brought in only modest numbers of captives or quantities of ivory, beeswax, and hides. Records for the later period, however, showed some striking improvements. Cleeve adhered to the same two strategies but produced notable increases in both the number of deliveries from Geregia and the number of voyages. Supplies of captives, beeswax, and hides increased substantially. Only the levels of ivory appear flat, suggesting supplies of it were inelastic at that moment. Cleeve also twice sent vessels for stores of sea salt and organized upriver voyages for locally woven cottons.[40]

A closer look at how Cleeve managed to achieve such an expansion of exports reveals that his strategies would not have been sustainable over time.

The lion's share of exports came in via the voyages upriver, which numbered around thirty or more. At least seventeen vessels went to Bur Saalum or all the way to the falls at Barrakunda, sometimes stopping at other river ports in between. Seven or more went coastwise south to Cacheu, and another seven or more sailed north to the Petite Côte. The logistics of handling these wide-ranging ventures, along with transporting goods to and from the far-flung factories, would be problematic even when the fort had its own coasting vessels on hand and in good repair. Since that was not the case, Cleeve had redirected incoming company ships, putting them in service to the James Island fort. Such blatant and repeated interferences in London's shipping schedules did not escape the notice of the Court of Assistants. Writing to Cleeve in August 1687, they chided him for having so many small vessels and men at work and for commandeering their own supply ships, all of which had incurred great expense without increasing ivory exports, which at that time were very profitable. They demanded to know exactly what he was doing and why, and they ordered him not to incur any more expenditures beyond what they thought their returns in sales could bear.[41] In other words, the company either could not, or would not, invest in the vessels and voyages it would have taken to expand the volume of their exports from northern Guinea.

Local wholesalers who regularly supplied exports to the fort on James Island were not numerous, but they serve as vivid examples of the commercial strategies these suppliers devised and followed. Some benefitted much more than others. One successful case was the family firm of Peter Vaz, a Luso-African merchant based at Cacheu, who appears to have had dealings with English companies, including the RAC, for twenty-eight years or more. Vaz was also a shipowner and sea captain and thus enjoyed the all-important advantages in coastal trading of flexibility and maneuverability. He had supplied beeswax and hides in the mid-1660s to one of England's earlier companies, but because of a thirteen-year gap in the records it is not possible to follow the full development of that stage in his career. By 1679, his account with the RAC refers to him as Captain. Over the next four years he served as a prominent and reliable individual supplier of exports to James Island.[42]

Vaz's handling of trade shows him to have been experienced, shrewd, and trusted by the company agents. He ran up a debt in their books over the latter part of 1679, taking out over 300B worth of overseas goods but bringing in only a single male captive valued at 30B. Almost half of the assortment he selected was in iron bars—intermediate goods that were valued extremely highly in Cacheu as a commodity currency and in the surrounding region as the raw material for producing capital goods such as agricultural tools or other bladed tools or weapons. The eight reams of paper—or approximately four thousand sheets—he took back home were undoubtedly put to good use in the Luso-African merchant community, enabling them among other things to continue making and exchanging records of debts and contracts among themselves and with other trading partners. Then, on his visits to the fort in January 1680, Vaz paid off all of his debt to the company by supplying them with seven captives, ivory, beeswax, and hides, to a total value of over 1,100B. Included in the assortments of overseas items he took home as profits from his sale were several hundred bars of iron and a fifty-six-pound load of cowries, the latter an indicator that some of his other trading contacts extended into the cowry currency zone in the interior.[43] It is likely that he invested most of the bars and cowries in advances to his own suppliers, in effect using credit to expand his operations in the African economies of Cacheu's commercial hinterland.

Over the next two years, Vaz continued to run a debt with the company, and the company allowed him to increase it and pay it down with regularity. The patterns of his trading activity over time show how successful borrowers like Vaz must have accumulated enough capital to exploit these RAC investments in producers who supplied the export commodities and captives they wanted. Just when the level of Vaz's debt was rising to the point where it looked like it might become a matter for concern, he would bring in enough exports to lower it and thus remain in good standing with the company agents. Other merchants based in Cacheu who also tended to run up very high debts with the RAC often let them stand, and company efforts to recover them almost always failed. Peter Vaz appears to have handled his debt and credit balances with more flexibility, perhaps having a longer-term relationship with the company in mind, and indeed he succeeded in building up a diversified import-export business both as a supplier to the RAC and as a dealer in Cacheu's most favored overseas goods. In addition to imported iron bars and paper, he sometimes dealt in personal weapons such as swords and, only rarely, firearms. Establishing himself as a reliable source of such valuable overseas merchandise would have also brought him considerable social capital—high standing, trust, and respect in his community. His contact with the fort at James Island also gave him access to imported shipping supplies such as tar for caulking the hulls of his trading vessels, as well as canvas and cordage for their rigging.[44]

In September 1683 the account that Peter Vaz ran with the RAC was taken over by a woman named simply as Jane Vaz, without the title senhora, and so presumably his daughter. At the time he owed a debt of 562B. What had happened to Peter Vaz—whether he had died or had decided to retire and pass his business on to a family member—is not clear. In any event, Jane Vaz assumed his debt to the company and put the account in her own name, taking out an additional ten yards of cloth for good measure. Showing she had a keen knowledge of current market trends, the cloth she selected was black bays, a lightweight English woolen cloth that was popular in Cacheu at the time. Also, and perhaps to demonstrate to the company that she would prove to be as trustworthy a business partner as her father had been, she brought in a representative assortment of their major exports—four captives, beeswax, ivory, and hides.[45]

From 1683 to 1688, Jane Vaz showed herself to be a capable and successful merchant. Like her father, she supplied the James Island fort with arrays of their major exports and took back to Cacheu well-chosen selections of the town's most favored overseas goods. And over time, the sizes and values of her assortments grew larger, eventually surpassing those of her father. The extant records indicate that exports he brought in only rarely came to values of 1,000B or more, and he never took out overseas goods totaling more than 500B; only once did he run a large debt of 2,000B, which he did not let stand for very long. Jane started her trade with the RAC in 1683, making four visits to the fort and keeping her exchanges modest in size. The following four years saw her establishing a pattern of regular visits and gaining in confidence. She made seasonal, well-timed deliveries to meet the schedules for incoming and outgoing RAC vessels, and in several instances the overseas assortments she took back to Cacheu were over 1,000B in value, more than twice the largest values of her father's. The exports she supplied were mainly captives, ivory, and hides, with only a few cakes of beeswax.

How Jane Vaz might have managed successfully to transport cargoes of captives provides an opportunity to consider some of the logistical hazards of slaving. She must have had a trusted team of male employees working for her at home and crewing her ship, packing and moving goods to and from ports and into and out of holds, probably themselves either enslaved people she owned or skilled professionals who were either salaried or working for hire. Certainly they would have to have been well armed. On at least two occasions, the number and demographic composition of her cargoes of captives presented threats of insurrection or escape—one cargo included twelve men and two women, the other twenty men and four women. Transferring that risk and potential loss of life on to the RAC fort was best done as quickly as possible.[46]

After a gap in the records between 1688 and 1692, the Vaz account shows a significant trend toward retirement from these risks. Jane became Senhora de Melo, having earned a term of respect in Portuguese creole equivalent to Lady, and having made a very good marriage to one Bernardo de Melo. Activity in her account shows her dealing in smaller assortments of exports and imports, perhaps to avoid increasing insecurities at sea and around the fort as Europe's War of the League of Augsburg spilled out into the north Atlantic.[47] Her supply of ivory appears to have been interrupted, and she was no longer dealing in hides. Also notable was a drop in the price of captives, from 30B to 25B. The last entry on her account came on September 30, 1693, at an uncertain time of transition on James Island as William Heath took over for late agent John Booker. She had known Booker well and was named in the codicil to his will as guardian over the slaves he had bequeathed to his child slave Hope, now freed and soon to marry William. Perhaps Senhora de Melo returned to the fort to witness the marriage in October. Whatever the case, on this occasion she departed James Island with a payment of 10B each for three caulkers whom she had lent to the fort for three and a half months' service.[48]

Hiring out members of the skilled labor force she managed was one more way Senhora Bernardo de Melo shored up her position as a prominent, reliable, and successful wholesaler in the Guinea trade. She was among many well-known senhoras prominent in trading towns along the coast and up the rivers, often from African or Luso-African families with trading networks in the interior who favored contracting marriages of their daughters to immigrant merchants. Some senhoras were thought to have been of slave ancestry, their European husbands supposedly having given them their freedom as a wedding gift. Children of such unions usually took the surname of their fathers. Senhoras became skilled merchants in their own right, and through their own success and their rights to inheritance, they were able to build up conspicuous wealth and property in the form of slaves, impressive "Portuguese-style" houses, trading vessels, and lavish creole wardrobes and jewelry. Their authority and expertise in supervising skilled male labor, slave and free, gave senhoras an especially valuable commercial advantage not generally available to the mass of ordinary women.[49]

That Cacheu wholesalers and shipowners such as Peter and Jane Vaz made their own deliveries to the fort relieved the RAC of significant risks and add-on costs. Sending ships to Cacheu was not an unreasonable option for them, as it was likely they would manage to return with desired assortments of their major exports. But they could also find themselves facing unexpected delays or, at times, terrible losses. On a voyage to Cacheu in August 1685, trading conditions had declined to a low point, with commodities in short supply and a new set of required customs and other charges that came to 10 percent, or twice the usual rate. The result was dangerously long times spent in port at Cacheu and smaller-than-normal return cargoes of higher-priced ivory and beeswax. Five months later the customs charges at Cacheu were back down and supplies of exports were up. But then a succeeding voyage to Cacheu, in November 1686, turned out to be a disaster. Three vessels left James Island, sailing together for protection, but that precaution did not prevent the seizure of one ship, the plundering and attempted seizure of another, and over thirty deaths among company personnel and captives as the small fleet headed back to the protection of the Gambia fort. Company books provide grim details of the losses: customs and other charges at the rate of 10 percent; a ransom payment of 1,554B to recover the seized ship; unknown amounts of export commodities stolen from two of the three ships; 19 dead among the 108 captives they carried; and 15 crew members dead or killed, including one of the ship captains.[50]

Company agents at James Island also welcomed individual traders and suppliers who traveled there from other locations on the mainland. One of these suppliers was António Silva, a Luso-African merchant who was based up Vintang Creek at Geregia. During the 1680s he became an important wholesaler for the RAC. Precisely when he had opened his account with the RAC is not clear, but by September 1680, when relatively consistent records begin to track his trading activity, he was running a debt of 1,424B. A year and a half later he managed to erase it, sending down shipments that brought his account balance up to a credit of 3,094B. His deliveries were well diversified across the four main categories of exports—ivory, captives, beeswax, and hides—and on occasion he supplied bulk amounts of locally woven cotton cloth and provisions of rice.

Being located in Geregia at the intersection of both the inland north–south and east–west trade axes placed him in an advantageous position for gaining access to all of these exports. Raw beeswax and ivory tusks collected south of the Gambia and along the Casamance River could be carried northward along the linked riverine and overland routes between Cacheu and Geregia. And once there, Silva and other merchants in Geregia, as in Cacheu, organized processing and bulking of the raw materials. Slaves prepared beeswax for export by melting, cleaning, and molding it into cakes, while ivory tusks needed to be sorted into lots by size. Geregia also offered Silva easy access to the lower Gambia and ports upriver where hides could be purchased in bulk and, at the right times of year, caravan merchants arrived with captives for sale.[51] For all of these reasons, generations of Africans and Euro-Africans engaged in the Guinea trade had populated and protected the town.[52]

Silva's and others' import-export businesses brought substantial infusions of overseas goods into Geregia and its environs. Iron bars figured prominently in the assortments he bought, despite their being unwieldy in size and cumbersome to load, transport, and unload. The eight recorded assortments Silva took back to Geregia between 1683 and 1688 together show that he imported at least twenty-seven tons of iron, most of it probably destined for yet other markets in port towns far up the Gambia River where he or a trusted agent—a slave or employee—purchased captives on still especially favorable terms of trade. Captives bought directly from caravan merchants were much lower in price than those bought from intermediaries, whereas the values of individual bars of iron remained higher upriver than on the coast. Some portion of the iron Silva carried off from James Island must also have gone to communities and ports along the way, as iron served as a currency in all sorts of transactions large and small. In addition to being important items in trading assortments, iron bars paid customs and other fees, labor in piloting and in loading and unloading cargoes, interpreting and other brokering services, and daily provisions. Overall, Silva's direct access to the voyage iron of the RAC gave him an advantage in purchasing power on the river and handsome profit margins when he then sold his captives to the company at the coastal price.[53] Presumably those margins left him a comfortable living beyond his costs.

Experienced Luso-African wholesalers like the Vaz family and António Silva were not the only local individuals who grew successful by trading with the RAC. A Muslim man named Siddiqui started by selling provisions to the company and then turned himself into an import-export wholesaler. Records of his account do not specify precisely where he lived, but he must have been based in one of the port towns near the fort since he dealt directly with the company on a regular basis and maintained an account with them for a period of at least nine years.[54] His case is unusual in that individual Muslim traders did not normally hold ongoing accounts with the RAC.

Two exceptions from the 1660s, however, give some idea of the commercial dealings that Muslim clerics sometimes had with England's earlier merchant companies. One was a "bicherine" (itinerant Muslim preacher) in Combo who sold them rice and at least once took out a small measure of spirits, surely to use in payment to laborers not of his faith. The other cleric, referred to as Sidi, probably lived on the northern shore in Albreda. He sold rice and cattle to the company and sometimes provided piloting services on their river vessels. On at least one occasion he purchased a captive from the company.[55]

Surviving RAC records refer to Siddiqui by name only and do not identify him as a Muslim cleric.[56] His trading activity can be tracked from November 1679, just after the ending of the rainy season, when he brought in a harvest of "clean" rice, that is, rice that had been carefully pounded to remove its husks for cooking. Over the next two years he continued to supply provisions to the fort, mostly rice—sometimes clean, sometimes still in the husk—and beef cattle, along with small numbers of hides. He chose an unusual and intriguing combination of goods and labor to take out in return. In February 1680, the middle of the dry season, he took out twenty iron bars, some brandy, and thirty locally woven white cotton cloths. He also "borrowed" two male captives in some sort of hiring arrangement financed by the company, perhaps to support his business with them. Later in the month he took out eight more iron bars and, in March, "borrowed" a third male captive.

Given the timing, it is tempting to assume that he took at least some of the iron bars to a blacksmith to be turned into hatchets or machetes for clearing land for the upcoming planting season, and the slaves' labor might have been sustained with the brandy. More iron bars could have served as payment for the smiths' skilled work in making implements for clearing, tilling, and harvesting. But why the cotton cloths? One possibility is the use of them as a commodity currency for purchasing provisions and also to pay for additional agricultural labor. It is possible also to consider the goods and labor together as a portion of a bridewealth exchange for Siddiqui himself, or for a member of his family, say, a brother or a son or a nephew. In any case, he returned the three captives to the company in September and October, after both the rainy season and the labors needed to take advantage of it had come to an end.[57]

Between 1683 and 1688, Siddiqui phased out supplying provisions to James Island and became a supplier of export commodities on his own. He was able to make this investment in part by working for the RAC, on a salary of 3B per month, most likely shuttling between the fort and the mainland with messages or deliveries of necessaries such as fresh water and firewood. For these services the company either sold or lent him a dugout canoe large enough and sturdy enough to transport loads weighing a ton or more. Out of his twelve recorded export deliveries, eleven included one or more captives, nine included hides, and six included ivory. Only two, in the earlier years, included provisions. Sizes, values, and complexities of the assortments of company imports he selected grew steadily over the period, indicating a widening in the range of his trading contacts and consumer markets. Luso-Africans' creole tastes in textiles included locally made cottons and imported India cottons, as well as linens and woolens from Europe. Siddiqui made it a point to keep five varieties of Indian cloth and eight types of yardage made in Europe on offer. He also bought substantial quantities of paper, amounting to at least eighteen reams, or nine thousand sheets, for the period of five years.[58]

Siddiqui's changing of business contacts with the RAC opens up questions about the varying roles and experiences of individual Muslims in the cross-cultural workings of the Guinea trade. His dealings with the James Island fort and with Luso-African traders suggest that he must have been or was becoming conversant in Crioulo. His assortments show that he was also adding European-style units of weights and measures to his commercial toolkit, such as the casks and gallons of brandy he selected, and the reams of paper, yards of English cloth, and skeins of crewel thread that he regularly chose. Being familiar with such measures and thus able to gauge or at least estimate the corresponding amounts and valuations of goods in currencies of account were skills that guided the movement and pricing of goods in the coastal trading sphere. The RAC issued notes of debt, receipts, and contracts, written in Portuguese or Crioulo, as proofs of pledged or past transactions, spreading the importance of literacy as a practice of doing business. Glimpses of these documented exchanges appear in the RAC records—for example, when individuals paid in a credit balance or took out a debit on the account of another person, or when they opened partnership accounts. On at least two occasions, António Silva took out overseas goods on a debt note specifying an amount the company owed. One was to the account of a prominent Cacheu merchant who had brought in commodities

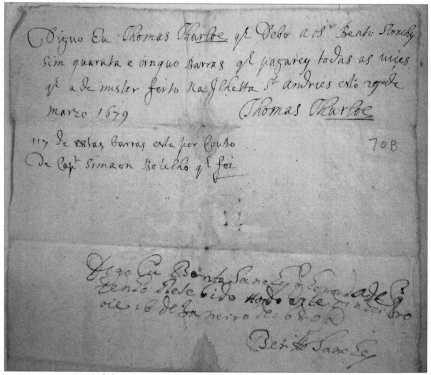

FIGURE 3.4 RAC debt note to Bento Sanchy, "Vinty Santia" Account. The practiced and sure hand of agent Thurloe contrasts with the not yet legible hand of Sanchy, illustrating the spread of literacy via the Guinea trade. The National Archives of the UK, T 70/830 (1679–80).

for export, the other was to the account of the RAC fort at Bence Island. Presumably, Silva had contracted to select and deliver specified assortments on their behalf. In other cases, Siddiqui was credited once on the account of Luso-African trader Bento Sanchy, who himself, in turn, was credited twice on the account of Senhora Isabel Diaz. Very rare surviving debt notes also show that although the RAC agents kept their accounting records in English, they were conducting their business transactions in Crioulo or Portuguese, as illustrated in figure 3.4.[59]

How many matching or other records of debts, credits, and contracts Siddiqui himself created is another question that leads to a consideration of the multiple interacting legal systems available for making money on the Upper Guinea Coast. He might have learned to read and write Arabic in the local Quranic schools, which La Courbe observed in his 1686 visit to the lower Gambia. The Frenchman wrote admiringly about the numbers of (presumably male) children who attended Quranic school at night, where they learned to read and recite Arabic and write verses from the Quran on special wooden writing boards. He claimed that almost all of the children were using the Arabic script to write in both Arabic and their own Mande language of Mandinka. One wonders whether Siddiqui had been able to progress in studies like these as far as the boys who so impressed La Courbe. Other aspects of Muslims doing business with the company might involve the degrees to which individual Muslim traders understood or followed Islamic commercial law. Whether Siddiqui knew about or had formally learned what legal experts in the Maliki school of Islamic law prevailing among Mandinka-speakers prescribed for credit, debt, contracts, and usury cannot be seen in the RAC records since they recorded his work with the RAC according to English accountancy. He evidently also engaged in—whether or not he also needed to understand—Luso-African practices regarding contracts and credit under Portuguese law.[60]

Siddiqui represents the intersection of Muslim commercial practice with the Euro-African sphere of the Guinea trade on the coast. His years trading with the company schooled him in the major Atlantic import-export markets in and around the Gambia estuary and how to profit by them. Against that background, it is hard not to see the final entry in what survives of his account on the last day of November in 1688 as a systematic closing of it. He made sure to be credited with the payments due him for over five years in service, and he sold the company a canoe valued at 30B. The assortment he took back home with him, an ample 1,484B worth of overseas goods, was twice as valuable as any other, and it included, tellingly, two young boy captives, perhaps to be trained as assistants in his ventures as an independent trader. They were joining Siddiqui's labor force of at least five of the RAC's adult male captives who were domiciled at his residence at that time in Combo, located conveniently nearby on the south shore at the mouth of the Gambia River.

Siddiqui must also have already purchased an even bigger canoe, since the iron bars in this assortment by themselves weighed almost four tons, more than twice the weights of his previous loads. And by then he had assembled a carefully selected inventory of overseas commodities that were tied to specific markets for the imports: the red cloth, cowries, skeins of woolen thread, copper bars, and brassware were particular to transactions up the Gambia River; and the European and Asian textiles, swords, shotguns,

shot, and gunpowder characterized transactions with Luso-African suppliers down the coast. Conspicuously left behind at the James Island fort
was Siddiqui's debt of 1,218B, four and a half times the size of debt he had
carried with the company in 1680.[61]

Senhoras and the Independent Traders

The royal charter granted to the RAC gave them a monopoly on English
trade to and from the Guinea Coast, but in actual practice the company
never managed to put that privilege into full effect. In addition to the intense competition they faced from other European companies and the
various local Luso-African merchant communities, none of whom were restrained by the charter, there were also many private English traders intrud-
ing, though their numbers and shipping activities are almost impossible to
track and assess over time. However, RAC records do provide suggestive
glimpses of individual private traders, including English ones. They were
responsible only to themselves or their individual investors, and only scant
records of them survive. Private trading was legally branded "contraband
trade," with the traders themselves dubbed as "interlopers," and it may well
be that such trade was especially significant in the company's domain in
large part because of the nearness of the Upper Guinea Coast in the north
Atlantic to Europe, North America, and the Caribbean. The career of Robert
Gunn in the Sierra Leone estuary is instructive, for it shows how individuals
slipped in and out of the formal categories of "company men," "wholesale
suppliers to the company," and outright "interlopers." Robert Gunn was all
three. A cornerstone of his career was his Luso-African wife and business
partner, Isabella, who survived him as a senhora, or *nhara* or *signare,* in the
various spellings of this title of respect.

Gunn can be tracked in the extant RAC records for Sierra Leone and
Sherbro over a period of seventeen years from 1678 up to his death in October 1695. For six of those years, 1678 to 1684, he was based at the Bence
Island fort on a company salary and then, for a time, remained an employee
at their Tassily factory far up the coast near Cacheu. He may have been a
son of Thomas Gunn, who had worked for one of the earlier English companies in northern Guinea in 1665–66, by marriage with a coastal woman
and therefore of mixed Anglo-African ancestry. Upon leaving the employ
of the RAC in 1684, Robert Gunn became a private trader and supplier to
the RAC and to others. The exports he delivered were mostly ivory, captives,
and wax, and he also sold rice, as well as several times providing cordage

and other shipping supplies for fitting and repairing company vessels. At least once the company purchased over two hundred locally made cotton cloths from him. After he died, his widow, by that time known as Senhora Isabella Gunn, opened an account with the RAC and carried on the trade until her own death almost two years later.[62]

Exactly when Robert and Isabella married cannot be definitively known, but Robert was the second of Isabella's three successive RAC husbands. Judging from the company records, it is likely that their marriage took place sometime in late 1680 or early 1681, for it was during that time that Robert Gunn's account shows him engaging in some unusual trading activity and making a major change in domicile. In October 1680 he contributed 3B worth of overseas goods on behalf of Isabella Thompson to Senhora Francisca Fernandez, a supplier of rice and other provisions to the Bence Island fort. It is not clear what Isabella's relationship was with Senhora Francisca. They might both have been rice dealers who traded with each other, with Gunn paying off a debt Isabella owed to Francisca. Gunn's formal payment on Isabella's behalf indicates not only that he and she knew each other but also that they had reached some kind of agreement or relationship, suggesting he was either doing her a favor or perhaps giving her a gift.[63]

For her part, Isabella Thompson was a member of the Luso-African merchant community in the Sierra Leone estuary, many of whom, including Francisca Fernandez, lived on or near the island of Tombo, farther up the estuary from the company station on Bence Island. Situated near the entrances to Port Loko Creek and the Rokelle River, both of which led inland to rice-producing areas and to more remote sources of ivory and captives, Tombo was propitiously located as a brokering point between the regional and interregional rice trade of the interior and the overseas Atlantic trade.[64] Portuguese and Luso-Africans from the Cape Verde Islands had lived there since at least the mid-seventeenth century, when the site was described as "a village of whites with a church dedicated to St. Anthony." How Isabella became Isabella Thompson, perhaps by marriage to either George or Thomas Thompson, both of them RAC employees, cannot be determined, but George engaged in trade in the same circuits where Isabella appears, sometimes purchasing rice for the company's store of provisions, perhaps from her or from Senhora Fernandez. Both Thompsons disappear from the company books in the months prior to Gunn's payment on behalf of Isabella. And Robert Gunn left his post at the Tassily factory and moved south, back to the Sierra Leone estuary, in the month following that payment.[65] His abrupt move and subsequent activity suggest his marriage to Isabella was solemnized around this time.

Gunn continued to work for the RAC on salary over the next several years. Gaps in the records prevent filling in the picture of what his position was and exactly where he was living, but he was very likely already engaging in trade on his own account using RAC vessels. In August 1682, he put his coasting skills to work commandeering the company's longboat for a delivery of overseas goods to the York Island fort. Once there, agents at Sherbro apparently allowed him to borrow the vessel for his own use, a commingling of company and private affairs that drew sharp complaints from London. Then, in early 1683, three of the company's smaller coasting vessels underwent major repairs and refittings, which laid the groundwork for a major milestone in Robert Gunn's life. He struck a deal with the agent at Bence Island to purchase one of these vessels with all its new rigging and fittings for the sum of 144B, to be paid in "good Negroes." Paying the company half that amount at once and also selling them some ivory, he then took out an additional 138B in overseas goods. Evidently he had put his ship and its cargo to good use by November when he paid off the balance in captives. Thanks to the company, he had the experience and capital equipment necessary to engage in private trade on his own account, and in late 1684 or early 1685 he stopped drawing his salary.[66]

Between 1685 and his death in 1695, Robert Gunn maintained his RAC account and his close ties with agents at Sierra Leone and Sherbro while also conducting business with other private traders. His was a pragmatic career that maneuvered among the legal categories of the Guinea trade at this time to his advantage—as an employee, then a supplier to the company, and eventually an independent interloper working as a contractor on the company's behalf. The trading he carried out with the RAC can be followed in what was recorded in his company account, and references to his contacts and contracts with other private traders appear intermittently in the company correspondence as well. Taken together, these records of Robert Gunn's career on the Upper Guinea Coast allow for a rare, and revealing, view of the dynamic interplay between private and company traders there. By continuing to work with the RAC, Gunn enjoyed privileged access to their incoming cargoes of valuable bar iron, swords, paper, and other overseas goods. His regular visits to both the Bence Island fort and the one at York Island varied in frequency over time, five or six in some years, two or three in others. There were times, too, when he was able and willing to offer them valuable assistance. One example occurred at Bence Island in early 1686 when the fort was short of coasting vessels and Gunn offered to lease his to them for a set time and fee. He also occasionally sold them vital shipping supplies. In short, Gunn made himself useful in a variety of ways.[67] The company, for its part, could not have operated without Gunn and doubtless other independent entrepreneurs like him.

Some of Gunn's business contacts with other private traders appear in correspondence between the forts and London, even as he was also supplying the company. Letters from Sierra Leone and Sherbro, written on the same day in July 1690, capture the complexity and legal ambiguities of Gunn's commercial operations, for just as the agent in Sierra Leone was complaining about the interlopers with whom Gunn was trading, the Sherbro agent, in contrast, made special note of how helpful he was to them. He was not above trading with characters of whom the company disapproved. The Sherbro agent in 1692 identified Gunn as one of the trading partners of an English interloper named Wilkinson, notorious in official circles, who was drawing off their own trade, selling exports to independent English ship captains, and tempting company employees to desert and join him, in defiance of the RAC charter.[68]

Gunn managed nevertheless to remain on good terms with local company agents, who called him in to Sherbro in 1693 to discuss an outstanding credit due to him from previous years. They settled with him for 645B in overseas goods. From that time to his death two years later, he supplied ivory, captives, and rice to the company while letters to London continued to grumble about the assistance he was giving to known interlopers. Officers in London found Gunn's behavior altogether perplexing, and at least once, in 1695, they wrote directly to him requesting his assistance in the ivory trade and wondering why he didn't prefer to work exclusively with the RAC. Dealing with interlopers was clearly profitable, however, for at Gunn's death in 1695 his personal estate included at least two midsized coasting vessels that he had bought with profits acquired during his career in the Guinea trade.[69]

Upon the death of her husband, Senhora Gunn inherited whatever property they had accumulated, including their remaining stores of imports and exports as well as their ships. Her contributions to their business in prior years can be only inferred, for it was Robert who had made the deliveries to the RAC forts, and the company account was in his name. But there is no doubt that her own commercial activity was significant, as evidenced by her having attained the wealth and dignity marked by the title of senhora.

It is probable that she followed the lines of other senhoras along the coast who often began their trading careers as dealers in rice. Rice was a women's crop.[70] One well-informed Luso-African observer provided a detailed description of the major rice-exporting area in the Scarcies River estuary, just north of Sierra Leone. There, cleaned rice could be purchased in exchange for salt and fine coral and glass beads. Women were also the main brokers of the rice coming from upriver, traveling to buy it directly from producers there and then having it hauled down by canoe to waiting ships, some of them owned by the brokers themselves, the senhoras of the coast. Women rice dealers were known to be remarkably adept in handling a variety of measures and methods of calculating values, earning respected reputations for being entirely trustworthy traders.[71]

The business activities of these seventeenth-century senhoras, an important group of contributors to the local trade, make fragmentary but valuable appearances in the RAC records from the late seventeenth century. Senhoras are well known in the late eighteenth- and nineteenth-century French and Portuguese sources, but the predecessors of these ladies of the coast living and working in this earlier period have been relatively overlooked, especially the ones documented in RAC records. An illustration of how and why the economic roles of such prominent players in the Guinea trade could be misunderstood or deemed as marginal is the selective treatment given "La Belinguère," a prominent and titled woman in the lower Gambia who was described by Michel Jajolet de La Courbe, the director of the French Senegal Company, after his visit with her in July 1686.

La Belinguère lived at that time in the town of Albreda, on the Gambia's north shore, in a "Portuguese-style" house with a covered porch for receiving guests. La Courbe called her a "famous courtesan" and daughter of a king, beautiful and well built, very hospitable, and fluent in Portuguese, French, and English. He was particularly impressed by the exotic dinner they shared, which consisted of chicken prepared two different ways, pepper-seasoned rice, warm flatbread, pineapple for dessert, and palm wine. Her attire—a man's wool jacket worn over a close-fitting Portuguese corset, with a skirt of an intricately patterned cotton *pano alto* ("high cloth") from the Cape Verde Islands, and a headwrap of fine muslin from India—was a richly selected and arranged visual representation of the whole of early modern Afro-Eurasian commerce and the cosmopolitan creole culture it created. La

Courbe was quite taken by her, and he alluded enviously to what he imagined to be the countless men she had conquered by way of her considerable charms, not to say also her wealth. He left her with an elegant gift of coral and amber beads, a gesture fitting for a woman of her evident fascination and stature.[72]

La Courbe's well-known description is as important for what it omits as for what it conveys. Understandably, his brief social visit with her was his central focus. There can be no doubt that this woman was attractive, charming, and displayed impeccable manners. Dinner was sumptuous and surely delicious. That she spoke three European languages indicated the range of visitors with whom she was intimate. But La Courbe did not mention her likely mother tongue, Sereer, or other West African languages she most likely spoke, namely, Wolof and Mandinka. And he had no remark on the prominence indicated by what she was called—"La Belinguère." The name indicates that she was indeed of royal blood, as it was a political title, *linger,* given to selected royal women in the Sereer and Wolof kingdoms just north of the Gambia River.

In Sereer and Wolof languages, the *linger* title was reserved for the mother or maternal aunt of a king, that is, for a queen mother, or for princesses. The title carried with it well-known rights and responsibilities. A *linger* was in charge of judging disputes and meting out punishments for women accused of illicit acts such as adultery or having children out of wedlock. She also exercised political influence as an advisor to the ruler and his court and apparently played special roles in certain public ceremonies. For performing these important services, a *linger* received income in labor, agricultural produce, and other resources from designated villages.[73] Not surprisingly, but not mentioned in either La Courbe's description or the dictionary definitions of the term, individual women who held the title of *linger* could also be directly involved in trade independently of their royal duties.

RAC account books show the trading activity of a *"be linger"* over a period of three years, from October 1680 to November 1683. Whether this woman was the same *be linger* who later entertained La Courbe in 1686 cannot be determined, but whoever she might have been, to see this glimpse of the life and career of an individual *linger* is revealing of the interlocking European and African networks on the coast. This one, at least, was not simply an object of male Europeans' desires, although she must have known how to kindle them. Just after the harvest of 1680, the *be linger* in the RAC books managed the bulking and sale of over five hundred pounds of clean rice to the James Island fort. That she had taken out an assortment of overseas goods totaling 33B in the month prior suggests she had formally contracted her rice deliveries with the company in advance. Among the items she selected were coral, amber, cowries, European textiles, and a ream of paper, all signaling her high social position and varied commercial ties. In 1681, she delivered provisions of millet and some cakes of beeswax, taking out still more goods in even larger debt to the company. During the last four months of her trading with the RAC, she brought in a single female captive, the only such time, and it is not unreasonable to wonder whether she had tried and convicted this woman in a Wolof or Sereer women's court. Her last four assortments of overseas goods—among them iron bars, coral, textiles, slippers, brandy, and a padlock—brought her final debt level up to 192B. At that point, and in an echo of Siddiqui's disappearance under similarly profitable circumstances, her trading with the RAC apparently came to an end.[74]

The *be linger* episode shows that aristocratic women on the Upper Guinea Coast, on their own initiative, entered into private trading agreements on their own accounts, including with foreigners. The same was true for senhoras who seem to have been heirs to their deceased or departed husbands' business operations. The company recorded their lives and careers incompletely, if at all.[75] Senhora Isabella Gunn, for example, became visible in the RAC books only after her husband died. But the profile and longevity of the combined accounts strongly suggest that they were in business together as a couple. Over the ten years of their private trading, they delivered mainly ivory, captives, and rice to the RAC. In the early years, their deliveries of rice were steady, but ivory was their most profitable item. Their sales of captives were infrequent, and their dealings with interlopers can only be guessed at. But over time there were notable signs of their success. The sizes and values of deliveries increased such that in 1695 Gunn managed to supply a potentially dangerous but probably profitable cargo of forty-five male captives valued at 1,260B. That same year they made two large deliveries of provisions of clean rice, which together amounted to an unprecedented six tons. Their business was on an upward trend, and at the time of Gunn's death, he left an unmet forward contract with the RAC for ivory.[76]

Isabella's possible roles in the business can be only inferred. Given other coastal women's documented prominence as wholesalers of rice, it seems safe to assume that she was instrumental in that part of the couple's business, and she may very well have also contributed to their stores of ivory, as did other senhoras. For his part, Robert had his ships to look after, as well as the members of his male labor force (employees and slaves), who assisted him in outfitting and navigating his voyages, loading and unloading cargoes, and, when necessary, guarding, monitoring, and tending to imprisoned captives. Isabella and Robert probably lived in or near Tombo, within the relative security of a community of mostly Luso-African merchants and their families, servants, and slaves. Their home and daily meals and upkeep, and care for any children they may have had, would have required a domestic staff, presumably managed by Isabella or a trusted employee or female slave.

Another component of their business that would have come under her purview was the hulling of rice, a skilled task done by women working wooden mortars and pestles. Not only was it likely that the Gunns occasionally had to buy rice in the husk, but sometimes they also had to sell it for a lower price as such. Turning their husk rice into clean would therefore have been a priority whenever possible. Hence the six tons of clean rice the Gunns sold to the RAC in 1695 becomes even more impressive considering the labor demands of hulling it, work done either by their own female slaves or those of their suppliers. Some of that rice went to provision two voyages that year for the RAC vessel *John*. First it fed the crew on a coasting voyage northward to the Pongo and Nunez Rivers to purchase captives and probably also some ivory. Then it provisioned the crew and 133 captives in the *John*'s crossing of the Atlantic to Nevis, where the ship arrived safely with 131 surviving captives to be sold into slavery.[77]

When Robert Gunn died in October 1695, the RAC was under siege in northern Guinea. Louis XIV had chartered a series of French companies to trade up the Senegal River from posts well north of the RAC operations. England and France were at war (War of the League of Augsburg, 1689–97), which precipitated conflicts between their respective African companies on the Upper Guinea Coast. Early on, in 1690, the RAC had taken the precaution of reducing staff at the dangerously exposed Bence Island fort, thus making York Island the main RAC depot for that area because of its relatively sheltered location farther down the coast. But there came a major blow to the RAC in July 1695, when the staff and soldiers at James Island were forced to surrender their fort to French warships, whose soldiers proceeded to plunder and then desert it. Agent Corker at York Island reacted to this loss with alarm. Just two days after writing to London announcing the death of Gunn, Corker wrote again, expressing his concern about the seizure of James Island fort and his hopes for recovering it. He had already taken action by outfitting three sloops, loading them up with cargo, and dispatching them northward to the Gambia, two of them leased to the RAC by "the widdow Gunn."[78]

Isabella's behavior after the death of Robert leaves the impression that she was a shrewd if also cautious businesswoman. She obviously had traveled the hundred miles south to York Island to deliver the news of his death in person, or it would not have been possible to have so quickly made an agreement with Corker to rent him two of her coasting vessels. In doing so, she publicly claimed title to her inherited property while following her late husband's example of providing just this kind of strategic logistical support to the RAC in times of need. She also had at least one other ship at her disposal, for she made a delivery to York Island three months later, in early February 1696, clearing out at least some of their remaining inventory of exports.

Her method of trading was markedly less reliant on company credit than that of Robert, and also that of the *be linger*. Robert had often arranged contracts in advance on paper and carried over large sums of credits and debts in his account, for which he kept receipts. The *be linger* had also accumulated a significant debt over her three years of trading, which the RAC probably never recovered. Isabella, on the other hand, made separate deals per class of export and settled each of them on the spot with assortments of equivalent value. In exchange for her February 1696 delivery of 1,391B in ivory, she took out exactly 1,391B in assorted overseas goods. And likewise, for the seventeen captives valued at 472B, she took out an assortment of goods totaling 472B. Her care not to carry over either a credit or a debt could simply have been a sign of her initial caution in conducting trade directly with the company, or it could signal a more general and ongoing wariness on her part that might have come from hard experience. Perhaps she was numerate but not fully literate and so did not feel comfortable engaging in paper-based trading. Whatever her method, she departed York Island with impressive stores of imported goods, including hundreds of iron bars, swords, metalwares, European and Asian textiles, beads, shoes, gunpowder, and six gray coats of the kind often worn by RAC grometos. Three months later, the wealthy widow married the Anglo-African Richard Bridgman, a former RAC employee.[79]

In June 1696, one month after her third marriage, Senhora Isabella Gunn brought in a note of credit, dated October 1, 1695, for the last delivery Robert

Gunn had made to the York Island fort. The export commodities he had brought in at that time—captives, wax, rice, and local cotton cloths—came to a total of 584B in value. Keeping closely to her cautious trading strategy, she took out only 533B worth of overseas goods in return, including some new items for her such as ribbons, hats, spirits, paper, padlocks, and men's thread stockings. That same day her new husband's brother, William, took out 17B worth of overseas goods at York Island, likely his payment for sailing her down to the fort. Among his goods were a light musket, shot, and gunpowder. There was no sign of further activity on her account until November, when someone withdrew 11B worth of cut tobacco from the RAC stores on her account, probably one of the Bridgman brothers. Her account then remained dormant for the following five months.[80]

In April 1697, Isabella made what would be her last recorded visit to the fort at York Island. Her business this time was to settle with the company for its purchase of one of her sloops, *William and Mary,* and to collect on leasing it and another sloop to the company for fifteen months. The company, in addition to paying for the purchase and rental fees, had also expended labor and supplies to repair the other sloop, *St. Antonio,* the one Isabella kept. The total due her amounted to 320B, which she matched precisely with an assortment of equivalent value in overseas goods, including iron bars, metalwares, padlocks, gunpowder, and handsaws. In May, the first anniversary of Isabella and Richard's marriage, Richard himself took out an assortment of goods on her account, worth a rather substantial 713B, which included such items for himself as men's slippers and shoes, tankards, brass chains, men's shirts, tobacco, pipes, and a small anchor, alongside the other trade items that Isabella customarily chose, such as swords, coral, crewel thread, fustians, and metalwares. Not long after, on June 21, 1697, agent Corker wrote to London stating that he had satisfied Richard Bridgman on the account of "the *late* widdow Gunn."[81]

Richard continued to trade on Isabella's account. But upon the death of the Sherbro king in July 1698, Richard was robbed and probably physically attacked by an angry throng of nearby villagers, who also set fire to his home, fields, and other property. Understandably alarmed by this event, he dictated a will, written and witnessed at York Island on October 12, 1698. It indicates that he had been under the care of a nurse, and that he had at least some wealth remaining in pounds sterling, most likely in London. Of that, £200 was to go to his father, £30 to his sister, and the rest was to be divided between his three brothers. The only personal property mentioned in the will was "the black girle," 4B in goods, and four good cloths he was leaving to his nurse, Emma.[82] Ten days later, Bridgman visited the York Island fort to select an assortment of RAC goods valued at 174B, clearing the balance of what the company owed on Isabella's account. Richard Bridgman's last appearance in the fort records showed him bringing in and taking out sundries on January 1, 1699, with no values given.[83]

How old Isabella might have been when she died and how she met her end cannot be determined. She was at least in her thirties and could have died from any number of natural causes, including complications during childbirth. She may have been killed by accident or by design, for it was a time of great insecurity and violent clashes on the coast. What can be said about her last days is that her substantial inheritance, the timing of her death, and the bold and suspicious behavior of the Bridgman brothers present an unsettling picture of the temptations and possible dangers of women's wealth and success along the Upper Guinea Coast.

Conclusion: A Large Cast of Diverse Characters

RAC account books mention a revealing variety of individuals who did business with the company in different ways, if only a small and intermittent selection of them. Foremost among them were, of course, the important local landlords—kings and officials—in the vicinities of the forts and outstations, at ports upriver, and at coasting destinations, along with masters of towns nearby. Depending on who and where they were, these local people—owners and stewards of the territories they allowed the company to occupy—might collect regular yearly rents or customs fees charged to the company, or they might create ad hoc income streams by offering special services to the company or by performing certain tasks or favors at negotiated prices. Examples recounted here demonstrate that these incomes could be quite substantial in their aggregate amounts and in some cases even exceeded the yearly salaries of RAC employees. The landholding authorities took their incomes in preferred commodity currencies and valuable overseas trade goods, as additional personal wealth or parlayed into social capital. Local people such as these were indeed "making good money" in the Guinea trade.

Others "made money" in trade in more overtly commercial strategies as suppliers in the import-export sector. The RAC records provide new information about these people. In addition to the suppliers situated in the coastal trading towns and stations visited by the company ships, others made deliveries directly to the company at its forts. Peter and Jane Vaz of Cacheu and António Silva of Geregia were two prominent examples from the well-established Luso-African commercial communities. More unusual was the case of Siddiqui, a Muslim man who worked for the company first as a hired provisioner and then leveraged that position into a place for himself as an independent trader in the import-export business. How much, if at all, he had connections to specialist Muslim trading families in the Gambia basin is not known. Finally, the women of the coastal towns, such as Senhora Bernardo de Melo, La Belinguère, and Senhora Isabella Gunn— as members of Luso-African commercial families and networks or as family members of prominent African authorities—also appear repeatedly in records of the company's Guinea trade. The RAC could not have done business without this large supporting cast and the many others hidden from view by their absence in the records of its operations.

CHAPTER FOUR

Company Property

Captives, Rebels, and Grometos

SLAVE LABOR remained much in demand on the Upper Guinea Coast even while demand for unfree labor steadily grew across the Atlantic with commercial agriculture on plantations taking hold in the Caribbean Islands by the late seventeenth century. American plantation labor was steadily becoming Africanized as the RAC supplied planters with enslaved Africans to replace indentured servants at work in their expanding fields of sugar cane, cotton, indigo, and tobacco.[1] At the same time, West Africans increasingly kept captives to work in land clearance, in food production, in extraction and processing of raw materials, in the workshops of artisans, in trade and transport facilities and their operations, and in creating and maintaining homes and households. RAC officers in London faced their own competing demands for labor as they dispatched ships filled with captive people across the Atlantic while also trying to satisfy the labor needs of their forts and trading posts on the Guinea Coast. RAC agents in Upper Guinea found themselves caught in the middle as they sought to balance directors' demands for captives for the plantations and their own needs for "company slaves" as laborers at their own forts or at Cape Coast Castle on the Gold Coast.

African captives on both sides of the Atlantic were for the most part people who had lost their freedom by being taken prisoners in war, by being convicted of a crime, by being held as debt pawns, by being kidnapped, or by being traded away from their homelands by merchants.[2] Company ships or coastal suppliers delivered them to RAC forts on the Upper Guinea Coast where company soldiers kept them imprisoned with little or no freedom of movement for eventual transportation across the Atlantic. Having been purchased by the company as an export commodity, they were inventory of considerable value as a trade good until delivery across the Atlantic turned them into valuable labor power to be purchased as the chattel property of masters. Whether local RAC agents and employees saw themselves as temporary masters of these people or as guards of prisoners must have varied from individual to individual and over time.

The company's years on the Guinea Coast during the second half of the seventeenth century was a moment when slavery as an institution was being reshaped by more and more commercialized social and political conditions throughout the Atlantic basin. Slave codes for regulating the lives, work, behavior, and punishments of slaves were being established in the Caribbean, which was a crucially important step in structuring the new, more modern order, although how much or how consistently those laws were enforced is open to question. New forms of corporal punishment were being invented as maiming and murder became masters' weapons of choice in asserting and maintaining control over people whom they treated inhumanely as

brute labor and replaceable property.[3] Punishments witnessed in Brazil and the Caribbean in the mid-1690s, illustrated schematically in figure 4.1, depict the gruesome methods of retaliation American slave owners might mete out on a repeated runaway slave. Flogging him while suspended naked from a tree, amputating his leg at the knee, or crippling him by chaining one of his ankles to his neck—these were among the newly devised alternatives to death by hanging.[4]

FIGURE 4.1 Corporal punishment of slave runaways, seventeenth c. Brazil (above) and Caribbean (below). François Froger, *Relation d'un voyage*, (Paris, 1700). John Carter Brown Library, Providence, RI. *Internet Archive*. Web. 16 Nov. 2016.

Unfree captives on the Upper Guinea Coast who passed through or lived and worked at the RAC forts and outstations experienced strikingly varied living and working conditions, although they also shared some of the most pernicious and defining characteristics of commercialized slavery. One of the classic features of the institution is namelessness. RAC men referred to the company's captives in their records only in such generic terms as "negroes" or "sale slaves," whereas "company slaves" were usually called *grometos*. That they were anonymous rendered them not only "natally alienated" but also meant that their lives and actions as individuals cannot be clearly identified and tracked over time.[5] The RAC records nevertheless offer invaluable glimpses of them and of how they insisted on demonstrating their personhood, as examples in the following sections will show.

"Sale Slaves" and Stages of Captivity

Most of the captives coming into company hands had been free people who were seized from their homes and families and then forcibly taken to some unknown place far away to be sold into slavery. This initial violent uprooting might occur during wartime or in times of relative peace, as individuals might be rightly or wrongly convicted of a crime, held against their will as collateral, or given as payment for a debt. It might also be that a slave would find him- or herself uprooted and transported once again during times of food insecurity or for reasons having to do with inheritance after a master's death; or it might be because of a family emergency or as a punishment of some kind. Within the RAC trading sphere on the Upper Guinea Coast, most captives reaching any of the main slave embarkation points— Barrakunda and towns in Saalum up the Gambia River, the port town of Cacheu, other ports of Joal and Portudale on the Petite Côte, anchorages at the mouths of the Scarcies, Pongo, and Nunez Rivers, the post at Samo up the Melakori River, and Tassily—came into company possession only after having been forced to travel long and arduous distances in groups of some size on foot by caravan, by boat, or both; others were marched there from nearby towns and villages alone or in twos or threes.[6]

Although it is possible that some captives were taken from their homes directly to the Atlantic shore in a few days, it was more likely that they endured much more protracted and complicated travels, forced for weeks or months into and out of caravans and changing hands from merchant to merchant along the way. The complexity of overland and riverine arbitrage trade in the interior regions (described in chapter 1) allowed for use of captives both as commodities for sale and as potential "beasts of burden" for commodities in transit. Also, leaders and traders traveling overland in caravans changed from one entrepôt to another. Independent merchants moved in groups, and those in an arriving caravan would make their sales each in turn, then purchase and pack up other goods before finally joining together in a new caravan to head toward their next desired destination. In this case, arbitrage trading meant that unsold captives might be forced through a succession of segments of trading routes. These might change or reverse direction several times when destinations were dictated by the best-known markets for other goods. Reaching an entrepôt, captives might be purchased to be kept as a slave to a local master, or they might be forced to travel on through yet another journey in captivity. Friendships or other attachments they were able to make among themselves, if any, were thus in constant jeopardy.

Immediate labor needs, gendered divisions of labor, and the sources and destinations of trade in other goods shaped the experiences of captives forced to traverse the hinterlands of Upper Guinea in the late seventeenth century. Far in the interior, female captives might be moved north toward the edges of the Sahara Desert, where specialized long-distance trans-Saharan merchants would select them for Muslim slave markets in North Africa, which preferred women and children. Or they could find themselves far from home and held in households or in fields during planting and growing seasons or doing unskilled or semi-skilled work for provisions traders, spinners, potters, leatherworkers, coastal salt makers, or dyers.

Males would likely be directed toward the Atlantic zone, where they were the preferred captives for heavy and monotonous tasks of planting and cultivating sugar cane or other commercial crops in the Americas. But rarely would their routes be a single or continuous one.[7] Demand for male labor in West Africa—for example, as soldiers, field hands, construction workers, weavers, bellows operators, charcoal makers, and miners—rose and declined in specific locales given the changing of seasons and circumstance. Thus, the captive populations of caravans fluctuated. Some were divided up for sale to work for a time, whereas others found themselves thrust into another caravan and setting off on yet another grueling march through unfamiliar lands. As social beings suffering the same fates and confined together for a time, they undoubtedly sought human connections of some kind throughout their ordeal. In other words, captives were not uprooted only once. They would be isolated and displaced again and again as they persistently sought to form alliances of friendship and trust among themselves, only to be torn away once again.

RAC trading records suggest that captives could find themselves working as slaves for a time in places where production of goods was expanding in the late seventeenth century for interregional commerce and for export into the Atlantic system. One major example of this flexible appropriation of the swelling flows of captive people was the development of centers in the Upper Guinea hinterlands that specialized in producing cotton cloth currencies. As this sample transcribed record shows (transcription 4.1), the company relied on cotton cloth currencies, especially in the purchase of provisions but also in a variety of other transactions with suppliers and in payments for labor. These textiles were plain white strips or whole cloths that circulated widely in standard-size units. Their fabrication generated an increasing demand for labor in the cultivation, harvesting, and processing of raw cotton fiber, as well as in the spinning and weaving of it. It cannot be accidental that these centers were located consistently in areas directly inland from points of slave embarkation, as the relatively low market prices of these currencies were most likely achieved by the incidental use of low-cost slaves en route to the coast in the various stages of production.[8]

The most obvious uses of male captives in weaving centers would have been in the preparation of fields for planting and also in the harvesting of cotton at the end of the growing season. Demand for male labor would also have extended into and throughout the dry season, when men's weaving workshops increased their numbers of looms to boost output. Unskilled and semiskilled men or boys might perform a variety of tasks, from the winding of cotton thread into long lengths of warp to be dressed onto the loom to the dressing of the loom and to the winding of thread onto shuttles for weaving. Some male captives might even have been kept and trained in the weaving of these plain cottons. Cotton currency often circulated in the form of large rolls of woven cotton strip as it came directly off the loom. Alternatively, it circulated as a semifinished portion of cloth with the strips sewn together according to standard measures. The labor of male slaves in tailoring workshops would have been useful at this stage as well. Some owners may even have invested in keeping and training skilled or semiskilled slaves to hire out to do such work.

Preparation of the cotton fiber was one of the major bottlenecks in textile production. Steady demand for imported English wool cards during this time signals that the labor-intensive work of preparing cotton for spinning

TRANSCRIPTION 4.1 COTTON CLOTH CURRENCY TRANSACTIONS, JAMES ISLAND, JANUARY–FEBRUARY 1679

Source: T 70/830, f. 109. TNA.

1679			# of cloths	Barrs
Jan.	9	To King of Barrow	10	5
	10	For Matts	10	5
	10	For Provisions	20	10
	12	For Provisions	2	1
	15	To Franciscoe Vere	10	5
	15	To Vinty Santia	4	2
	17	For Provisions	2	1
	19	For Provisions	3	1:3
	19	For Provisions	24	12
	20	For Provisions	5	2:3
	20	To Padler	5	2:3
	22	For Provisions	4	2
	22	For Provisions	23	11:3
	23	To Ambrose Headly	4	2
	23	For Provisions	16	8
	30	For teeth and wax	1	:3
Feb.	2	For Provisions	16	8
	3	To Cidikey	30	15
	4	For Provisions	19	9
	6	To Doktor for the use of the Negroes	1:3	
	7	To Lewis Deas	3	1:3
	7	To Domingoe Mora	1	:3
	12	For Provisions	10	5
	14	To George Manchitt	2	1
	15	To Will. Padison	2	1
	16	For Provisions	51	25:3
	19	For Provisions	10	5
	20	To Ambrose Headly	4	2
	20	To Oliver Scott	1	:3
	24	For Matts	6	3
	24	For Sundries	7	3:3
	24	To Tho. Boaz	2	1
	25	To Profit and Loss for the use of the Negroes	2	1
	25	For Provisions	30	15
	25	To Joseph Hide	4	2

was being carried out on a large scale by women and girls, many of whom were probably slaves. The RAC shipped several hundred pairs of English wool cards yearly into the Upper Guinea Coast, especially to the James Island fort. Local suppliers of rice and ivory regularly selected wool cards in their trade assortments, up to twenty pairs at a time, which could then be put to use in coastal or inland workshops.[9] Spinning could be done on a large scale in areas of intensive production or in smaller domestic settings to contribute to household income of townsfolk with access to cotton fiber.

La Courbe described an example of the latter in 1686 as he made his way around the lower Gambia and its tributaries surveying possible trading prospects for the Compagnie du Sénégal. Traveling up Vintang Creek to the town of the same name, he was favorably impressed with the setting and took note of the town's dwellings and their features, which were a mixture, like its population, of Luso-African, Manding, and Bagnun cultures.[10] After settling in for a short stay, he made a visit to the master of the town and then to a Luso-African woman who was married to one of the town's most prominent merchants. As he approached their home, he saw her seated on the porch surrounded by several of her black female servants or slaves who were spinning cotton.[11] Cotton thread being produced in the home of a prosperous town merchant, presumably under the supervision of his wife, indicates the high degree to which labor in textile manufacture was integrated into the domestic economies of northern Guinea. Periodic RAC requests to their factors to send back to London cleaned cotton fiber or cotton thread met with little success, no doubt owing to its importance in the production of cotton currencies, which were used in all sorts of personal and company transactions. RAC attempts to have imitations made in England repeatedly failed, leaving the company dependent on their West African suppliers. It would be at least another century or more before Britain would be able to produce on its own cotton textiles acceptable to West African consumers.[12]

Captives who continued their marches overland or those who found themselves once again forced into caravan travel would have had every reason to sink into despondency. Journeying by caravan was difficult and dangerous enough for people who had chosen to travel, but for unwilling captives it could be devastating and often deadly. As encampments on the move, caravans took on complex and shifting compound organization and structure. Led by knowledgeable and experienced leaders called *silatigui* in Mandinka, single caravans were usually composed of several separate merchant groups, each one with a head merchant, his assistants and armed guards, porters, pack animals, trade goods, and, in many cases, captives for sale.[13] As slow-moving targets on the road, caravans had to be well defended and organized in order to fend off possible attackers or robbers, although merchants' incentives to keep their captives alive could be overwhelmed by unexpected and threatening circumstances.

Added to these ever-present risks from their surroundings were the internal threats of theft, resistance, or escape that accompanied the forcible transporting of resentful men and women. As a safeguard, captives were coffled to form a single line, that is, tied or held together in some way, usually by rope or leather straps at the neck. Hence for captives the rough and dangerous paths of caravan travel were particularly hellish. Having no control over their bodies or their mobility made them extremely vulnerable and dependent on others, initially strangers, to stay alive. There was shame and humiliation to be endured for being naked or in rags, for living in filth, and for having to relieve themselves in public, and there was also the fear of punishment or abandonment for slowing down the coffle because of illness or fatigue. Even worse, a merchant might offset the cost of a captive's daily ration of food and drink by forcing him or her to take on the work of headloading trade goods or caravan provisions to the next stop.

Entrepôts on the Gambia River such as Jour and Barrakunda, upriver 100 and 250 miles, respectively, saw regular seasonal arrivals of slave caravans, which attracted merchants from the coast who had the experience and wherewithal to make the upstream journey. It was not an easy ascent, requiring skillful maneuvering through tidal currents in the lower reaches and changing wind patterns farther inland. What made the trouble worth the risk were the profits that came from price differentials between the coast and interior, especially for captives. Thomas Weaver, the senior RAC agent at James Island, planned one such company venture in February 1704. His instructions to the ship's captain were to ascend the river to the town of Jour, in Saalum, and to assist the company men there in purchasing slaves brought there by caravans. Agent Weaver specifically urged him to make sure that the "negroes" were fed and cared for to avoid sickness and to keep guards on board to prevent any uprisings or escapes. Above all, they were to complete all transactions, loading, and provisioning as quickly as possible.

After only one week spent upriver, agent Weaver had to order the expedition back to James Island. A fire that had started in the thatched roof of the fort's storehouse got out of control, spread to and set off the gunpowder in it, and destroyed the company's entire inventory of trade goods. All the stock they had left was upriver in the ship. Undeterred and unwilling to let the opportunity pass, however, Weaver sent another vessel upriver once the fort was sufficiently repaired and supplied. The *Postillion* set off for Jour on March 26, reaching the town three days later. "Slaving" the *Postillion* would take all of April and half of May, evidently from dealing with the many small-sized cohorts of slaves arriving there.[14]

RAC accounts of this venture provide vivid details of cross-cultural trade at the meeting of these two commercial zones—the West African interior and the Atlantic basin. The intense nonstop buying and selling that Francisco de Lemos Coelho had apparently witnessed upon the arrival of Jahaanke-led caravans at Barrakunda in the mid-seventeenth century (described in chapter 1) was not in evidence on this visit to Jour. During the month and a half of transactions, the RAC men dealt with at least three different caravans. In addition to the usual payments of customs fees and offerings of gifts to town officials and dignitaries, they gave presents to the *silatigui* of each caravan on its arrival and again on its departure after having completed its sales.[15] They also paid small fees to caravan merchants for assisting them in negotiating transactions. Purchases of captives were gradual, occurring in small lots of one or two at a time or occasionally up to seven or eight. Almost all the captives the RAC purchased were males, as specified by their orders from London.[16] Trading for provisions took place throughout to feed company men, crew, and the growing numbers of sale slaves, who on this occasion were being held on the ship rather than onshore. One purchase of thirteen fowls was intended for an unspecified number of "sick men" presumably among them. Despite evident concern for their survival, if not also comfort, at least one male captive died on board.

Other details in the report of this venture bear on the commodities they also required. A portion of the company trades was for ivory and wax, along with gold they also purchased or were given as gifts by the merchants and others. But they primarily bought sale slaves whom they carried back to James Island. Of the ninety-nine surviving captives, ninety-four were men, three were boys, and only two were women. The suppliers were from two distinctly different categories of sellers—overland caravan merchants and local African and Euro-African traders. The local traders varied, consisting of eleven individuals, four of them men and seven women. Included among the men was a king, or *Bur,* of Saalum (or his representative) and his heir apparent, the *Bumi*. The two remaining men were senhors, that is, prominent local male merchants, and all of the seven women were senhoras, three of them with Portuguese names and another whose name might also have been Portuguese. The other three senhoras bore the surnames of their English husbands or fathers, who were former RAC employees at James Island.[17] These local traders sold the company only one or two captives each and at higher prices than the caravan merchants. Whether these individual traders were selling local captives or slaves of their own at the higher coastal price, or whether they were selecting prime caravan captives and selling them to the RAC at a markup, the reasons for this price differential are unclear. Whatever the case may be, the average price of captives sold by the caravan merchants in the interior came to about two-thirds of what local traders charged on the coast. These differences in pricing are consistent with the principle that captives were cheaper at, or nearer to, their place of capture, which made the seasonal availability of caravan captives at least potentially worth the costs and risks of a voyage upriver.

Prices for captives on the Upper Guinea Coast differed slightly by locales and also over time. At Gambia, prices were generally higher than at Sierra Leone and Sherbro, and in all places prices were higher in times of relative peace and stability, indicating drop-offs from larger numbers of captives taken in times of war.[18] Records show that the valuation of captives on the coast at this time had no clear and consistent differentiation by gender, as can be seen in this sample listing of prices for women ranging from 25 to 26B and for men a wider range of between 16 and 30B (transcription 4.2). What regularly made a difference in price were the physical conditions and ages of captives. Prices for caravan captives purchased upriver also fluctuated, women from 14 to 17B and men from 15 to 19B, which speaks to the heavy toll that the overland journey exacted on the bodies and psyches of some of them.[19] Prices for captive "boys" and "girls," presumably preadolescent children, were lower, and again with no clear gender differential. Slaves who were considered too old for heavy labor or to promise a long-term return on investment for them, and therefore unacceptable, were sometimes shipped across the Atlantic anyway, provoking angry complaints from RAC agents in the Caribbean. One example from the early 1680s concerned a shipment of 114 captives from Sierra Leone, which arrived in Barbados. The RAC's local agent described the human cargo of the *Two Friends* as "indifferent" with "many elderly among them," almost half of the men being forty to fifty years old. Sierra Leone's factor admitted as much in his letter accompanying the group, but he blamed the company, insisting he could not get better slaves because of the lack of overseas goods provided to the Bence Island fort.[20]

TRANSCRIPTION 4.2 SLAVE PURCHASES, JAMES ISLAND, AUGUST–DECEMBER 1706

Source: T 70/835, "Slaves" Account. TNA.

1706			#	*Barrs*
August	28	1 woman Slave	1	26
September	4	3 men Slaves bought of John Masceda	3	75
		1 boy bought of ditto	1	20
		2 men bought of Mr. Godineau	2	32
		1 woman bought of Mr. Defains	1	25
	23	1 man bought of Mr. Godineau	1	25
October	14	1 boy bought of Mr. Plunkett	1	25
	24	1 man bought of King of Phony	1	25
	25	1 man bought of ditto	1	25
	30	1 man bought of Seignora Desea	1	23
November	6	1 man bought of King of Bara	1	30
		97 Slaves for which given a Receit to Mr. Dakins		
		4 Slaves said to belong to Mr. Chidley		
		11 Slaves purchas'd at Jour by Mr. Adcock		
December	1	1 bought of Anthony DeGear	1	25
Oct.	15	7 men and 3 women Slaves returned by Mr. Adcock	10	282

Most captives purchased at the upriver entrepôts and RAC outposts were taken to the company's island bases on the coast to await shipment. Company records, like other sources on the slave trade, are noticeably—and revealingly—silent about their day-to-day experiences as individuals and as groups. Brought in by suppliers or on company vessels, they arrived intermittently from embarkation points inland or elsewhere along the coast. The island became their prison until the arrival of RAC ships destined for the Caribbean, and they customarily would be held in irons and under armed guard. Sporadic inventories of the contents of company storerooms there give faint indications of the conditions of their imprisonment and the ways they were forcibly restrained. Shackles, collars, and handcuffs, all made of iron, refer to the captives' ankles, necks, and wrists, where they would be bound and then secured by chains to another captive or to a fixed anchoring point—floor, wall, or post. Sporadic shipments of prisoners' irons from overseas were supplemented when necessary by company smiths who worked up shackles on the spot from bar iron.[21] Occasional requests for branding irons suggest that branding of captives was not yet fully or systematically practiced. Floggings, which must have been meted out on returned runaways, were usually not recorded. One exception is an account of an attempted escape that described the alleged ringleader as a repeat offender who was publicly punished with one hundred lashes.[22]

Additional material evidence speaks indirectly to the RAC men's ongoing fears of having to serve as prison guards and temporary slave masters. At Sierra Leone and Sherbro, the well-established use of brass chains rather than iron ones indicates an awareness on the part of company agents that captives might find a way to file or hammer through chains that were made of corroded, rusting, or imperfectly refined iron. Word of the efficacy of this precautionary practice evidently began to spread beyond the company forts and factories to local suppliers of slaves and provisions, who increasingly selected dozens of brass chains in their assortments.[23] Company letters overtly expressed anxieties about the possibility of escapes, thefts, and uprisings. RAC agents sent urgent requests to London asking them to send more soldiers to protect and secure themselves and the factory from possible acts of aggression by the sale slaves they accumulated while waiting for company ships to take them abroad. Some requests were prompted by costly recent direct experience, such as the testy remarks agent Booker sent from James Island in 1693 after an insurrection on the vessel *America,* instructing London to make sure that masters of slave ships followed their directions and carried more and stronger irons to better secure the "negroes."[24]

Though living conditions at the RAC forts cannot be described precisely or definitively, a plan of James Island and its fort and outbuildings, dating to the time of its capture by the French in July 1695, allows good inferences to be drawn (see figure 4.2).[25] Located about a mile from the nearest (north) shore, the island was a low-lying rock formation that at high tide measured only slightly larger than the size of an American football field. Encircling the island stood a palisade of thick logs as protection from erosion and easy attack.[26] Semicircular cannon batteries guarded the island at its north, southwest, and southeast corners, shielding the small fort situated at its center. The fort's imposingly high exterior walls surrounded an interior space

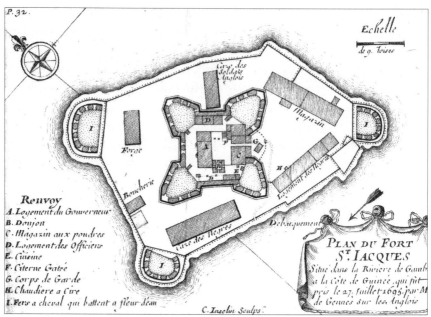

FIGURE 4.2 Plan of James Island and the fort, 1695. François Froger, *Relation d'un voyage* (Paris, 1700). John Carter Brown Library, Providence, RI. *Internet Archive.* Web. 16 Nov. 2016.

of only 5,300 square feet, where the chief agent, company officers, and their personal "house slaves" lodged. Construction of walls around and within the fort combined brick and stone masonry. Also inside the fort were an armory for storing gunpowder, a water cistern, a tower, and a kitchen shed. A guard post flanked its entrance.

Buildings outside the fort were made of less permanent materials such as wood and adobe brick. Among them were the company storeroom for overseas trade goods, lodgings for soldiers, and another building for housing the company slaves or "grometos." Standing outside the fort's southern wall was the building that served as a jail, or barracoon, for holding sale slaves. It is not clear how long any of these outbuildings depicted in the plan had been in use before the fort's capture in 1695. Earlier company records show passing references to agents sending men out in sloops to gather stones for construction or repairs and shells to make lime cement. Company men, assisted by grometos, engaged at times in making bricks on the mainland.[27]

Based on dimensions for the buildings drawn on the plan, the grometos and sale slaves look to have lived in structures of about the same size, and the structure for company soldiers was much smaller. But the sizes of their populations differed markedly. The average number of soldiers living on James Island in the 1680s was twelve, with the figure going up to between twenty-five and forty-eight in the mid-1690s, when England and France were at war. So in times of peace, at least, each soldier would have had about an eight-foot-by-eight-foot storage and sleeping space, or just slightly larger than the average jail cell. No wonder then that they often spent most of their time serving at outposts or on company vessels. The RAC grometos at James Island during the 1680s usually numbered around twenty-five, thus leaving each of them with about the same amount of space as the soldiers. They, too, had at least some freedom of movement and spent time running errands or working on the mainland. As for the sale slaves, the conditions of their continuous forced confinement were far from livable. At times when the RAC had its full capacity of two hundred sale slaves on hand, each would have been cramped into a space of three feet by three feet, or nine square feet, only slightly more than the eight square feet prescribed as the minimum allotment of space per slave on slave ships in a regulation passed in Parliament in 1799 to ameliorate overcrowding.[28] When the number of sale slaves was around one hundred, each one's space came to four feet by four feet, or sixteen square feet, only a quarter of the space allotted to soldiers and grometos. Being confined as prisoners, sale slaves had little to no freedom of movement, which meant that their time on the island would have been next to impossible to bear.[29]

The generally poor state of health common among sale slaves left them especially vulnerable to diseases. Weakened by hunger and dehydration and with what little clothing or covering they had in tatters, their exposure to cold and rains could impose a heavy death toll. RAC agent Horde at James Island wrote to London in June 1680 at the onset of the rainy season that they had lost thirty of their sale slaves over the past twenty days. Their close quarters heightened risks of spreading any contagious affliction. Agent Booker wrote in 1693 that a terrible outbreak of smallpox was raging among the "negroes" and that he dared not ship them until it subsided. Malaria and dysentery were also frequent maladies.[30] Records noting intermittent and rare instances of amelioration serve mainly to amplify the sale slaves' general and ongoing social degradation and precarious physical condition.

Agents at James Island occasionally made payments to individuals who had taken care of and cured sale slaves who had fallen sick. In the middle of the rainy season in September 1686, the master of Juffure on the north shore received a payment of 5B in goods for overseeing the care of five captives who had been suffering from unspecified illnesses. The next September another 5B went to someone, perhaps again the master of Juffure, for bringing some sick "negroes" back to health. Then, in November 1688, the successful curing at Juffure of nineteen sick "negroes" drew a reward of 17B and 6 ounces of amber. There were also several recorded instances of the RAC distributing cotton or linen cloths to ailing sale slaves, but these dispensations were irregular and fewer in number than the monthly allotments of cloth that had been given to captives between March and July 1666, presumably in preparation for the coming rainy season.[31] There were infrequent efforts to tend to the health of sale slaves at Bence Island as well, though with less successful results. In the years 1679 and 1680, there were three recorded deaths of sale slaves who had been sent out to be cured, two at Tasso Island, and one in the houses of the company grometos. A local gentleman (or his wife or female servant) received reimbursement for feeding and caring for four captives who fell sick during the rainy season of 1680, which the company paid with cloth and brandy.[32] It is not possible to estimate the daily provisions of food and drink given to sale slaves, but it can be assumed that although everyone at the forts experienced times of food scarcity, theirs were more frequent and debilitating.

Contrasting sharply with these few and scattered indications of care are the frequent notations of captives' daily deaths. Given that records of mortality were kept only irregularly and imprecisely and that the numbers of sale slaves were in a constant state of flux, the deaths by diseases and other causes presented here allow only very approximate estimates of the rates of fatalities. Nevertheless, they are a reminder that the reality and high risk of death were ever present during the time captives spent on the Upper Guinea Coast, as well as during their Atlantic crossing.

Recorded deaths varied from year to year and by seasons, and they also showed differing patterns for the three RAC forts. Relatively consistent records of captives' deaths exist for James Island for a three-year period in the 1680s, each death recorded as a financial loss to the company rather than in terms of its human cost. From the end of September to the beginning of the next September for three years in succession (1683–86), the numbers of deaths of captives show wide variations. For the first of these three years, twenty-three men and nine women died, whereas for the last of these years twenty-three men and four women died. The middle year shows a doubling of men's deaths to fifty, with six women also lost. During the rainy season, deaths increased slightly. Some months went by with no deaths recorded; other months showed one or two deaths. The month of August during the rainy season of 1685 was the deadliest, with eleven captive males dying. RAC forts at Bence Island and Sherbro were less involved in buying and holding captives, resulting in lower numbers of deaths overall. Two years of relatively consistent figures for Bence Island (1679–80) show death tolls of eight men and four women one year, and fourteen men and two women the next. There, too, deaths went up slightly during the rains. Sherbro, which was combined administratively with Bence Island in the 1690s when England was at war with France, shows similar figures. Over two years between 1695 and 1697, twelve men and two women, and then eleven men and one woman among the sale slaves died.[33]

Comparative slave studies help sharpen our understanding of slavery as a major institution in world history. Analyzing and comparing gender differences, for example, demonstrates how men and women had differing experiences of slavery, including different rates of mortality. Rough mortality rates can be calculated by gender for James Island and Bence Island using the above figures, along with informed estimates of the general sizes of the populations of male and female captives held at each of the forts (table 4.1). Averages from data sets in other studies, although none of these data sets are directly applicable, can provide a general basis for comparison. For example, the mean percentages of loss among slaves transported across the Atlantic in the seventeenth to nineteenth centuries came to 11.9%, and for voyages in the seventeenth century alone the figure was almost twice as high at 22.6%. But these percentages are not per-annum figures. Annual mortality rates of West African men who served in the African squadron of the British Royal Navy were sixty-five per one thousand in the 1830s and twenty-two per one thousand in the 1860s, but their physical health and shipboard conditions were far better than those for slaves.[34] In comparing the scattered available years from RAC posts on the Upper Guinea Coast, and assuming equal periods of times spent on the company books, one sees that rates of deaths for both men and women at James Island appear to have been higher than at Bence Island. The gender patterns differed as well, with higher death rates for men than women at James Island and the reverse at Bence Island. The demographic pattern of slightly higher death rates for men on the transatlantic crossing is not consistently in evidence here, and the very small and irregular sample cannot explain it.[35]

TABLE 4.1 ESTIMATED ANNUAL MORTALITY RATES FOR CAPTIVES,
JAMES ISLAND AND BENCE ISLAND

	EST. VARIATION		AVERAGE	
	Men	*Women*	*Men*	*Women*
James Island	11.5–50%	8–36%	31%	22%
Bence Island	6–14%	10–28.5%	10%	19%

Source: Three sample years for James Island, 1683–86, in T 70/546; two sample years for Bence Island, 1678–80, in T 70/360. TNA.

When records permit, rough estimates of the deaths of RAC men alongside those of male and female captives allow a comparison between the two groups of men, namely, free Europeans and unfree Africans. Europeans were well known to have extremely high death rates in tropical Africa given their susceptibilities to malaria, which RAC men called the "country sickness," and other tropical fevers.[36] Figures for the early 1690s show that for the year November 1, 1692, to October 31, 1693, at least twenty-six RAC men out of a staff varying in number between sixty-two and eighty-six died on James Island. The company recorded fifty-seven deaths among the male sale slaves for that same time period out of a number generally varying between one hundred and two hundred. Among the smaller population of captive women, varying between twenty-five and fifty, there were seven deaths. Estimated average mortality rates for each group came to 36% for RAC men, 43% for male sale slaves, and 21% for female sale slaves (see table 4.2).[37]

TABLE 4.2 JAMES ISLAND—COMPARATIVE ESTIMATED ANNUAL
MORTALITY RATES FOR RAC MEN AND CAPTIVES,
NOVEMBER 1, 1692, THROUGH OCTOBER 31, 1693

	Est. Variation	*Average*
RAC Men	29–43%	36%
Captives, Male	28.5–57%	43%
Captives, Female	14–28%	21%

Sources: T 70/546, 547, 1442. TNA.

This mortality rate for RAC men is comparable to the 47 percent rate estimated by Davies for James Island in 1705, which he based on the total number of men entering the company service for that year and the number of deaths reported. His figure, a rate for the first twelve months, was higher, however, probably because those men were all new to the coast, or "raw," as the RAC veterans put it.[38] In contrast, the RAC men included in my sample were a mix of individuals who had spent different lengths of time on the Guinea Coast, some of them perhaps having acquired immunity to malaria and other illnesses. One figure though in particular stands out—the higher mortality rate for men who were captives, higher than that of the RAC men, and twice as high as the death rates of female sale slaves. Disaggregating the captive population by gender not only deepens our appreciation of gender differences in rates of mortality but highlights the death rates of male captives, which this sample suggests were also extremely high. It suggests also that RAC forts on the Upper Guinea Coast at this time could be called a "black male captive's grave."

Not all sale slaves who managed to survive were put on ships destined for the Americas. Some found themselves sold off to local people on the mainland, usually for provisions. For example, in May 1666 the Company of Royal Adventurers agent at James Island had paid for a cow with one woman; later on in July he included a slave in a payment for rice. At Bence Island in April 1680, the RAC agent paid two men and one woman in exchange for 6,120 cwt. of husk rice.[39] Less rare were the instances when captives were put on vessels to serve the captain or crew, or were sent to London to serve the friends or families of RAC employees. Shipping patterns for James Island between 1683 and 1688 show that two-thirds of the thirty outbound voyages were intended for the Caribbean or North American mainland, with the other third sailing to London.[40] Records between 1679 and 1704 show that ship captains headed to the Caribbean purchased or took as commission at least thirteen male captives, and other ships bound for London carried off at least thirty-five men, several boys, and a girl.[41]

The great majority of sale slaves, however, ended up as cargo on ships crossing the Atlantic, primarily to the Caribbean. Bound in irons below deck and usually packed prone on rough wooden platforms, their floating prisons must have seemed a sure death sentence. Lying in their own and others' filth for the average crossing time of five to six weeks, doused only occasionally with seawater to temporarily lessen the stench, captives who survived experienced an even starker state of degradation.[42] Even on the ships the horrors could vary ever so slightly. Table 4.3 presents provisions data from fourteen vessels loaded up with captives and provisions and destined for the middle passage. It shows just how precarious the captives' per-diem food allotments were, such that any delays in the crossing might threaten them with starvation. The data show variations among individual vessels in the provisions for captives and a general standard of supplying each of them with about one pound of rice or millet per day, which came to less than one-third of the daily two thousand calories necessary for long-term survival. Data from 1797 suggest there had been some improvement over the intervening century, as ship captains by then provisioned slave ships with about two pounds of rice per captive per day, a still-insufficient amount providing only twelve hundred calories.[43] As the table shows, some captains, usually those with more experience, purchased additional food such as fish and beef, and some provided brandy. In one case they supplied the captives with cloth coverings. However, these small differences would have had little to no effect in minimizing the general food scarcity that captives on slave ships suffered in the late seventeenth century while crossing the Atlantic.

Rebellions and Runaways

The chronic deprivations and harsh life-threatening conditions forced on captives did not succeed in weakening or destroying the spirits of all of them. In various ways, as individuals or in groups, some managed to muster the energy to plan and act out rejections of their captivity. The most dramatic examples were insurrection and flight. Between 1681 and 1704, the RAC recorded six instances of uprisings, although there must have been others.

The first of these in November 1681 was a major insurrection carried out by the sale slaves being held on James Island. Described by agent Kastell in a letter to London the following January, the event provides rare evidence of captives, nearly all strangers to one another, organizing and acting together to refuse their captivity and to insist on choosing for themselves the manner and timing of their deaths. As such it was a powerful expression of their human dignity. The mostly male prisoners were at the time a conspicuously large majority on the island, numbering 105. Kastell noted that there had been only 19 white men, fewer than the usual number for the 1680s, which ranged between 25 and 35. Their numerical advantage might have been noticed by some of the captives, whatever their states of health. A reference in Kastell's description to the "negroes' houses" indicates that at that time they were dispersed in a number of dwellings, creating an obstacle to communication that they obviously overcame. How they communicated with one another would also have been a challenge since they had come from diverse

TABLE 4.3 JAMES ISLAND—PROVISIONS LOADED ON SLAVE SHIPS (1684–88)

Voyages database	Destination	# slaves	Rice/millet per slave	M.P. days[a]	Rice/millet per slave per day	Daily calories	Other provisions
9884	Virginia	130	44.6 #	37 or 58	1.2 # or .77 #	454	fish, tobacco
21024	Virginia	190	26.8 #	37 or 58	.72 # or .46 #	271	
9863	Virginia? Md.?	217	66.3 #	37 or 58	1.79 # or 1.1 #	649	
21028	Virginia	250	59.2 #	37 or 58	1.6 # or 1 #	590	
21052	Virginia	137	69.3 #	37 or 58	1.87 # or 1.2 #	708	fish, brandy, tobacco, cloth
9835	Virginia	233	71.2 #	37 or 58	1.92 # or 1.2 #	708	
9877	Jamaica	230	44.7 #	47	.95 #	590	1600 fish
9675	Jamaica	207	43.4 #	36	1.2 #	708	2000 fish
9857	Jamaica	200	45 #	35	1.3 #	767	
9846	Jamaica	200	45 #	32	1.4 #	826	brandy, tobacco
15259	Barbados	181	37.5 #	37	1 #	590	brandy, 2 cows
n.a.	Barbados	194	38.6 #	ca. 37?	1 #	590	brandy
9833	Antigua	110	37.3 #	76	.5 #	295	brandy, 2 cows, tobacco
21014	Nevis	200	40 #	38	1.05 #	619	2 cows

[a]Middle passage voyage, # of days. For Virginia, the middle passage was normally to Barbados, where they probably took on provisions for the voyage up to Virginia.

Sources: T 70/546. TNA. And Voyages Database. *Voyages: The Trans-Atlantic Slave Trade Database* (2009). Accessed 12/19/2014.

backgrounds and undoubtedly spoke different languages. That many of them were probably multilingual would certainly have helped in planning and coordination, and perhaps many of them shared some knowledge of a lingua franca such as Mandinka or Crioulo. It is even conceivable that they had begun to create their own pidgin during their confinement on the island, enabling them to include so many individuals in the organizing and execution of their uprising. As linguists who study pidgins and creoles have shown, linguistically diverse groups of people often work out rudimentary means of communicating when quartered together over long stretches of time. Their plan was particularly bold and effective, for all the men had formally sworn an oath to rebel and to "drink the blood of the white man."

At three in the afternoon on November 24, they assaulted their captors. Kastell did not specify what weapons, if any, they had or what tactics they used to try and overpower them. The fighting lasted for four hours and must have involved fierce hand-to-hand combat, with captors armed with cutlasses, pistols, and other weaponry. How the struggle proceeded and reached a hiatus is unclear—perhaps they were all overcome by sheer exhaustion—but a palaver between the two groups ensued, with the captives insisting that they had rebelled with the intention to die, "and die they would." In this case, we are given some indication in the records of the motives behind the rebellion. The captives' vivid and powerful statements about swearing their oath and pledging to die together come across as something close to the tone of their own fiercely defiant voices despite having passed through filters of translation and interpretation as related by agent Kastell. In choosing and swearing to fight to the death, the rebels were expressing a core of inner freedom.

With the standoff, a long and uneasy night followed, thirty-four captives having been killed and forty wounded. In the morning, help came from the mainland. Kastell warned the remaining rebels that they would soon die, but they resolved to stand their ground. How the company finally managed to round them up is not clear, but Kastell and his men put the survivors in irons and so ended their insurrection. Kastell claimed that he did not order those who were left killed, but it is probable that some terrifying punishment was served on at least one of them as a deterrent.[44] This was not the only insurrection of captives in the area of the James Island sphere, but it apparently was the only one that took place on the island itself.

One likely effect of the rebellion was that the RAC was put on notice as to just how disastrous it could be to hold large numbers of male captives together on the island for extended periods of time. Their factories along the river were probably as important for holding their sale slaves in small numbers in dispersed locations as they were for buying them. But setting up more factories did not end uprisings, for at least four occurred on board vessels trading up the Gambia River. In March 1684, the agent at James Island had sent out five vessels in differing directions, one northward to the Petite Côte, one to purchase salt at Folan, and three on the river, either trading or supplying the company's out-factories. As the RAC longboat was making its way back down to the fort from a port in Saalum with a shipment of captives, they rose up in rebellion. In quelling the uprising, the company killed one male slave, and one woman somehow managed to escape to the riverbank.[45] The following year brought another insurrection, this time in September aboard a company vessel at Tankular on her descent down the river. She was carrying at least thirty-six captives, probably purchased at the upriver factory at Jemasar. They rose up, and this time the RAC crew killed eight of the rebels. The surviving captives were probably then loaded onto the *Coaster*, which was anchored at James Island at the time, preparing to sail to Jamaica.[46]

After the uprising of 1685, the RAC established an outpost at Tankular and staffed it at least through 1689. Why they did so is not entirely clear. Tankular was an occasional supplier of rice but not of very many captives, if any at all.[47] It is therefore worth considering the timing of this new post, especially in relation to the uprising. It is fair to assume that the experience of these unpredictable and violent rebellions and the threat of future hand-to-hand combat on their river vessels would have made a deep impression on the company men. To them, setting up a permanent post at Tankular would have made sense for strategic purposes. Keeping one or two armed guards at this spot could not guarantee that there would not be another insurrection on the river, but their presence at least could have been a deterrent or provided reinforcements in the event. In any case, even these sporadic rebellions, though each one was quelled, created extra worries and added costs and delays to RAC operations.

A company listing from November 1688 of "slaves abroad" shows a dispersal of the sale slaves on hand to various locales on the Gambia River. At the same time, a potentially dangerous number of ninety-seven male captives and seventeen female captives had been assembled on James Island. If the thirty-four men and nine women who had been sent elsewhere had remained on the island, they would have made the total number of sale slaves there even greater and riskier, suggesting that dispersing captives to prevent uprisings may have been a deliberate strategy. Small groups of them were kept in places on the mainland, such as at Juffure, Sika, and Albreda on the north shore and Combo and Brefet on the south shore. Upriver, another male sale slave had been entrusted to a local supplier with security given by the company factor at Jemasar. Nine men and three women were on the *Fortune,* a company vessel stopped for provisions at Tankular. Other individuals were ill and being treated, but most were doing work of some kind, all of them probably experiencing living conditions better than they would have endured on the island.[48] In other words, these sale slaves were not only dispersed but were also conditionally unbound and enjoying limited privileges.

While RAC agents were trying to limit the number of sale slaves kept on James Island, company demand for exports, especially captives, remained as strong as ever, intensifying the pressures on agents on the coast to manage them. Agents stepped up their trading activities during the 1680s by sending out vessels on coasting voyages and upriver and by reestablishing outposts at promising locations. Jemasar and Jogery, just downstream from Saalum, and Barrakunda far upstream, had been staffed early on, and they regularly provided captives in small lots. From October 1683 to May 1687, these three posts combined sent down 160 male and 21 female captives. In March 1687, the recently revived post at Mangegar in Saalum provided its first shipment of 228 men and 3 women, far larger than the others. This factory, under the management of William Blow, became an important supplier of captives to James Island over the next five years.[49]

After over four years at Mangegar without major incident, the insurrection on May 21, 1691, of captives on board the *Charles* must have come as a dreadful shock to the RAC staff and the vessel's crew. The size of the cargo is not given in the surviving record, but the sale slaves delivered by the Mangegar factory were usually substantial in numbers and overwhelmingly male. One can only speculate about how the captives managed to communicate among themselves to plan and execute their rebellion. The season of the year might have been an important factor. May was caravan time, and the captives, even if they had come from several different caravans, could have nevertheless already formed alliances.[50]

Or the rising might have been more opportunistic. Keeping a watchful eye on their captors, they might have noticed and been encouraged by the relative inexperience of the vessel's captain, Lambert Helmont, who had never before spent time trading on the Gambia River. He had been stationed at Bence Island and Sherbro in the 1680s and became master of the *Charles* in 1684. Although he made at least one Atlantic crossing to Jamaica and back, he apparently spent most of his time coasting in the Bence Island trading sphere. His only two visits to James Island in 1686 were brief. He had informed the company that he intended to return home to England in 1687, but for unknown reasons he never followed through and remained at Bence Island. He was then among the large influx of RAC men brought up to James Island in July 1690 to protect it from French invaders. Less than a year later he was piloting the *Charles* up the Gambia River to load up captives at Mangegar for delivery back to James Island. Details of the insurrection have not survived, save for its financial cost of seventeen sale slaves to the company. Thus, it is not known how and when the captives rose up and whether they engaged in combat or simply jumped overboard. The Mangegar factory continued in operation for at least another year, and the *Charles* remained on the Gambia River captained by William Blow. Helmont returned to Sierra Leone.[51]

With the outbreak of war between England and France in 1689, trading had been interrupted and the coast had become even riskier than usual. It was in this context that a major insurrection took place in 1693 on board the *America* while it was anchored at James Island in preparation for an Atlantic crossing. Three years earlier the RAC had transferred forty company men and seventy grometos from Sierra Leone to James Island to better defend their main position on the coast. Even so, John Booker, the agent there at the time, wrote to London to complain about their lack of arms and the poor quality of what remained of their gunpowder and to lament the low morale of his men. However, he was just then getting caught up in the fervor of war and wanted to engage the enemy. He proposed to the company that they should send out a force to take the French forts at St. Louis at the mouth of the Senegal River and on Gorée Island off Cape Verde, which would bring major advantages to their trading operations. In December 1691, agent Booker himself took the initiative by convincing Captain Brome of the *America* to take him and an armed force of company soldiers to go after a French ship at Bissau, which he claimed was a spy ship. By the end of the month he was writing excitedly to London about their success in seizing the crew and captain, his cargo, and the ship as a prize. He wrote again in January that he had enough RAC men on James Island to guard it but that he thought it might be advisable to send more ships out to take further actions against the French.[52]

Meanwhile, the *America* had departed for the Caribbean and from there back to London. It arrived again at James Island in late November 1692 together with the *Ann*, both ships laden with cargoes that must have buoyed the spirits of all the company men at the fort. In addition to overseas trade goods they brought strategically important supplies, tools, and equipment for operating and defending their station. Booker managed to convince the captains of the *America* and *Ann* to take him and a force of armed RAC men up the coast to seize control of the French forts. He was encouraged by the presence among their French prisoners of a Huguenot officer who had served at St. Louis and was willing, being a Protestant, to offer the RAC his expertise in piloting around the bar at the mouth of the Senegal River. The RAC force took St. Louis on January 1, 1693, renaming it William and Mary Island and leaving a former Gambia agent in charge of a new RAC factory there. The taking of Gorée was more difficult, but it too finally fell into the hands of the RAC. Realizing that he would be unable to staff and secure both islands, Booker chose to demolish the fort at Gorée and confiscate its contents. The plundered commodities from both French forts—mainly ivory and Senegal gum—were loaded onto the *Ann,* which sailed to Sherbro for wax and then on to London in March.[53]

In writing to London about the success of the Senegal and Gorée expedition, Booker mentioned rather ominously that during their maneuvers he came down with an illness and that he hoped to return home. However, he had much work to do on the island, and the *America* encountered troublesome delays in loading up with captives. Some were ill, and Booker took the precaution of waiting for them to recover before putting them on board. Records for the number of captives held are cryptic and irregular. Captives had been taken from the French forts as legitimate wartime plunder, and some may well have ended up in the hands of individuals as their own shares of the spoils of war. Other "plunder negroes" were held by the company to be sent aboard the *America.* They, and perhaps others, had been kept on James Island since the return of the RAC ships in February, a perilously long period of about seven to eight weeks. During that time, the *America* had been dispatched to the Petite Côte for more captives, returning on April 22 with 53 men, 19 women, and 3 boys. On April 23, an enormous and very risky human cargo of 421 captives—280 men, 99 women, 18 adolescent boys, 15 boys, and 9 girls—was finally taken onto the ship soon to depart for Jamaica.[54]

Losing no time themselves, the captives rose up in rebellion the next day. Details of the insurrection are few. It is not clear how many of them took part, precisely how many were injured or died, or how long it took to quell them. One brief note in the company accounts charges the captain with twenty-six pairs of "negro irons" and twelve swords, suggesting that the captives had not been very well secured and that the crew initially had not been sufficiently armed. Another passing comment is especially significant for its specification of the common origins of the leadership of the uprising and their rivalries with others in the group. Booker wrote to London that "the Jolofs rose" and "the Bambaras side with the Masters [of the ship]." Booker was of course viewing these two factions among the rebels through his own subjective prism, assuming that the "Bambaras" by not rising up with the "Jolofs" were therefore siding with the RAC.[55]

A less Anglocentric line of thinking about this division among the captives that doomed the revolt is to consider why these two factions existed and what might have kept them from forming an alliance. As separate ethnolinguistic groups, they were factions of Wolof-speakers from near the coast and speakers of Bamanakan from much farther into the interior, or perhaps they were captives sold by these groups. They might also have seen themselves as divided irreconcilably by religion, with Muslim Wolof-speakers and polytheistic Bambara each considering themselves hostile to the other. They could also have seen themselves as divided historically and geopolitically, that is, the militarized Wolof states centered in the lower Senegal region versus the militarizing Bambara polities far inland in the upper Niger basin. Members of each group might well have assumed that their rightful status was to be masters, not slaves, while believing the other group to be clearly subject to enslavement. In short, that they failed to find common cause points to the kinds of deep ethnic, cultural, and political divisions in western Africa that heterogeneous groups of slaves had to overcome in staging unified insurrections on the Upper Guinea Coast or aboard the ships taking them to the Americas. Historical memories and social barriers of all sorts, including multiple languages unintelligible to most of their companions, would have been major obstacles to overcome if groups of captives were to see themselves as sharing a motivating grievance and then acting on it. The remaining sale slaves would certainly have recognized their common fate as they found themselves bound together in a ship crossing the Atlantic. The *America* landed in Barbados in May 1693, with just over four hundred having survived the middle passage and another forty or so in the hands of the captain as his "plunder negroes." Those whom he did not sell at Barbados went on with him to Jamaica.[56]

The sixth recorded insurrection gives another glimpse into how the enslaved experienced their captivity through the cultural backgrounds they brought to it. In this case, on the *Postillion* during its voyage up the Gambia River in April and May 1704, the captives converted a misguided company effort to entertain them into a cover for rebellion. The ship and crew, having purchased ninety-nine captives and loaded and provisioned at the river port of Jour, began their journey back down the river on May 17. Also on board were a Maninka xylophone (*bala*) and drum, both of which the RAC agent in charge of the voyage, Chidley, had purchased, intending to use them to "divert" the sale slaves during their Atlantic crossing. His aim was to follow a common practice during Atlantic crossings whereby crew members would periodically bring slaves up on deck and force them to exercise to music played by one of the crew. The instruments, the players, and the music were normally European and therefore unfamiliar—or even alien and meaningless—to the captives. That Chidley had purchased musical instruments familiar and motivating to his captives proved to be for him an almost fatal mistake.[57]

In letters to London from upriver and in a deposition he filed later in the RAC's investigation of the incident, John Tozer, the ship's captain, described how he became uneasy about the voyage as soon as he and Chidley began loading captives on board. He had advised the company in early May that his ship could not take on more than 110 captives, judging the males from the Gambia River to be one and a half times the statures of any others in Guinea. Adding that he had never carried more than 60 men, with another 50 women and children, he expressed concern that at Jour they were taking on mostly men. He had good reason to be worried. According to Tozer, and against his advice, Chidley had turned over the *bala* and drum to the captives for the voyage downriver.

Perhaps shading his account with the convenient knowledge of hindsight, Tozer claimed that he told Chidley it was unsafe for the captives to have music while still on the river and that he had asked Chidley to give the instruments to him instead. Chidley apparently refused Tozer's request and insisted that the slaves should have music even on the river. On May 28, the captives rose up to the sounds of the *bala* and the drum. Tozer blamed the insurrection squarely on the music, calling it "noise" that prevented the crew from hearing the captives somehow managing to break free of their irons. The unbound captives then were able to storm seven of his men, knocking them down with wooden staves. Tozer and crew fired their muskets at the rebels and advanced with drawn cutlasses, forcing them to jump overboard. The crew recovered most of them, but thirty-one lost their lives in combat or by drowning. Another died on the voyage downriver, probably from wounds sustained in the battle.[58]

What the captives themselves had heard was not, of course, simply "noise." And "noise" was not how La Courbe characterized the *bala* music he heard in Albreda on the lower Gambia in 1686. Visiting there to trade for ivory and captives, he met with the master of the town, who welcomed him to join his entourage of Muslim teachers and town elders, all seated on mats in the refreshingly cool shade of a tall tree. A musician soon arrived to entertain them with a *bala,* and La Courbe took a keen interest in the design and construction of the instrument, from its carved and polished flat hardwood keys of different sizes and pitches to the hollowed-out gourds of different sizes underneath them serving as resonators. The musician played it melodically by hitting the keys with small batons. La Courbe was surprised and very impressed by the pleasing sound of the music, and he used the correct words for distinguishing the instrument, *bala,* from the person who plays it, *balafon.*[59]

But what the restless captives on the *Postillion* had heard was far more inspiring and meaningful than La Courbe's uninformed experience of the music as merely "pleasant." The *bala* is an ancient instrument associated with the heroic time of the founding of the Mali Empire in the first half of the thirteenth century, and its historical and cultural significance cannot be overstated. The *Sunjata* epic, a Mande oral tradition recounting the legendary story of the empire's founder, includes an episode in which Sunjata's personal *jeli,* the bard or praise singer who confirms the nobility of Mande aristocrats, is sent out on a diplomatic mission to seek peace with their mortal enemy, the blacksmith king of Soso. The bard is taken prisoner but is able to sneak into the king's secret room where his powerful sacred *bala* is kept. He quickly masters the instrument and charms the Soso king by playing praises to him. He is then forced to become the king's *jeli.*

Much later, when Sunjata becomes ruler and culture hero of the Mande peoples, his *jeli* returns to him, bringing the *bala,* which henceforth became associated with Sunjata's many magico-religious powers. In public recitals of the epic, a *jeli* would sometimes accompany himself with a musical instrument, either an *nkoni* (lute), a *kora* (harp), or the *bala* (xylophone). Mande peoples over a wide geographical area in West Africa know and celebrate this history, an empire their ancestors created seven or eight hundred years ago and that flourished for two centuries. The epic and the instruments bind speakers of Mande languages together around a remembered and recited glorious past.[60] So it is not surprising that the captives rose up to the potent sounds of a *bala* and a drum, perhaps invoking praises of heroic figures and legendary events.[61] By this interpretation, there was among the captives at least one skilled *bala* musician, a reflection of the able individuals from many walks of life hidden within every group of captives who in company records appeared only as nameless inventory, undifferentiated except by the prices they might bring upon disposing of them.

RAC agent Weaver wrote about the insurrection to London, having interviewed Tozer, and recounted to them his particular version of the event. He also explained how he was preparing the *Postillion* for its Atlantic crossing, loading her with provisions and making up for the lost captives. Echoing Tozer, he confirmed that the ship was small and the slaves so very large that, when it returned to the island, he had dismantled one of the platforms below deck to fit them all in, with the result that she could carry no more than one hundred slaves. Weaver added that experienced river traders told him that they had learned to associate trading at Jour with misfortunes of one kind or another. In the future, Weaver wrote, having been so informed, he would send for slaves to be brought from there to James Island divided into lots of ten or twenty at a time and in small vessels for better security. When the *Postillion* arrived in Virginia, eighty of the one hundred captives embarked had survived—twenty had either died of illness, drowned, or been killed.[62]

Escapes of captives were more common than rebellions, although RAC records provide only irregular indications of how such events occurred at particular times in and around each of the three island forts. Captives arriving on the Guinea Coast were for the most part very far from their original homelands and families, making it next to impossible that they would be found and ransomed by relatives or friends.[63] Still, even though they were in unfamiliar territory, some risked their lives and ran away. They did so as individuals or in small groups and mostly during the dry season when exposure to the elements was not so forbidding as during the rains. Some neighboring communities were known for harboring runaways, such as the town of Buje up the Casamance River and a locale upriver from Cacheu.[64] But tragically, many of the escapees ended up being caught by strangers who chose to return them to the RAC in exchange for bounty payments in overseas trade goods. Escapees would have been conspicuous and easy to identify as captives owing to their emaciated, weak, and unkempt physical conditions and their partial or complete nakedness.

James Island was an especially effective site for holding imprisoned captives securely, for it was situated in the waters of the lower Gambia at a spot where the river swelled to almost five miles in breadth. Escape by swimming or stealing a boat looked to be almost impossible. Even so, some slaves made valiant attempts to get away, although not all of them succeeded. One such incident involved two captives who escaped the island, probably commandeering a canoe or other small craft for making it across the three miles of water to the river's southern shore. They were wise to avoid the closer northern shore, where numerous company employees and allies lived in Juffure and neighboring towns. They managed to cross safely only to be recaptured by residents of Fogny, whose king transported the pair back to the fort to receive the company's reward of ten gallons of brandy.

Other captives had better luck. For a three-year period between 1683 and 1686, RAC factors made a rough estimate that fifteen male slaves had succeeded in running away at different times to various places in the vicinity of the James Island fort. One daring male slave drowned in his attempt to flee the island in December 1686. Other individuals seized much more opportune moments on the mainland, such as the several captives who managed to escape the RAC factory up the Gambia River at Barrakunda. One male captive on James Island saved himself from a life of exile in England by escaping from the *Dolphin* as it was being loaded with a cargo of ivory, wax, and hides for London.[65]

The fort on Bence Island in the Sierra Leone estuary was over a mile from the nearest mainland and also about a mile away from adjacent larger islands such as Tasso. Yet there was also traffic of small craft moving around the islands in the estuary, which presented opportunities of escape that were not lost on all of the company's imprisoned captives. Over a five-year period between 1678 and 1683, recorded escapes numbered twenty-two, most of them from the Bence Island fort itself. This number may seem small, but it is remarkable that any captives continued to make the attempt after witnessing other escapees regularly being caught and returned by local people. Out of the twenty-two escapes, only seven appear to have been possibly successful. One young Muslim girl ran away, spending a month and a half hiding in some nearby woods until finally being found and returned to the company, evidently weakened by her isolation. She soon died, reportedly from a combination of starvation and exposure. Escapes from the RAC out-factories and coasting or river vessels were more likely to be successful in part because soldiers guarding captives in such situations were not always as attentive and well-armed as they were at the forts.[66]

York Island at Sherbro presented yet another set of challenges for captives planning an escape. Sale slaves there were fewer in number overall as the export trade on this part of the coast was mostly in dyewood and ivory. Nevertheless, records show a small but steady trickle of captives who made escapes from in and around the fort. York Island was very close to the mainland and also adjoined the large island of Sherbro, which offered marginally more promising opportunities for running away. The sparse early records from the 1680s show that a male captive of about thirty-five years of age ran away from York Island in 1684, and a woman escaped from the company's Gallinas factory farther down the coast. More consistent and detailed information from a later four-year period between 1693 and 1697, a time when slave exports there were slightly higher than normal, shows thirty fugitives. Fourteen of them were eventually caught by local people and returned for bounty payments. Four of the ones who succeeded managed to get away from one of the company's sloops in February 1697 while it was on a coasting voyage. Payments of bounty for returned slaves were generally much higher at York Island, leading the factor there to complain to company officials in London that the local people were demanding exorbitant amounts for bringing back runaways.[67]

"Company Slaves"

In addition to "sale slaves," the RAC recognized another category of people they bought as "company slaves" or "grometos," who were owned by and worked for the company at its stations on the Upper Guinea Coast. The historical sources characterize grometos (or *grumetes*) variously in terms of their positions and status, which appear to have varied widely. An example of these ambiguities is Coelho's mid-seventeenth-century account where one chapter described grumetes in the vicinity of Bissau as semiskilled non-slave workers, whereas two chapters later he described a man who sailed around the coast in an old vessel with very little property of his own except for a few young grumetes, or deck-hands, who were slaves. Others describe grumetes both in terms of their family ties as Luso-African descendants of Portuguese men and their local African wives and in terms of their important roles as "free servants" in commerce, especially as handlers of cargoes and work boats.[68] Apparently the workforce staffing commercial operations along the coast contained both local residents and captives from the interior, varying in their numbers from port to port and from time to time.

The so-called grometos in the RAC records were enslaved, although with greater freedom of movement than slaves the company held for sale. They were also paid regular salaries or allowances for supporting themselves. At the same time, however, they were considered properties of the RAC and were sometimes listed as such in inventories. What the grometos themselves might have thought about their duties and rights is difficult to sort out from RAC records. For the most part, company agents selected their grometos out of the groups of imprisoned sale slaves by releasing them from their irons and taking them out of confinement, then redefining them in the account books from commodities to assets.[69] This transaction was a purely internal bookkeeping convention with no offsetting exchange of goods, although from the perspective of the captives, grometos would have been seen as having been released from their captivity. However, these bookkeeping details created very real problems for some company employees. In 1703, for example, the agent at Bence Island sent a letter to London expressing concerns about his commission on the sale of captives to be sent to the West Indies. He had recently loaded eighty onto a vessel that went on to the Gold Coast and feared that some of them would be designated as grometos by agents at Cape Coast Castle. If so, they would not be counted as parts of his sale, thus reducing the commission owed him.[70]

Despite their uncertain status, male grometos received RAC salaries comparable to those paid to company soldiers and sometimes additional payments by task. Their duties could entail considerable freedom of movement, such as assisting crew on board coasting vessels or running errands alone in small craft. Grometos at James Island piloted canoes upstream to engage in the river trade and also to handle exchanges of letters between the fort and their outposts and local suppliers. Grometos at the Bence Island fort at times were paid to do work on the large nearby island of Tasso, where the company carried out agricultural experiments and building projects. Grometos were also given the occasional gift of cloth or brandy and occasionally were even entrusted with the difficult work of searching out and catching runaways.

Nevertheless, some grometos found reasons and times to run away. A grometo killed James Leads, a carpenter at James Island in the early 1680s, while assisting him with chopping wood in the forest in March 1685. In 1683, one of the Bence Island grometos stole away with the company canoe. At

Sherbro one grometo man slipped off, taking with him a boy from among the sale slaves. Late in December 1693, a group of fifteen male and three female grometos ran away from York Island very well armed with four muskets, four shotguns, and two pairs of pistols. However, the grometos' valued and sometimes trusted positions in the company workforce did not protect them from severe punishments. On one occasion, Bence Island grometos were caught stealing overseas goods from the company storehouse and had to witness the public execution of their alleged ringleader, who was singled out as an example to the others.[71]

Female grometos on the Upper Guinea Coast were also on salary, but RAC records do not indicate whether they were also paid by task. They were apparently few in number, but it is also very likely that other women among the sale slaves gained similar privileges as informal companions of company personnel. But given the directors' strong disapproval of any hint of sexual relations of agents or other employees in their stations and factories, this would have been strictly off the written record. Since pounding rice and winnowing the husks was and still is a specialized skill of women in the communities they came from, the female grometos' public work duties likely included processing rice or millet that came to the forts still in husk.[72] The women kept by the company might very well have had other duties in food preparation, cooking, cleaning, and washing, and perhaps they also were put to work at times processing and cleaning wax for shipment to England. Some were domiciled in nearby towns and out-factories, where they would have participated in the usual household, agricultural, and artisanal work such as spinning and indigo dyeing.

Tending children when necessary was another of their responsibilities, as evidenced in a sample listing made at James Island in 1688, where four of the six female grometos listed had children in their care, either their own or others' (transcription 4.3). Some were known by European names, others by names that appear to refer to geographical places (Gamboe, Cumboe), or their home communities (Belanter, Beaffada).[73] Occasional listings of "company slaves" by age and gender suggest they formed friendships, attachments, and even "family" groupings. One inventory from the RAC factory at Tassily in 1683 included four male grometos—Christopher, Bettow, Saggy, and Anthony—and one woman of unclear status called Yamboy. The two children also listed, a boy and a girl, may have been hers, perhaps by one of the grometos. A later inventory from York Island listed fifty grometo men young and old, seven grometo boys, a male child two years old, fifteen grometo women young and old, three grometo girls, and five female children. Some lived at the company forts to advanced ages. At the onset of the rains in 1683, the agent at Bence Island "freed" three elderly women—Camessa, Monta, and Repunga—considering them "not serviceable nor fit for sale."[74]

TRANSCRIPTION 4.3 GROMETOS AT JAMES ISLAND, 1688

Source: T 70/832, "Slaves" Account, loose leaves. TNA.

Secundoe
John Berreca
Belanter
Jack at Barraffatt
Domingoe
Antho.
Sarrah and Gelloone, onboard the Smack
Gamboe the Bumberse onboard the *Benj.*
Marron the Bidgigoe
Great Tomber
Little Tomber
Jack the Carpenter's assistant

New Gramettoes:
Burrow att Barraffatt
Salleff
Oachia Jun.
Kommo the Bricklayer's assistant
Mamadoe
Mansar with Mr. Quine
Bcaffada att Socar in Lcw off Oachia Segn.
Little Secunda
Mandingoe
Anthony Jun.

[women]:
Tomasey
Cumboe   with 2 Children and a wt. Child
Isa   with 3 ditto
Adam   with 1 ditto
Cumboe Sissee   with 1 ditto
                                    with 1 ditto
Polonia in Lew off Yewle

On the Upper Guinea Coast, free blacks and grometos who considered themselves free, especially men, could all too easily face losing their freedom in Atlantic labor markets hungry for human property. RAC factors at Jamaica reported that a company ship had stopped for water at the Portuguese island of Principe, where it took on board two free black men to work as sailors. At the time of writing, the ship had left the men ashore at Jamaica, either sold or soon to be sold, apparently for not having the proof of their free status acceptable to authorities there.[75] And on more than one occasion, people on the mainland took captive both company men of color and grometos and held them for ransom.

Being either known or recognizable as an employee of the RAC might protect grometos from being sold off the coast as slaves, but being ransomed was in itself a potentially terrifying experience. Captain James Jobson sailed up the Gambia River to Cantor in September 1684 to exact damages from people there who had killed two of his crewmen the previous February and imprisoned four of the company grometos. How long they were held is not clear from the records, but the compensation he demanded came to 100B, payable to the RAC in captives. A free black company man named John White was held at ransom for three weeks in May and June 1688. He was one of the crew on board *Little Lady Mary* trading in the Rio Grande area when the vessel was seized by a French ship with the loss of five of the RAC crew. White apparently jumped ship and made it to the mainland, where local people captured and held him. How much ransom the company paid is not clear, but he was returned to James Island, where he drew out the balance of his salary, which came to a total of 150B in overseas goods. Grometos who ran away and were returned garnered bounties for their captors much higher than company agents paid for fugitive sale slaves. Four of the James Island grometos who deserted a company vessel in 1692 were recovered for a total payment of 97B in goods.[76] This ransom fee comes to just over 24B each, which is five to ten times higher than the bounty payments made for escaped sale slaves.

Grometos were recognizably set apart from sale slaves by their dress. That they were clothed at all was in stark contrast to the captives' nakedness. Men in particular were regularly given tailored garments that elevated their status and connected them directly to the RAC. Local men's tailored garments, such as the long cotton tunics and trousers made in Cape Mount and its hinterlands, did not usually enter the wardrobes of RAC grometos. Instead, RAC agents gave them either ready-to-wear garments made in

Europe or European-style suits made to order by a local tailor, usually from woolen yardage woven in England.[77] Grometos were company men and visibly, sometimes ostentatiously, so. In 1686 in preparation for a voyage to Montserrat the agent at James Island had fourteen yards of woolen cloth made up into six suits for the grometos, who, properly dressed in "European style" with their European hats, might pass in the English Leeward Islands as protected from captivity.[78] Stories like the fates of the Principe free blacks detained in Jamaica or worse underlined the hazards in the Caribbean for Africans less gentlemanly attired.

More often, though, male grometos were given ready-made garments from Europe. There were at least two reasons for this preference. One was that it was easier and less time-consuming for the agents simply to select a garment from inventories on hand than to order one made locally. The agent at Bence Island explained another reason in a letter to London in 1670. Agent Pierce requested that the company send livery for the grometos as an alternative to having clothes made for them because the grometos apparently were selling their garments to local people. In Pierce's thinking, they knew they would be given replacements since the company could not bear the shame of having their employees appearing naked or poorly dressed in public, and he added that if their grometos sold distinctively tailored imported uniforms, he could easily identify who was trading with them.[79] How much of a problem grometos' selling their clothes might have been cannot be determined, but the company books show regular entries for cloth coats, livery coats and trousers, grometo suits, stuff suits, and hats given to mark male grometos, and plain and patterned cloths given to the women. Company officials in London complained to their agent at James Island in 1692 that he was spending too much on hiring grometos and far too much on clothing them.[80]

After 1698, the RAC lost its monopoly when England opened its subjects' Africa trade to "separate" traders, that is, merchants and captains unaffiliated with the company who paid a 10 percent duty on goods they exported from England. Starting in the early 1700s, directors began an effort to exert greater control over the labor and sexual behavior of their employees and their company slaves. Instructions to the agent at James Island in 1702 ordered that the grometos they had or might buy for company service should be given names and be included in the listing of current employees, along with the particulars of their ages and their deaths. The company agent at Bence Island was similarly told to record the names of the "company slaves" and also to train them in occupations most useful to the company, such as carpentry, bricklaying, spinning, weaving, dyeing, and crewing boats and ships. The directors went even further in imposing greater regulation of their characters and behavior, stating that the so-called company slaves were to be made Christian, were to have only a single wife, were to learn English, were to be branded on the right breast, and were not to be sold away. In one of the rare direct references to the daily violence of captivity, they added that their "company slaves" were not to be beaten.[81] It is unlikely that agents on the coast followed these rules.

Conclusion: Enduring and Defying Captivity

In western Africa and on the Upper Guinea Coast, captives and their labor were sold and cruelly harnessed to increase the wealth of others. Substituting for willing family members or employees deserving of respect and compensation, they were forced to yield savings in costs and generate incomes for people of all sorts even before overland caravans delivered them at entrepôts in the interior or at embarkation points on the coast. Markets, trade routes, and the movement of commodities determined their travels and shaped their lives. Within the confines of their enslavement, the people in chains had a considerable range of destinations—outcomes of the many and varied parties who managed to make use of them along the winding courses they followed. Merchants took advantage of their coffled captives by forcing them to work as porters in caravans moving in all directions in West Africa's vast forests, savannas, and deserts. Captives might find themselves purchased for seasonal work along their ways, laboring in fields and forests or in workshops carrying out such preparatory tasks as charring wood or cleaning cotton or rice. At the RAC forts, a runaway captive might break free and make it to the mainland only to be caught by villagers hoping to cash in on the bounties the company paid for returned escapees. A lucky few among the sale slaves might be selected and unchained to serve as company slaves, remaining in Africa and earning for themselves small salaries. Except for rebels, the captives themselves made none of these vital decisions over their own lives. Others controlled where their bodies would go, how they would be treated, and what they would do. And the vast majority caught a last glimpse of the continent as they descended into the insufferable stench of the dark holds of RAC vessels bound for the Americas.

Though the people living in captivity suffered constant degradation and were deprived of elemental human respect, they were not passive victims.

The recorded instances of captives' rebellions and escapes remind us that they nonetheless reclaimed themselves and their mobility by repeatedly seizing opportunities to experience freedom, even if merely for a moment. And they insisted on acting as social beings. Within the groups into which merchants or masters or RAC men forced them, they likely also formed alliances and attachments, thereby asserting their humanity, as the Jolof rebels on the *America* and the Maninka musicians on the *Postillion* made very clear. Sporadic references in company records only hint at what must have been frequent efforts on the part of captives to form relationships and communicate with one another in the interest of creating both some semblance of a social existence with others who cared and a chance at a different, hopefully better future. Some, like the male sale slaves who swore an oath to rebel and die together on James Island in 1681, exercised the freedom to choose an honorable death. Survival itself was a significant self-affirming achievement of captives in the face of the indifference, neglect, and brutality the company imposed on them. How they endured day by day the physical, emotional, and psychological toll exacted by captivity can hardly be imagined.

CHAPTER FIVE

Free Agents and Local Hires

Managing Men in Northern Guinea

ONE OF the most obvious difficulties the RAC faced was the enormous geographical scale of the pan-Atlantic trade they were trying to integrate, which involved operations and employees on three distant and distinctive continents. On the Guinea Coast, it faced competition from other European companies and private traders and also what a leading scholar of these operations dismissed as the "shortcomings" of RAC employees who worked there. Continuing his survey, he enumerated several internal obstacles that he believed seriously interfered with the day-to-day business of early modern Atlantic commerce. He acknowledged that the RAC in London had very little control over their numerous and far-flung employees, handicapped further by their inability to ensure that agents kept accounts consistently and accurately over time. As a result, they had no choice but to leave much of what went on to the discretion of their men on the African coast, men whom they also seldom gave sufficient rewards to behave as loyal RAC employees.[1]

This chapter focuses on who some of these RAC employees on the Upper Guinea Coast were and what dilemmas they faced in attempting to carry out company business. A central theme is how they created their own individual career paths spontaneously on the spot and how much and in what ways they appear to have succeeded in gaining personally during their periods of employment with the company, often in outright defiance of its dictates. By following what they did and how they fared, we also can see the limited extent to which company plans and policies formulated in London translated into local practice on the Upper Guinea Coast. RAC agents often ignored rules against foreign and English "interlopers" and against consorting with local women, and they were generally prone to taking matters into their own hands when confronted with unanticipated circumstances, which was often. And there were contradictions and changes in RAC regulations and requirements that made it difficult for their employees to act at all without violating one or another of them, which led to disputes, open conflicts, and in some cases desertion. Perhaps the most important of these was the inherent contradiction between the company's prohibition of private trading by employees and how RAC directors in London arranged payments of salaries on the Upper Guinea Coast. From 1680 onward, RAC employees had to swear under oath that they would not engage in trading on their own accounts. But since most of them had to draw on their salaries in trade goods rather than cash, private trading was all but inevitable, and some company men amassed impressive personal estates.

There were a number of other employees whose careers took quite different turns. Some English men in the Gambia sphere left the company and married local women, making the Upper Guinea Coast their chosen home, where they traded in partnership with their wives. Their independence renders them all but invisible in company records save for the rare instances when their wives appear as suppliers of exports in RAC accounts of trading voyages. English men in and around Sierra Leone and Sherbro worked both for the company on salary and for themselves as private traders, and various of their male children followed them along these paths, sometimes causing consternation among directors in London. Still other RAC employees were West African men who signed on with the company to supply them regularly with provisions and information services without which the RAC staff on the Upper Guinea Coast would have suffered even greater losses. If company directors in London recognized the contributions these local hires made to the day to day operations of their forts, it is not evident in their records.

Living on "Country Money"

The RAC paid salaries to their men on the Guinea Coast in two different ways. The method reserved mainly for higher-paid agents and factors was to pay part of the sum in pounds sterling to wives, relatives, or acquaintances back in England and the balance to the men on the spot in what they recognized as "country money," that is, overseas goods sent out from

England and West African commodities and commodity currencies. The other method of payment was to pay the full amount in "country money," which was the case for the majority of company men: soldiers, artisans, and local employees. The home payments generated their own sets of problems for the men themselves, for their families, and for their employers in London. In 1691, for example, agent Booker at James Island wrote a letter to London requesting the company directors to stop payments from Peter Gally's salary to his wife in England so he could receive all of it locally, as he had learned that she had married another man after he left for the Guinea Coast.[2] Keeping track of payments made and balances due was an ever-present burden not easily managed. One sees this in the wide variations in coastal practice, where men overdrew their accounts to enrich themselves at the company's expense while others who died had years of back pay still due to them and their families.

How salaries paid in "country money" led to and even encouraged private trading of RAC employees can be better understood by following the process in sequence: from quoted cash valuations of salary rates to examples of the forms in which they were paid and then to the various possible ways that company men from England could spend their "country money" on consumer items, labor, services, or exports in the Guinea trade. The RAC quoted salary rates in pounds sterling, with salaries on the Guinea Coast comparable, for the most part, to compensation in England. Soldiers, for example, were on salaries averaging about £12 per year, artisans worked on contracts ranging between £20 and £30 per year, and agents' pay was usually around £50. These rates varied over time and could be revised at the discretion of local agents.[3] Agents then converted these salaries from pounds sterling into the local currency of account on the Guinea Coast. For the Upper Guinea Coast, bar iron served not only as a local commodity currency but also as the RAC's currency of account for valuations of goods, tasks, services, and salaries. The usual conversion rate was six shillings to one bar, with local values expressed in RAC accounts as bars, shillings, and pence, the bar replacing the pound in the notation. Some company "writers," or scribes, were in the habit of rounding off account entries simply to bars for convenience, as shown in this sample transcribed record (transcription 5.1).[4]

At RAC forts and stations on the Guinea Coast, agents engaged in a "truck system," or "trucking," meaning they paid out salaries to most of their workforce in overseas goods, commodity currencies, or both. These payments in goods all but forced employees to violate their oaths not to trade on their own

TRANSCRIPTION 5.1 RAC CURRENCY OF ACCOUNT ON UPPER GUINEA COAST: BARS, SHILLINGS, AND PENCE

Source: T 70/165 January 1696. Gambia, Cacheu Debts. TNA.

Cachauo Debts, January 1696 [rounded off to Bars]
Santais de Vidigall as pr Receipt of 771 Barrs off which 294:4:6 hath been paid

Remains due	479:1:6
Antho. Gomes pr. bill	.85:0
Bibiana as p. bill 3097	
trusted by Mr. Booker. . . . <u>18</u>	3115:0
John de Masado p. bill.	.85:0
trusted by Mr. Walrond just before Gambia was taken more	514:
Martus de silva as pr bill	20:
Barnaby Lopus Ditto	35:
And	60:
Manuel de pena as p bill	19:
Francisco vaz ditto	1409:½
and owes besides	36:
Diogo Coiles as p. bill	.212:
Lewis Depena. . . . . ditto	30:
Francis Dias . . . . ditto	343:
and 36:	
Migill Barbon Francia. . . . ditto	10:

To: de Masado for 71 cwt Wax
To: Soris Fragaso 25 cwt Wax

Barrs	6188:4:6

accounts. The example of a free black seaman named Valentine, who was employed on several company ships in the 1680s, illustrates that his salary rate in pounds sterling was converted into a rate in bars and what kinds of goods he selected when drawing on his salary. His account shows his annual salary rate quoted in pounds sterling as £11:13:1 (pounds:shillings:pence), which converted into bars at six shillings to one bar came to 38B:5:1 (bars:shillings:pence), on which he took out imported goods worth 20B:3. The assortment he selected included one bar of the metal plus brandy, sugar, beads, cowries, 2 ounces of coral, and tobacco.[5] He could have consumed some of these items himself or shared them with friends or traders, whereas the bar of iron was a potential intermediate good if paid for services to an artisan or laborer. Alternatively, the commodity currencies in the form of bar iron, coral, beads, and cowries together could have been exchanged to purchase a boy or girl captive or another export if Valentine managed to strike the right deal. In short, the practice of drawing on one's salary by taking out goods gave employees access to overseas goods and local commodity currencies that in turn enabled them to engage in private trading.

John White, another free black seaman, used the RAC trucking system to support himself at various times over several years. White arrived at James Island in May 1684 on the *Sarah* from London. He had already been paid in London a small advance of 7B in unspecified goods or cash, and he apparently spent the next twenty-eight months on the Upper Guinea Coast on ships sailing up the Gambia River or on coasting voyages to Cacheu. When he returned to the fort, which he did intermittently, he drew only modest amounts of overseas goods on his salary: September 1686, 2B in beads and a dozen knives; September 1687, 10B in beads; and June 1688, 11B in beads and coral.[6] On board ship his personal daily needs may be presumed to have been taken care of without him spending from his salary, though details about individual crew members were hidden in RAC accounts, which listed single aggregate expenses for all members of crews for ships' voyages. If he had additional earnings from working by task for other employees, these amounts would have been off the company's books.

In other words, John White was living on company overhead at sea, and on land he was spending beads, coral, and table knives from his salary as the coastal equivalent of small change for incidental expenses. Items such as these were acceptable as payment for food and drink or for services provided on the mainland by washerwomen, for example, or male canoe paddlers. Ledgers for James Island consistently show company men and other individuals regularly taking out modest amounts of beads and cowries, clear indications of the widespread acceptance of these commodity currencies in daily transactions.[7] In May 1688, when French privateers or warships seized the RAC's *Little Lady Mary*, John White escaped only to be captured and held hostage by people on shore for several weeks, during which he was unable to draw on his account. RAC records show the balance of salary owed him for the period May 1684 to May 1688 as coming to 150B, but there is no indication of how or by whom he was freed or what the ransom was. He was back on James Island in June, and one can only wonder why he withdrew the entire balance of salary owed him in unspecified overseas goods and what he did with them. Shortly thereafter, he resumed his career serving the company on coasting voyages, mainly to Cacheu. His death was recorded in July 1692, with no notation as to whether there was a balance of salary owing to his estate.[8]

Although White's account leaves no suggestion that he was involved in personal enrichment at the expense of the company, accounts of other employees do present examples of the forms and complexities of wealth they accumulated in the early modern Guinea trade. In the last weeks of his life in 1693, agent John Booker dictated new bequests and instructions about handling his estate in a codicil to his will. They offer a picture of the intercontinental social world he had lived in, enriched and enlarged by commerce. As RAC agent, he ordered black wool suits to be made up for company officers, soldiers, and commanders of vessels. To his "Negro-man," António Lopez, he gave unconditional freedom, and he bequeathed two captive "Negro-girls" to Betty, the young Euro-African daughter of "Billingary."[9] Two of his close RAC associates, the company scribes Richard Black and Charles Davall, were given 100B each in the form of goods of that value to be taken from his own personal stores on the coast, while £100 was to be given in cash to the London merchant Richard Hutchinson. Booker thus distributed his wealth in a variety of forms, reflecting the variety and locations of his holdings. Some material goods were to be worked up by a local tailor into a special collective gift to staff on the island, other items were to be directly selected there by individual recipients, and still others were to be liquidated and turned into cash or bills of exchange in pounds sterling. A substantial lifetime annuity of £25 and passage to England to collect it marked Hope Booker's manumission and impressive inheritance from Booker as a truly Anglo-Atlantic phenomenon.[10]

Booker's codicil also offers a window onto the considerable amount of personal wealth an RAC employee could gain by participating on his own and off the books in the Guinea trade. But trading off the books leaves few if any surviving traces and so is next to impossible to assess with accuracy. Rough estimates of Booker's personal estate, or portions of it, are all that we have to go on. My own estimate of the value of Booker's bequests in his codicil began by estimating the worth of goods not given a value—the suits for company men and the individual captives he itemized—based on their usual coastal prices in bars. This figure, added together with bequests valued in bars, could then be converted into a figure in pounds sterling. Adding that amount to bequests that were valued in pounds brings my total estimate for this portion of Booker's estate to at least £721. William Heath made an inventory of the remainder of Booker's estate on James Island after these bequests had been honored and gave it a total value of £1,340:13:01. This amount, plus my figure for Booker's bequests, comes to a total estimated value for Booker's personal estate of £2,061, the equivalent of thirty-seven years of his £55 annual salary. Thus, it is reasonable to assume he had been engaging in private trade.

For the purpose of transferring their profits and wealth to England, RAC men like Booker and his successor, Heath, had to create their own personal networks of merchants in England and elsewhere abroad who were not directly associated with the company in order to conceal their profits from private trading. The complex and shadowy paths of such liquidations made it close to impossible to make reliable assessments of the sizes and values of deceased RAC men's estates. But those with experience in the Guinea trade knew quite well how much wealth it could bring to a canny trader working on his own account. The deaths of John Booker and William Heath illustrate this problem and the sometimes-irresolvable legal disputes that arose as executors administered the estates of RAC men. In this case, the accounting difficulties were compounded by the competing interests of the particular individuals involved, especially those of Hope Heath and Humphrey Dyke. Each of them had had a long-standing relationship with John Booker—Hope, as his child slave whom he sent to school in England in the 1680s, and Dyke, as a contributor to Booker's sizeable £1,500 bond for promotion to RAC agent and as executor in Booker's 1688 will. The personal relationship between Hope and Dyke complicated matters further, for it was Humphrey Dyke and his wife, Elizabeth, who had brought Hope into their home in Stepney to care for her during her pregnancy and the birth of her daughter.[11]

William Heath's death at sea in December 1695 set off repercussions well beyond the court complaint contesting William's marriage to Hope. As executor of Booker's will, Humphrey Dyke struggled to administer Booker's estate and was mystified by its complexities. Then, having received a copy of Booker's 1693 codicil, Dyke found himself drawn into more far-flung merchant networks and repeatedly frustrated in his efforts to track the flows of goods among them. Matters worsened for Dyke in January 1696, when Hope Heath consented to let him administer her late husband's estate as well, for it caused the commingling of Booker's and Heath's estates to become more apparent. Dyke himself at various times had sold or exchanged goods for both of them. But he discovered that he was only one figure in a wide constellation of merchants with whom Booker and Heath had worked. And how much of all the varied properties was Booker's and how much was Heath's could not be determined.[12]

Nine months later, in November 1697, Dyke formally registered his mounting frustrations in a stormy bill of complaint at the Court of Chancery. With the discovery that Booker and Heath had had dealings with the merchant Richard Hutchinson, his estimate of the sizes and values of their estates grew by an order of magnitude. Dyke claimed that at the time of Booker's death, his possessions included about four hundred ounces of gold, forty thousand Spanish silver dollars, pieces of wrought plate, jewels, rings, household goods, and other items together valued at around £50,000, or the equivalent of £6,100,000 in today's currency.[13] He did not explain from whom he received this information or how he had come up with his total figure. But he alleged that Hope had seized most of Booker's estate at James Island and divided it up there, putting part of it away for safekeeping with "relations" and giving another part to her soon-to-be husband, William Heath, and then later, after her marriage, bringing the rest of it to England, where she allegedly turned the remainder over to Hutchinson. Dyke accused Hope and Hutchinson of deliberately withholding information about these items or any bills of exchange or other transactions that Booker and Heath had had with Hutchinson.[14]

How to interpret this striking change in Dyke's manner and tone? One factor that must have aroused his suspicions and set off these accusations surely had to be Hope's recent decisive actions. In the spring or summer of 1696, not long after giving Dyke permission to administer her husband's estate, she changed her residence from Stepney, where the Dykes lived, to the parish of Leyton, home of wealthy London bankers and merchants, including Richard Hutchinson. Then in May 1697, she and Hutchinson filed a belated response to Samuel Heath's claims to his brother's estate, and in it, Hope withdrew her permission to Dyke and asked the court to remove him as administrator of her husband's estate. It was her wish to take up that position herself, which she claimed was rightfully hers as William Heath's widow. For his part, Hutchinson stated he had joined with her in responding to the complaint because Hope had expressed concerns to him that she was not being well served.[15] In other words, Hope had requested and received alternative legal advice from Hutchinson, whom Dyke would surely have recognized as a more experienced and much wealthier merchant competitor. Two months later Hope married her second husband, Samuel Meston.

Dyke's suspicious outbursts can be understood not only as a symptom of the intrigues built into the process of tracking laundered personal estates amassed in trade abroad, but also perhaps as a personal reaction to Hope's deliberate change of residence, close alliance with Hutchinson, and assertions of her independence.

With the death of Humphrey Dyke in 1703 came still another round of allegations and controversies in London over Booker's estate. Booker's 1688 will had named Dyke's child Elizabeth as legatee, perhaps as part of Dyke's agreement to put up part of the security bond for Booker's promotion to RAC agent. With Dyke's death this daughter, now Elizabeth Boucher, was hoping to see the settlement of a legal complaint that she and her husband had brought against her own mother, Dyke's widow. It was Elizabeth's view that amongst her father's possessions as Booker's executor was a residual amount from the estate to the value of £5,500, which her mother held as widow and heir but that should be hers. Although the widow Dyke submitted in court that what residual there was came to £769 at most, she nevertheless settled with her daughter and son-in-law for a much higher sum, presumably to put the matter to rest.[16] Elizabeth Dyke Boucher and her husband received £2,605, the equivalent of £393,355 in today's currency.[17]

Whatever the sizes, composition, and total values of Booker's and Heath's personal estates actually may have been, these records of suits and countersuits and the information they contain demonstrate that RAC agents on the Upper Guinea Coast could, and sometimes did, amass considerable wealth on their own accounts and in violation of RAC regulations during their terms of employment at James Island. To be sure, the wherewithal to come out as well as Booker and Heath did was not within the reach of every man who worked for the company, honestly or not. Agents, factors, and scribes who kept the accounts and had direct access to the company stores were the ones best positioned to help themselves. And given the dangers and difficult conditions they faced in their work and the unpredictable deliveries of supplies, provisions, and logistical support from the company, it is not surprising that employees engaged in private trading despite company prohibitions, considering evasion perhaps as a means of awarding themselves the level of compensation to which they felt entitled.

Careerists, Company Disputes, and Fraud

Booker and Heath had learned the ropes of private trading from Alexander Cleeve, who preceded Booker as RAC agent at James Island. Cleeve's career ascended by his intensifying of RAC export trades and on the strength of an audacious accounting fraud based on a nonexistent supplier named "Francisco Lopus." Cleeve's time spent at the James Island fort was not very long, and he had the good fortune of working there during the relatively peaceful decade of the 1680s. Cleeve had arrived from London as a "raw" recruit in April or May 1680, although he must have been very quick to learn, for just short of a year later he had become second in charge of the fort under agent Kastell. And already he was requesting an increase in his salary. Then, upon the death of Kastell in August 1683, Cleeve assumed the position of RAC agent at James Island in charge of the company's stores and records, which gave him the opportunity to create his fraudulent accounting scheme.[18] In calculated respects what records he kept were relatively thorough and accurate in detail. His fraud consisted of financing company men's trading on their own accounts, offering them regular access to company stores in violation of company rules, and then masterminding an ingenious cover-up. To hide this illegal activity from officials in London, he invented a fictitious "local trader" named Francisco Lopus whose account in the company books stood for the company's share in all the ongoing trades that were being carried out secretly by RAC employees (probably including Cleeve himself). And "Francisco Lopus" became an astonishingly successful trader indeed. Directors in London did not discover the fraud until a year after Cleeve returned to England.

Cleeve organized and managed the Francisco Lopus account for a five-year period from September 30, 1683, to November 30, 1688.[19] It chronicles on an almost monthly basis the aggregate credits and debits of RAC men on the Lopus account throughout these years, but there is no way of tracking what each one kept or did with their own individual shares. Overseas goods went out, and coming in to the fort were the major exports of captives, ivory, wax, and hides, along with provisions of cattle, rice, and millet, local cotton cloths, and on one occasion a canoe. The price differentials recorded among the incoming numbers of captives indicate that they were being purchased in two main ways: regularly and in small numbers along the coast (at higher, coastal prices); and seasonally, in much larger numbers (at lower inland prices up the Gambia River) at times when overland caravan arrivals were due to arrive.

To gain a sense of how productive the Lopus account was, the supplies of exports delivered on the company's books by RAC factories provide a useful gauge for comparison. In September 1685, the two factories at Geregia and Bur Saalum, combined together, supplied the fort with captives (twenty-one men and four women), ivory, wax, and hides to a total value of 2,667B, while the Francisco Lopus account for that same month shows larger numbers of captives (eighty-five men, five women, and one boy), and ivory, wax, hides, cattle, and millet coming in to the fort, together valued at 2,989B. Thus, a significant part of Cleeve's strategy for intensifying the export trade was to encourage RAC men to trade for themselves, in violation of their oaths. And the strategy succeeded. By the latter half of the decade, the values of Francisco Lopus's monthly deliveries had doubled on average, owing largely to the addition of nine or ten salaried grometos to the alleged team of Lopus traders.[20] Exactly how much the participants were profiting for themselves at the same time remains opaque, but they would have had access to gold and captives up the Gambia River and their own outlets other than the company for sales of these and other exports.

Meanwhile, Cleeve's correspondence with officers in London gave no sign that anything was amiss. His reports and requests exhibit a growing level of expertise in commercial matters and a desire to do well for the company. Assuring them that his contracts on trust to Luso-African traders in Cacheu would be to their advantage, he offered them an estimate that the fort should be supplied with 20,000 bars of iron per year to purchase an increased stream of exports. Early on he was acutely aware of how important it was to pay close attention to the particular qualities of overseas goods, as he sent samples of textiles and beads to London so company directors could see what would sell. An inkling that something might have been wrong appears in an August 1687 letter from London in which they questioned Cleeve on why he was redirecting their incoming ships and putting them in service nominally to the fort.[21]

It was not until Cleeve had returned to London with his books that someone discovered the fraud. In a letter to Booker, Cleeve's successor, in January 1690, RAC officials explained that their discovery of what they called the "Francis Lopus" account actually represented and reported what had transpired in an argument they had about it with Cleeve. When he was confronted with their charges, Cleeve not only admitted what he had done but insisted that the company had neither suffered nor been wronged by his unusual method of accounting. Clearly, what they considered to be an "intolerable abuse" was, to Cleeve, merely creative accounting to evade a counterproductive company prohibition on underpaid employees fending for themselves while allowing them simultaneously to trade for the company. Some signs of Cleeve's scheme remained at James Island in the form of debts owed to the company, most likely from withdrawals of overseas goods on credit he and the other RAC men had allowed to their export suppliers. Booker reported to London that he was unable to recover what "Portuguese" traders in and around the river owed to them and that there would be no hope of collecting on other debts left behind by agent Cleeve.[22] Nevertheless, as can be seen in this sample transcription, the company made intermittent and chronically unsuccessful attempts to recover debts owed them over the coming years (transcription 5.2).

TRANSCRIPTION 5.2 RAC GIFT OF A PUNCH BOWL TO THE GOVERNOR OF CACHEU

Source: T 70/51, f. 85. TNA.

From RAC London to the Governor of Cacheu

African House, London   1 May 1701

To the Gove'r of Cutchoe

SIR,   The Bearer hereof Capt John Prowde Commdr of our ship the Evans frigatt having formerly been in your River is Encouraging us to fit him out for those parts . we have according to his advises laden a sortable cargoe proper for that Trade no wayes doubting but p yr favour he may meet with an agreeable dispatch , We have given the Captain orders to make demand of severall Debts wch we finde standing out , wch were contracted before our Factory in the River Gambia was Seized p the French p our Agents Castle, Cleeve, & Booker your favour in pcuring the payment of the said Debts is desired , Wee have lately made large Consignments to our Factory in the River Gambia and doe Resolve to Continue so Doeing , that our Agent there may be able to supply the Natives of that River & Traders of yr parts with goods proper for those Markets , We shall give directions that our Agent Correspond with you and doe hope their will be the Same good understanding as was in our former Agents time   Sir we have by Capt Prowde sent you a Silver Punch Bowle , of which your acceptance is desired so wishing you all health and prosperity   We remain

Yr Lo. Friends

John Evans Sub Gr

Thomas J. Pindar   William Jelliffe

Wm Hamond   Jos: Jorye   Sam: Dashwood

Jon: Andrewes   Ralph Lee   John Nicholson

Cleeve continued to work at times for the RAC in London while also maintaining his own private interest in the Guinea trade. At some point just after his return home, he made a modest investment in RAC stock.

And despite the deception he had carried out in the company books, officials clearly recognized his expertise and valuable experience on the Guinea
Coast, for he was elected to serve on the RAC Court of Assistants, first
for three consecutive years (1696–99), and then for eight consecutive years
(1700–1707). At the same time, Cleeve set himself up as a merchant, and
after termination of the company's monopoly, he operated for three years as
a "separate trader" based in London, sending voyages to Africa loaded with
consignments of goods coming to a total value of £10,471, the equivalent of
£1,531,000 in today's currency. This ample investment put him in a select
group of three "separate traders" in London who, between 1702 and 1712,
made yearly investments in Guinea voyages that exceeded £3,000 in value.[23]
Unfortunately, his costs and what profits he made cannot be calculated, nor
is it possible from the surviving RAC records to know much more about his
career as a separate trader or how long it lasted. What is clear even from the
limited moments in it we can see is that he managed to amass much more
personal wealth than one would expect from the salary he earned for six
years as RAC agent, which was somewhere between £300 and £400.

The quite different and rather less successful experiences of another RAC
employee, William Quinn, illustrate how European employees could get
caught up in international intrigues on the Guinea Coast, especially during
times of war in Europe. It is not clear when Quinn first came to James Island,
but in August 1680 the recently arrived Cleeve wrote to London that then-
agent Kastell was putting him in charge of the RAC outpost up the Gambia
River at Bur Saalum. Quinn's company account while on duty there over the
next two years shows that he took out small amounts of brandy on occasion
and made small purchases at the estate sales of company men who had died
on the coast. At some point he relocated to serve as factor at the post of Geregia, twenty miles up Vintang Creek, where he worked through January 1688.
During this period Geregia, together with Mangegar and Jemasar up the
Gambia, were major suppliers of exports to the James Island fort. Geregia
was for the most part a provider of hides and above all beeswax, though it
also sent down some captives and ivory. Quinn was given a substantial raise
in January 1686, from his starting salary of £35 to £60 per year, an indication
of how much agent Cleeve appreciated his performance.[24]

But a dramatic reversal occurred two years later in January 1688, when
Quinn realized that he had come under suspicion by the company of sym-
pathizing with the French and publicly declared himself to be no longer
its employee. As he resigned his post, he turned over the store of company

goods under his care to the local king, seeking his support and protection based on their landlord-stranger relationship. Wisely, the king remained neutral. A standoff ensued that lasted throughout the year as Quinn refused to come to the James Island fort to settle the debt he then owed to the company. After evading several attempts to capture him, Quinn finally surrendered himself in February 1689 and was put on board the *Margett* bound for London. By that time, agent Booker reported in a letter to RAC officials that there had been certified complaints taken out against Quinn. He also charged him with destroying company records at Geregia that, according to Booker, would have revealed his correspondence and proof of his allegedly close relations with French traders. In other words, Quinn was accused of being not only a debtor but also a traitorous French spy at a time of deteriorating Anglo-French relations in Europe and on the African coast.[25]

Quinn's supervisors, wary of his alleged secret dealings with French shippers, and in an atmosphere of strong anti-Catholic and anti-Irish sentiments in England during the lead up to and aftermath of the Protestant "Glorious Revolution" of 1688, became increasingly hostile toward him during the months before war broke out between England and France in 1689. Historians have written that Quinn had been considered untrustworthy even before then, as early as the 1686 visit of La Courbe, of the Compagnie du Sénégal, to the lower Gambia. During that visit, La Courbe did not call at the James Island fort, but he did make stops on the north shore at Albreda and Juffure and traveled up Vintang Creek to Geregia. There he supposedly met with Quinn and received valuable commercial intelligence from him.[26] But La Courbe's description of his travels around the lower Gambia mentioned no meeting with William Quinn.

La Courbe recorded details of his arrival in early July 1686 at the river's mouth, where he lodged first at Albreda on the north shore. There he received generous offerings of the local hospitality, which he enumerated with great care, from the warm greeting and invitation he received from town officials to the pleasurable entertainment of *bala* music to his lavish dinner with the enchanting La Belinguère. On the following day, he toured the nearby town of Juffure and visited the RAC's fortified house and garden there, staffed by soldiers William Heath and William Hollingsworth. Conversing with the Frenchman in Crioulo, the two invited La Courbe to join them in sharing a silver punchbowl brimming with a rich concoction of spirits, citrus juice, sugar, and nutmeg. Passing the punch around and toasting to one another's health with each turn in succession, they drank the bowl dry. It was on this convivial occasion that La Courbe queried his hosts if it was possible to travel by land from the south shore of the lower Gambia to the town of Cacheu. They replied yes, of course, a number of Englishmen had done just that. La Courbe wrote in his journal that he resolved at that very moment to leave his company's ship so he could explore this overland route to Cacheu.[27] His eagerness stemmed from the fact that such knowledge would be extremely important commercially, for this connection would give French merchants a potentially valuable "back door" access route for tapping into Cacheu's hinterlands and the port's productive networks of export suppliers.

The captain of La Courbe's ship loaned him supplies, staff, and a work boat to take him on the first leg of his journey, which was to ascend Vintang Creek to Geregia. After traveling upstream for about ten hours, they reached the town of Vintang, where they spent the night. On the following day, they reached Geregia at dusk and set about paying respects to town officials and arranging for lodging. Before retiring, however, La Courbe and his companions took time to visit the RAC house where Quinn was factor in charge. Describing him as a man of the "Irish nation" who spoke very good French, La Courbe noted that Quinn was actually not present during his visit. Instead, his assistant, a soldier named John Kemp, entertained the French visitors. La Courbe was favorably impressed by the trade that went on at Geregia, and especially by the volume and high quality of beeswax exports. But at least on this occasion he did not meet with William Quinn.[28] According to his journal, it had been the RAC men at Juffure who supplied him and the French company with strategic information about the land route to Cacheu and access to its suppliers of Atlantic exports.

Quinn's forced departure from James Island in February 1689 would have him arriving in London sometime around April or May. What immediate dealings he had with the RAC or anyone else in London cannot be determined, but at some point the company had him arrested for the debt he owed it, and he was imprisoned in the Wood Street Compter, a notorious debtor's prison within the City of London. He managed somehow to maintain himself there despite its violence and daily extortions until January 1691, when the RAC Court of Assistants agreed to refer his case to the company's Committee of Law. After signing a bill that acknowledged the amount of debt he owed the company, Quinn was released that February.[29]

It remains uncertain whether or how Quinn cleared his debt or what his whereabouts were over the next several years. However, the company hired him back sometime before June 1695. He signed on this time to work at York Island, where company rules and regulations were far more relaxed, and he resumed his career in trading, no doubt privately as well as for the company. His salary of £4 per month was less than he had made when he had been promoted to factor in charge of the Geregia factory, but for the southern forts it was a respectable sum. Judging from his regular quarterly withdrawals of goods, it appears likely that Quinn was not at the fort itself but posted to one of the mainland factories. Perhaps following the example of some of his coworkers who will be discussed further on, he was supplying himself and locals with the elements of creole dress by selecting European-style shoes and clothing, sewing materials, and African-made and imported textiles. Brass basins, important equipment for the workshops of local salt makers, were also among his usual selections.[30]

Quinn made at least one voyage north to the lower Gambia in late December 1696. He and his coworkers Wilford Ridley and Joseph Flavell managed to purchase a cargo of ivory, beeswax, and sixty-five captives, but they lost ten of the captives—six died and four ran away—while preparing for the return voyage. Another thirteen died on the way back to York Island. Three of the RAC crew deserted and went over to the French, taking with them over 400B worth of overseas goods, and Ridley died soon after their arrival at York Island. Quinn was listed as a factor at York Island in June 1697 and died the next month, once again in debt to the RAC, owing 273B.[31] During their time spent on the Upper Guinea Coast, both Cleeve and Quinn made money on and off the company's books and left behind debts to the company that could not be collected, but that is where the similarities between their career trajectories end.

Thomas Corker, who had worked at York Island since early 1684 and served as agent there from May 1693, experienced a sharp reversal in his RAC career almost as dramatic as Quinn's.[32] He was able to keep secret from the company his marriage to a prominent local woman, helped in part by the more sheltered location of the York Island fort, and during his time as agent he seems to have managed the fort and kept accounts relatively well. When war forced the merging of the Bence Island and York Island forts in 1690, Corker was put in charge of managing them until peace was restored. But officials in London had an ambivalent view of Corker. His leniency and pragmatism toward matters of personnel and employee behavior, his appreciation of the expertise of such free-wheeling local Euro-African traders as the Tuckers and Skinners, and his decisions to cooperate from time to time with so-called interlopers won him no admiration from company officials.

Even so, in the years just after the 1695 surrender of James Island to the French, they tolerated his efforts to send vessels northward to keep up an English presence on the lower Gambia, and they neither rejected nor accepted his periodic offers to serve there. They did, however, express growing frustrations over his decisions about local staffing and salaries at their southern forts and outposts. Instructions from them in January 1697 were to send an account of all the "mulattos" he had on hire, how it was that they came to be working for the company, what work they did, their ages, and what salaries he paid them. Meanwhile, Corker clearly had ambitions to become agent at James Island whenever the company managed to restore and reoccupy it. It must have made a favorable impression in London when Corker's June 1697 letter arrived in which he announced that he had purchased a sloop and sent it up to Gambia to recover debts owed to the RAC by Portuguese merchants who lived upriver. And just four months later, he himself set sail from York Island to the Gambia River on one of two ships he had outfitted and supplied for a trading venture up the river as a bold audition for the future position of agent at James Island.[33]

His persistent attention to regaining the RAC's Gambia posts paid off. In December 1697, London wrote to Corker that since peace between England and France had been restored (by the Treaty of Rijswijk of that year), they could go ahead with plans to resettle James Island and repair damages that the fort had sustained. Corker's offer to serve at Gambia had finally been accepted by the RAC, which they confirmed the following month in a long letter of instruction explaining what company ships Corker could expect to arrive next at York Island and where they should be sent. Typically, their overly optimistic expectations were impossible for anyone to meet. Corker was to settle his affairs and make arrangements to relocate to James Island while simultaneously training new staff at York Island. With the estimated arrival there of the *Rebecca* and *Sherbro* in March, Corker was to assist his York Island successor in conducting an inventory of the fort and its goods, give him instructions on how to supply the *Rebecca* with a cargo for London, and clear his own account books so they could be sent on the homeward voyage. He was instructed also to select which men among the employees at Sherbro would accompany him north to Gambia—seamen, soldiers, bricklayers, carpenters, and sawyers—and "Twenty Young Lusty Negroe Men for Gramettoes." On arriving at Gambia, he was to give notice to local kings about the company's return and inform upriver merchants as well, encouraging them all with presents as he saw fit. For rebuilding and repairing the

James Island fort, its outbuildings, and storage rooms, Corker was instructed to enlist laborers and work boats of local merchants for procuring and transporting sufficient quantities of construction materials, such as stones, oyster shells, and timber. This rehabilitation of the fort was to be done as quickly as possible so that upon arrival of a company ship with overseas merchandise Corker could immediately set about purchasing a cargo of ivory, wax, and hides for London. Accompanying these instructions were friendly letters to their on-again, off-again Euro-African employees Matthew Skinner and Richard Bridgman with presents of a sword and gun for each.[34]

But 1698 turned out to be a year of signal defeat for RAC officials in London, with disruptive ripple effects in northern Guinea. Although questions challenging the company's monopoly on England's trade in Africa had arisen in the House of Commons for years, this year's session ordered up a bill to terminate it. Starting in early January, petitions for and against the monopoly poured in from all quarters. Each side in the debate had their own energetic and vociferous supporters campaigning publicly and among political circles in Parliament. Rumors about the company's impending demise quickly reached the Upper Guinea Coast, embellished by private traders in high hopes that an end to the monopoly and perhaps the company itself was within reach. Some of the more devious among the ambitious interlopers spread word that the company was facing bankruptcy, which generated fears among local RAC employees that they would never be paid the salaries owed them. Local kings and merchants had their own responses, and acted out in retaliation for unpaid "customs" and debts owed or moved quickly to form new alliances in fear for their futures. Meanwhile, events in London progressed steadily. By early July, an act of Parliament ending the RAC's monopoly privileges had passed both Houses and been given royal approval.[35]

The second half of 1698 was an especially trying time for the company and its plans for recovering from its wartime losses and restoring its trade in northern Guinea, but now without the protections of its former charter. Added to the changes in staffing at Sherbro/Sierra Leone and the resettlement and rebuilding of James Island was the task of explaining how this new act of Parliament would affect the way RAC agents were to deal with legitimation of the "separate traders" on the Guinea Coast.[36] Letters with instructions went out in duplicate on any ship that might be stopping at one or another of their forts. Corker's whereabouts during this uncertain time are not entirely clear. He had much to do at York Island in transferring management of the fort on to his successor Francis Bowman, and when Bowman died in mid-July, that process had to be discontinued. Corker took it up again in August, having recruited Robert Loadman to succeed Bowman, and the two of them proceeded to conduct an inventory of the company's York Island stores. Behind the scenes, Corker must have had family issues to sort out regarding his move, particularly how to handle future support for his wife and son or sons. Corker's whereabouts remained uncertain to London, as letters went out from there through October 1698 addressed to him at Gambia and to Corker and Bowman jointly at Sherbro, sounding increasingly worried at having received no word from either of them in response.[37]

Second in charge at James Island was to be Paul Pindar. He had arrived there only recently in late 1698 or early 1699, and he wrote to London on March 4, 1699, that he was expecting Corker to arrive any day. One report from a company crewman who had been helping guard the fort at Sierra Leone stated that Corker had proceeded north to Gambia on a former pirate ship, but it gave no date for when this took place. Corker arrived probably in early to mid-March during a period of several weeks when Pindar was away from the island. And soon, unbeknownst to officials in London, their plan for resettling James Island and above all their choice of Corker as agent and Pindar as second would expose and exacerbate a deep social and experiential divide between company officials in London and its employees at their forts on the Upper Guinea Coast. When Corker and the newly arrived and rather straitlaced Peter Pindar finally did meet, it set off a major cultural clash and confrontation that proved to be disastrous for all concerned.[38]

It is difficult to gain an accurate sense of Corker's behavior as he assumed his new post at James Island since most of the records of it were written from Pindar's harshly critical perspective. Perhaps Pindar felt more self-consciously determined than usual, knowing that his brother Thomas had a prominent position on the RAC Court of Assistants and would be carefully watching how events on James Island unfolded. In any case, when Pindar returned to the fort, he found Corker there celebrating and wielding a grandiose vision of the authority of his new position with relish. Outraged at what he called Corker's "profligate" spending, Pindar wrote up a damning account enumerating Corker's excessive expenses over March and April. And even though Pindar was an extremely hostile witness, it cannot be denied that Corker had indeed run up a substantial personal bill with the company, totaling 34,739B by Pindar's estimate. Among Pindar's charges, Corker owed his employers for casks of spirits he and his guests consumed; for additional rum, brandy, sugar, and wine he served as punch; for barrels of gunpowder he expended daily on firing salutes to guests and to arriving and departing ships; for overseas goods he allowed his employees to take out from the company warehouse; for gifts and finery he awarded to his forty grometos; for export goods he requested from outstations for his own account; for presents he lavished on local officials and visiting ship captains; and for his personal appropriations of property from the estates of deceased employees. It is unlikely that Pindar, just arrived from London, made up all of these familiar practices on the coast.[39]

From Corker's perspective, however, he was simply carrying out his instructions for establishing a strong RAC presence in the lower Gambia. These salutes, toasts, feasts, and gifts were among the costs of doing business in the Guinea trade, and he had previously succeeded with similar extravagance at York Island. On the other hand, it is not at all certain from Pindar's charges that Corker was embezzling enormous amounts of RAC property. An indirect reference in one of the RAC London letters to Pindar indicated that officials there had heard from Corker that he had seized one or two vessels trading on the Gambia River. It is not clear if they were owned by Portuguese traders in debt to the company or by English "separate traders" or others. In any case, it appears Corker may not have fully understood the new act of Parliament, for under the older regulations the RAC was allowed to seize such ships and Corker, as agent, would have been entitled to a share in the plunder. As for the allegedly boisterous and generous conviviality, in the creole culture of northern Guinea ostentatious hospitality was an important feature of trading. And being on friendly terms with all sorts of people, from local kings and suppliers to coworkers and competitors, was a well-established and reasonable strategy for reducing risk, one that had served Corker well at York Island for over fifteen years.[40]

February 1700 brought the beginning of the end for Thomas Corker. He was formally discharged and ordered back to London to settle his accounts, and the company appointed Paul Pindar his successor at James Island and Thomas Gresham as Pindar's second (transcription 5.3). Letters informed RAC men at York Island, Corker's former posting, that they were not to allow him or any of his allies to seek refuge in any of their forts or stations. One wonders what thoughts and memories of James Island and the lower Gambia, if any, passed through the mind of Alexander Cleeve as he and the others in London on the Court of Assistants discussed recent events on the northern Guinea Coast and came to their decision to send out these orders. As it happened, Corker returned to England as ordered, arriving at Falmouth in late spring or early summer of 1700. He died not long after. Peter Pindar also died that spring at James Island, and his successor there, Thomas Gresham, died in early 1701. Fire destroyed what work they had accomplished in rebuilding and repairing the fort and other structures on James Island, and over the next decade the remaining near-ruin was occupied only intermittently. Meanwhile, trading continued at the two forts to the south, though not always smoothly, and starting in June 1708 the list of soldiers on staff at York Island included one Thomas Corker, "mulatto." This Thomas Corker served there at least until 1713 and represented the second generation of Corkers employed by the RAC. Their many descendants would prosper and become the prominent Caulker family of modern Sierra Leone.[41]

TRANSCRIPTION 5.3 THOMAS CORKER ORDERED TO LONDON

Source: T 70/50 London to Corker, 20 February 1700, f. 55. TNA.

London 20 February 1699/00

AGENT Thomas Corker

These are strictly to Require and Command you Immediately to Surrender and deliver up unto Mr Paul Pinder Mr Thomas Gresham Mr John Walter Mr Wm Hacker Mr Tho: Hide John Proud Thomas Williams Daniel Tilsley Nat:l Pyle Thomas Brooks John Clarke Or so many of them as can be present   Our Castle and Factory upon James Island in the River Gambia and all goods and Marchandises Guns Stores Ammunition and Provision and every other Matter or thing whatsoever therein or thereto appertaining or belonging. Also all the out factories and the Goods and Marchandises therein of wt kinde or Nature soever Also all our Ships Vessells Boates and Cannoes & all the Goods Marchandises Gunns Stores tackle amunition & Provisions and every other Matter or thing whatsoever in them also all books, accts papers whatsoever and all out standing Debits all which the Persons above Mentioned are by us Impowered and authorized to Receive, you are hereby likewise Required and Commanded to Embarque and Proceed for England upon our first ship that shall be dispatcht home directly to discharge your accounts with us and to ahnswere to such Matters as is alledged against you and hereof you are not to fail.   Wee Remain

J. Jorye

C. Whitcomb	J. Morgan	Urban Hall Sub Govr
C. Balle	A. Cleeve	John Evans D. Govr
R. Lee	W. Fazakerley	Wm Jollife
		Thomas Pindar

Such disconnects between RAC in London and their employees on the Guinea Coast are understandable in large part because of delays in communication, with letters between them taking months to arrive, if they arrived at all. Decisions in the Gambia sphere or at the southern forts might have to be taken on the spot, leaving no time for seeking advice or sending requests for assistance. But agents there also deliberately acted on their own, sometimes repeatedly overriding company rules and policies. It is not hard to understand why London had so little effective control. Company letters from London display how overwhelmed the directors were not only by the pan-Atlantic scale and complexity of operations on two parts of Africa's long coastline and in multiple American ports but also by a great and growing cultural distance between them and their agents in northern Guinea. Successful trading on the Upper Guinea Coast required building complex local social networks and adapting to their hosts' protocols and cultural mores, all of which the London men deemed as either bewildering or at times unseemly, and often excessively costly. RAC men who learned to thrive in the Guinea trade were well aware that the coastal creole culture did not fit well with the proprieties expected of them by London, and they acted accordingly. Breaking and bending company rules and evading detection could be attractive and profitable options, even at the risk of an interrupted career with the company. Distant RAC directors in London often strongly disapproved of and even punished employees such as Cleeve, Quinn, and Corker, but they kept them on or hired them back nevertheless, admitting only implicitly their dependence on men whose "offensive" behavior was an effective adaptation to trading protocols on the Guinea Coast.

"Living as Portuguese"

Throughout the monopoly period, staffing fluctuated at the RAC's three Upper Guinea forts as men died or left the company and as new replacements arrived from England. Visiting ships and crews also turned up and stayed before sailing on, perhaps for weeks or even months. Company agents sometimes took advantage of their temporary presence to enlist them to assist in trade or, on occasion, to take some direct action against the French or other intruders on their behalf. The captains of company ships were the company's go-betweens, carrying cargoes, passengers, invoices, bills of lading, letters, and official instructions between London and the company forts. They also served as informants, passing informal information along in both directions, sometimes serving as sworn witnesses to events in dispute, and reporting on the conduct of RAC men and others on the Guinea Coast. The island forts were not isolated, self-enclosed enclaves of Europeans. In addition to having a variety of visitors, coming from afar and also from nearby, company men spent time away from their island base, sometimes for long stretches, on voyages up rivers or along the coast or manning one of their outposts. In the case of James Island, records for a five-year period in the 1680s show that at the very least, half of the English company men were away at any given time, either at outposts or on vessels and not at the fort itself (table 5.1). It should be noted here that since the 1680s was a time of peace between England and France, these absences did not compromise the security of the fort.

TABLE 5.1 LOCATIONS OF RAC EMPLOYEES IN GAMBIA TRADING SPHERE (1684–89)

Date	# of men on James Island	# of Outposts	# of men at Outposts	# of men on Vessels[a]	Total # of men off island	Total # Men
18 March 1684	25	7	11	29	40	65
31 May 1684	28	7	9	99	108	136
30 Sept. 1684	21	7	13	33	46	67
15 Dec. 1684	28	8	9	27	36	64
4 Aug. 1685	26	5	7	36	43	69
8 Feb. 1686	29	6	8	38	46	75
24 June 1686	37	5	9	80	89	126
25 Jan. 1687	28	4	10	59	69	97
24 June 1687	29	7	12	77	89	118
3 Feb. 1688	30	6	10	49	59	89
30 June 1688	32	6	12	23	35	67
12 Feb. 1689	37	6	11	38	49	86
17 July 1689	32	5	11	38	49	81
Averages	29	6	10	48	58	87.7

[a] Highly variable, because it includes men and vessels in from overseas that were diverted to engage in coasting or local trading.

Source: T 70/1441. TNA.

Others settled into a practice known as "living as Portuguese," which had been established by some of the first European merchants on the Guinea Coast and its offshore Atlantic islands in the later fifteenth century. These men chose to remain permanently in West Africa, work there as locally based Atlantic merchants, marry local women, and raise families of Euro-African children. James Island agent Booker took up the practice as a policy he was trying out for certain selected employees, knowing full well that RAC in London would object to their employees living with women. He justified the strategy by emphasizing how it would improve the company's trading contacts and access to commercial intelligence. He first cleared Benjamin Bull to live on the mainland, insisting that residence there would be in the company's best interest. Two months later he cleared four others—Captain Cornelius Hodges, Benjamin Hodges, Jeffrey Baldwerd, and Joseph Flavell—to live "as Portuguese" under certain obligations spelled out in an indenture contract, copies of which apparently do not survive. Booker reassured the company that the men were required to live close to the island at Brefet on the south shore so that they could easily come over with their grometos to help defend the fort if there was any emergency or attack by French ships. His rationale for "settling" these men was that he knew little about events in the countryside that might affect trade because of the "lack of white men" living there.[42] What he might have meant, more precisely, was he could not rely on men already there for honest, current, and accurate information. But what remains unexplained is if and how "living as Portuguese" differed from sending employees out to be in charge of an outpost.

The career of Benjamin Bull demonstrates how company policies, including "living as Portuguese," encouraged employees to act entirely in their own self interest. Bull started his employment in July 1683 as a soldier at James Island, on a salary of £12 per year, or 40B. Over the next three years he was promoted to corporal, then sergeant, and then, in a striking career change, was made factor in November 1686 at a starting salary of £30, or 100B. During that period, his account shows him taking out small amounts on his salary only eleven times, four of them as selections of items from the estate sales of deceased comrades on the coast.[43] There is absolutely no indication of how he was able to gain the knowledge and experience to be promoted to the position of a factor in charge of managing company trade. The most likely possibility can be inferred from the timing of this early phase in his career, which corresponded to the term of agent Cleeve at James Island and his Francisco Lopus scheme to encourage, organize, and reward private trading by company men. Bull was probably among the employees who took part in the fraud, thereby learning how to conduct trade on the Upper Guinea Coast successfully and thus qualifying himself as factor. In a contradiction typical of life in northern Guinea, he acquired valuable expertise and earned a promotion by violating the prohibition of the very company that promoted him for doing so.

He started his new job as factor trading up the Gambia River with William Wells on board the *Sherbro*. Then, over most of 1687 and 1688, he was stationed as factor at the RAC post of Jemasar, located upriver on the south shore just below Saalum. In November 1688, the ending balance of his account in Cleeve's books shows the company still owing him 353B of his salary, so it is likely that he was taking part in the Francisco Lopus fraud for the company and trading for himself with "interlopers" or Portuguese traders upriver. He had no need of a salary that must have paled in comparison with his illicit profits. If so, and as was the case with Robert Gunn, it is not possible to track his own independent trading or his income. He remained with the company, however, and next moved down to the river's mouth, serving as factor for a company post at Barra through 1689 and into 1690, when Booker cleared him to "live as Portuguese." Since he had already been living off the island as a company factor, it is not clear what distinction Booker was making about Bull's new living and working arrangements. It may have been an unstated acknowledgment of Bull's marriage to a woman named Elizabeth, who was known to the company later as Senhora Betty Bull.[44]

This possibility of a marriage "Portuguese style" certainly makes sense in the context of Benjamin Bull's subsequent activity at Barra as a rice trader, perhaps in a partnership with Elizabeth. In 1692, he delivered 60 cwt. of hulled rice to the fort, worth 120B, and in the first quarter of 1693 he took out a selection of commodities, currencies, and capital goods that were essential in the river trade: 20B in large amber; 30B in cowries; several reams of paper; fifty-two skeins of crewel (worsted embroidery thread); and a pair of woolcards for spinning cotton. These were the last entries in Benjamin Bull's account, and he was not listed as an employee in the James Island nominal rolls for the years 1692–94. Presumably he joined his wife Elizabeth in independent trade. If at that time he had any wishes to maintain some connection with the RAC, they would have been dashed the following year by the surrender of the James Island fort to the French. In October 1699, RAC officials in London wrote to the agent at the recovered fort at James Island expressing their disappointment at learning that Bull had left the company. Where and how much longer he lived cannot be determined, but in 1704 his wife or widow, Senhora Bull, sold the company a boy captive on a trading voyage up the Gambia River.[45]

This small handful of RAC employees who were allowed to "live as Portuguese" were not alone in marrying local women on the Guinea Coast. William Heath, by then a company agent, was careful to keep his marriage to Hope Booker, and her pregnancy, concealed from officials in London. The career of William Blow presents another example, one which shows some parallels with that of Benjamin Bull. Both of them started out with the company in the early 1680s, and both became factors managing company trade. Blow served as a lieutenant based at James Island. His starting salary is not available, but in July 1683 he was promoted to factor. His annual pay increased from £40 per year to £50. In contrast to Bull, he was much more attentive to drawing out salary payments from the company during his first several years, making withdrawals more often and in larger amounts. But he, too, must have been taking part in trade off the books as part of Cleeve's scheme, for once he began serving as factor the recorded withdrawals on his salary decreased sharply. Meanwhile, he was engaged in working on trading voyages up the Gambia River and also to the Petite Côte, acting at times as supercargo in charge of negotiating prices and managing the logistics of Euro-African commerce and its complex labor force.[46]

Blow took on new responsibilities in January 1687, when he was put in charge of reviving the RAC outpost at Mangegar, up the Gambia River at Saalum. He was stationed there over the next five years, regularly supplying the company with large cargoes of captives. It may well have been during this time that he met and married another Euro-African woman named Elizabeth, who, like Elizabeth Bull, became a senhora and appeared as a supplier of exports in the RAC records of their 1704 voyage up the Gambia River. Since he did not draw on his salary, Blow must have been doing very well trading on his own account. By November 1688, the RAC owed him over 900B. There is no direct record of how he reacted to the slave insurrection on the *Charles* when it was anchored at Mangegar in May 1691, but he then left the post, perhaps as a result of that shocking and violent event. From 1692 to 1694, he remained upriver, spending most of his time in ship-based commerce, commanding the *Charles* up and down the river, and moving goods between ports on its banks, apparently without mishap. Then, in late July 1695, he was among the contingent of RAC men who surrendered James Island to the French. He is not listed in subsequent company records, but a Senhora Betty Blow sold a slave and some ivory to the RAC in May 1704.[47]

Marriages between RAC men and local women became more visible in company records of the southern forts at Sierra Leone and Sherbro as their Euro-African sons followed their fathers into employment with the company. One prominent example was Zachary Rogers, whose three sons worked in varying capacities in the York Island sphere. They were the original ancestors of the extended Rogers family in Sierra Leone (later thought to have been founded in the eighteenth century), who remained prominent and powerful throughout the twentieth century. RAC records of this seventeenth-century story of the father and sons take the history of the Rogers family farther back in time to the 1660s, when Zachary Rogers worked for the Company of Royal Adventurers.[48] Seven years after his death in February 1681, his son Simon was working on RAC vessels based at Bence Island as a boatswain, quickly advancing to the position of sailor. He went on to serve as a gunner on the coasting vessel *Charles* on its voyages southward to Cape Mount, but he abruptly left the ship when it and the *Berkeley Castle* were ordered north in July 1690 with a contingent of company men to defend the James Island fort. He preferred to remain behind at York Island and moved to the better-sheltered and more informally managed fort there, serving as a gunner for at least the next two years.[49] His brother, Zachary Jr., was already there, and his other brother, Samuel, joined them on the company payroll in 1692. Zachary Jr. and Samuel then worked at the York Island fort or at one of its factories at least until December 1699, when records stop. When RAC officers in London ordered their agents in northern Guinea to designate which of their employees were "mulattos," both Zachary and Samuel were listed as such throughout the 1690s (transcription 5.4). The two brothers managed the Gallinas factory for a time, but after that their careers cannot be tracked.[50] Records are sparse by the end of that disrupted decade and do not resume until after 1710. The RAC Home Ledger for 1698–99 lists a debt of over 100B owed by Zachary Rogers's three "children."[51]

Both Zachary Jr. and Samuel focused their later trading on the coast south of Sherbro, where they supplied export commodities intermittently to the RAC but mostly dealt with separate English traders as well as private traders of other backgrounds. Trading was rough and risky on this part of the Upper Guinea Coast, but their well-placed positions in local society and fluency in local languages helped both of them build successful careers— Zachary at Gallinas and Samuel at Cape Mount. They expertly managed

Source: T 70/1442, f. 13. TNA.

Factors: Henry Gibson
John Cumberbaich
Thomas Corker
Matthew Skinner

Belonging to the *York* sloop:
Capt. John Jeffery
John Williams
David Scott, his servant

Belonging to the *Stanier* sloop:
Capt. Richcard Charley
William Lovegrove, his servant
John Carter
Peter Foster

Thomas Clarke, bricklayer
Robert Davis, Sargent of the Island
Charles Eaton, Master of the *Sherbro*
Symon Rogers, Gunner of the Island
Thomas Cunstable, House Carpenter
John Swann, Steward of Provisions
Thomas Cranson, Chyrurgion
Richard Bridgman, Gardener
William Bridgman, Gardener
John Billings att 3 Barrs per month, Souldier

Malattos:
Peter Tucker, Storekeeper att 4 Barrs per month
James Darby, Sould. att 3 Barrs per ditto
Zachary Cumberbaich att 3 Barrs per ditto
Joseph Tucker att 2 Barrs per ditto
Henry Scott att 1 Barr per ditto
Zachary Rogers att 2½ Barrs per ditto
Samuel Rogers att 1 Barr per ditto
Symon the fisherman att 2 Barrs per ditto
Black Henry, Shipp Carpenter

their dealings on trust, taking company goods out and building up debts to levels that infuriated the RAC officials in London. One attraction that the RAC enjoyed over the private traders was their ready supply of European-style finished clothing, which marked free and successful merchants no matter their complexions. Samuel, for example, pledged the company a cargo of camwood in 1722, taking out a full outfit of tailored menswear and a pair of shoes. Zachary was described as having a large household of many slaves and servants, and it was likely he who was the immediate founder of the prominent and extensive Gallinas clan of Rogers. However, he is not remembered in the oral histories of the various branches of the Rogers family, which do not go back that far in time.[52]

John Cumberbatch and his sons John Jr. and Zachary present yet another example of a Euro-African family derived from company origins. John Sr. was based at Bence Island from at least April 1679 through 1680. The Bence Island records do not indicate his position or salary rate, but he took out several small assortments of goods on his wages due. The next record of him comes in 1684 from the fort at York Island, where he spent the next thirteen years until his death in April 1697. He held the position of factor at the company outpost on the Bum Kittam River, just south of the fort, supplying mainly camwood and ivory. How often he might also have dealt with private traders cannot be determined. Interestingly, it was only in the last year of his life that he made deliveries of captives to the RAC fort: a male and a female in September 1696, and three females in March 1697.[53] It is not clear whether he died of natural causes or illness, or if he was a casualty of the violence of the trade in captives.

His account activity shows a distinctive pattern of payments he made out of his salary to persons or family back in England via notes payable by the company in pounds sterling. In some years he made one or two such payments, in other years none at all. There is no clear answer to the obvious question of just who the person or persons he was supporting might have been. Amounts of the payments varied widely, ranging between £5 and £29 each. Three notes sent off to England in August 1682 on the *Two Brothers* came to a total of £31, and his order for three separate notes suggests that they were made out to different individuals. He may have had a wife or dependent relative, owed debts to merchants or tradesmen, or perhaps maintained John Jr. in England for training or schooling.

Another pattern in John Cumberbatch's account was his regular withdrawals of assortments of two distinctly different types of trade goods. One set included items characteristic of the trade in commodities and commodity currencies on this part of the Guinea Coast, such as various metalwares, beads, cowries, and brandy. The other set were items of European-style dress along with supplies and capital equipment for producing tailored creole-style clothing.[54] He was either selling to a local tailor or had a tailoring workshop in his own home. Items of European-style dress he regularly took out were slippers and shoes, men's thread stockings, various types of hats, and occasionally men's shirts. For the tailoring of creole-style clothing, he also selected a wide range of textiles, some of them being very long pieces of yardage, including various linens and woolens from Europe, different types of cottons and silks from Asia, and dyed and patterned cloths made in West Africa. Sewing equipment and supplies included needles, thread of varying types and colors, dozens of silk buttons, other types of buttons by the barrel, ribbon, scissors, and sewing and stitching silk. The clientele of such a tailoring business would likely have been a cross-section of local men and women who wished to be seen as worldly, fashionable, and recognizably involved in Atlantic trade. In addition to his private trading conducted with others, Cumberbatch must have made a good income from tailoring or supplying local tailors. When he died, the company owed him 535B from his 640B salary over the previous four years.[55]

Zachary Cumberbatch, John's son, was one of a number of men working at York Island who appeared on a separate listing of employees designated as "mulatto," as requested by RAC officers in London (see transcription 5.4). Despite these men's long-standing family connections with the company, they were viewed with suspicion and, at times, outright hostility. Their contacts with private traders were one source of irritation, and so was their skill in managing high levels of debt. Local RAC agents, on the other hand, held them in very high esteem. During Corker's time as Sherbro agent in the 1690s, he had tried to explain in his letters to London why it was so important to keep "the mulattos" in service. In one instance, he recommended Senhor Matthew Skinner to them by name, noting that Skinner had a long track record with the RAC (and, of course, with others) and describing him admiringly as a major merchant both in the area and at Cape Mount. Corker referred to Euro-African men like Skinner as "seasoned" and stated emphatically that one such veteran was worth more than five newcomers.[56] Nevertheless, company officials in London were not impressed, perhaps a symptom of their inability to face the fact that they had little to no control over their employees on the Guinea Coast and often did not even know who they were.

Zachary Cumberbatch's posting to the York Island fort lasted for at least eleven years, from February 1689 to 1700. Early records for him are patchy. Some of the blame for this obscurity lies with agent Gibson, who neglected to keep a journal of trading during his term from 1689 to 1693. Zachary went on to work for a time on the company vessel *Sherbro,* crewing with three other "mulattos," including Zachary Rogers Jr. In 1692, his salary was listed as 3B a month, or just under £11 per year. Cumberbatch's account in 1693 and 1694 shows him taking out modest amounts of goods—a mix of consumer items and commodity currencies such as cowries and iron bars—and only infrequently. Then, in the latter half of 1694, when Zachary was probably in his early twenties, he drew out trade goods worth the full balance of his salary still due to him from Gibson's term as York Island agent, a considerable sum that came to 109B. The assortment was extremely well chosen, consisting of the major commodity currencies—iron bars, cowries, and beads—and preferred goods such as metalwares and textiles that could be put to use either as household consumer items or as intermediate goods in production or artisanal work. A case of spirits and a shotgun with gunpowder and shot added special value to the mix. Given his youth at the time, it is tempting to see this transaction as marking a special event, perhaps serving as one of a series of bridewealth payments to the family of his future wife in a community nearby on the mainland. If so, he would have been following in his father's footsteps.[57]

Over the next five years, from 1695 to 1700, Zachary rose to become a successful merchant on the Sherbro coast. He and fellow "mulatto" Robert Davis lived away from the fort as managers of the RAC factory at Gay, and they sent clean rice to York Island in June 1695 and a shipment of ivory in February 1696. Zachary took out goods on his salary at three-month intervals in 1696, the total amount coming to 130B, or the equivalent of £39. If that amount represented his yearly salary at that time, it had more than tripled over the past four years. After the death of his father in April 1697, he continued on at his post, taking out small payments only once or twice a year. Company accounts give no indication as to how his father's estate was handled. In any case, it is probable that Zachary was dealing with private traders as well as supplying the RAC, for in the final surviving record of him, he was listed as Senhor Zachary Cumberbatch and, following his father's example perhaps again, was serving as factor in charge of the RAC outpost at the Bum Kittam River.[58]

The local roots and longevity of Euro-African men, often styled "Portuguese" or "mulattos" in company accounts, made them valuable sources and employees for local agents and even for London directors who so often struggled to find personnel they could trust to make money on the Upper Guinea Coast. Their value to the company lay, ironically, in their abilities to operate independently of its policies. At times when desperation exposed the grim reality of their helplessness, RAC directors would try to woo one or another of these independent traders back into their employ by sending a fawning letter offering him "friendship" and the gift of a pistol and sword.

Local Hires

Still greater reliance on local networks on the coast came from the failure of RAC officials in London to sufficiently supply their employees on the Guinea Coast with overseas trade goods, shipping supplies and equipment, a wide range of workmen's tools, medicines, and other basic necessities for their daily upkeep and operations. Foremost in their failures from a local employee's perspective were the company's shipments of food provisions. These were made up of staple items, following on the protocols established by the Royal Navy: a basic diet that consisted of dried beans and biscuits, flour, salt, vinegar, salted beef, and spirits, all packed for shipment and storage in barrels, casks, or sacks. However, the London firms contracted to supply these items often proved to be unreliable, either in meeting orders in a timely manner or in the quality of the products and their packing.[59] Ship captains had their own special set of provisioning problems, especially in feeding their free black crewmen, who complained bitterly of having to go "without food" whenever they had to subsist solely on English salt beef and biscuits. Irregular arrivals of ships from London, coupled with uncertain availability of other sources of food supplies in the Cape Verde Islands, meant that RAC agents on the Guinea Coast often had to rely on local foodstuffs to get by.[60]

Organizing and carrying out the provisioning of RAC forts, outposts, and voyages thus became yet another of local agents' many responsibilities. In northern Guinea, they established company gardens on the mainland, guarded and tended by company factors and grometos, to provide fresh produce, while bulk provisions of millet, rice, and salt came in from coasting voyages or from local suppliers. Bulking centers were set up from time to time in mainland locales where the most desired fresh provisions could regularly be had. And in some cases, agents would hire local suppliers on monthly or yearly salaries to assist them in the essential and ongoing business of provisioning.

One such provisioner of the James Island fort was a Muslim man named Mamadu. He was hired to be keeper of the company's cattle and served in that position from at least February 1681 until March 1688.[61] In hiring Mamadu, agent Booker was following a practice that was common in the Senegambia region, whereby cattle owners would often hire specialist Fulbe herders like Mamadu to manage their livestock (described in chapter 2). Such men were expert not only in pasturing and watering large herds but also in breeding, weaning, and raising calves. Husbandry of the larger, *zebu* breeds of cattle was particularly demanding. These animals required attentive care, for they could be raised only in areas free of the tsetse fly, carrier of the parasite that causes bovine sleeping sickness. Cattle purchased by the RAC at James Island, however, were most likely from the smaller *ndama* breeds, which are resistant to the parasite.[62] The company records misleadingly refer to all of their cattle as "cows," ignoring the fact that adult females made up only a fraction of the herds. Although the exact location where Mamadu tended the company's animals was not given, it was certainly close by, most likely in the kingdom of Combo on the south shore at the mouth of the Gambia. That area was well known as a land of plenty, where cattle, goats, and fowls thrived and where the RAC usually had a factory at Banyan Point for buying rice and millet.[63]

A general description of Fulbe herders and their settlements, written in 1730 by an RAC employee at James Island, gives some idea of the services that Mamadu provided to the company. Cattle were allowed to pasture during the day in the open savanna and also in the rice grounds after harvesting. They were kept under close watch, mainly to prevent them from damaging fields still under cultivation or from wandering off into the woods. At night, herders would pen the cattle in their settlements for protection. Fulbe settlements were large and spacious enclosures, encircled by a thick hedgerow that protected their homes, their fields of cotton, and a clearing large enough to hold all of their cattle. A guard tower stood at the center of the pen, with a ladder leading up to a sheltered platform. Planted into the ground around the tower were wooden stakes, to which the cattle were tied by ropes. At nightfall, after milking time, several armed men climbed the tower to stand watch, ready to ward off attacks by thieves or wild carnivores.[64]

Records of the provisions store at James Island for the 1680s show how infrequently they were receiving shipments of English salted beef and how steadily they made purchases of local cattle instead. Mamadu therefore must have played a major role in helping maintain the RAC staff at the fort and their visitors. The number of cattle purchases in the 1680s is comparable to figures reported in 1730, which estimated an average intake of two hundred head of cattle per year. That report also remarked on the ample quantity and quality of their fresh provisions, noting that a beast was slaughtered every other day for meat and that fowls were purchased daily for those who preferred an alternative source of flesh. Greens and a variety of fruits came from the company garden at Juffure, and there were oysters to harvest on the northwest shore of the island when the tide was low. There was no mention of salted beef or biscuits being on the menu for meals served inside the fort, although dried provisions may have been the fare of soldiers and other lower-level employees.[65]

Mamadu's salary in 1681 was 6B per year and had risen to 10B per year by the time of his final withdrawal of goods in March 1688. He visited the fort only once or twice a year but probably made more frequent deliveries of cattle to the company post at Juffure, where grometos held them for transport on company vessels to James Island. He was particularly fastidious about keeping his account balanced or with some of his salary still owing—there is no evidence of him running even a small debt with the company. The goods he selected as salary payments were varied and well chosen. He invested in a musket in February 1684, presumably for himself or an assistant to guard the cattle at night. He selected bars of iron on three occasions: six bars at the end of April 1685; five bars at the end of March 1686; and for drawing out his last salary of 20B for two years, he took out ten bars of iron and a shotgun.[66] The regular withdrawals of iron bars raise the question of how he might have used the bars—whether he paid iron out to men for performing labor, or whether he took it to a smithy to be worked into tools for clearing land, tending crops, or building projects. Mamadu's March 1686 selection also included beads and copper rods, which could have been intended for making purchases upriver or as part of a bridewealth payment on behalf of a brother, son, or nephew. Mamadu did not select any European-style clothing, undoubtedly because he and his associates preferred the ample white cotton shirts and trousers made by Fulbe spinners, weavers, and tailors. And keeping strictly to his Muslim faith, he did not take out any brandy or spirits. His departure, just a year before England and her allies went to war with France, was well timed. If he had stayed on, being allied with the RAC and living in the vicinity of heavily armed French men-of-war might have exposed him to seizure and perhaps to captivity and enslavement.[67]

RAC agents at Bence Island and York Island also had to provision their forts, vessels, and outstations. Located far to the south of the James Island fort, four hundred miles and five hundred miles, respectively, they usually received the "leftovers" of overseas goods, shipping and trading equipment, as well as provisions and other supplies from London. They also had to contend with environmental conditions entirely different from the open savanna around the Gambia River. Dense rainforests covered the coastal hinterlands from Cacheu to Cape Palmas, making large-scale cattle herding impossible. They had the advantage of a longer growing season, which lasted from about mid-April to mid-November, and years of Atlantic trade had expanded their tropical Afro-Asian foodways to include American crops such as maize, pineapple, pumpkin, and sweet potato. The Sierra Leone estuary, especially, had long been a favored provisioning stop for Portuguese vessels returning home from voyages to the Indian Ocean or the Lower Guinea Coast and Angola. Sixteenth- and seventeenth-century observers noted the ready availability of fresh spring water easily accessed on the shore and the wide variety of fresh provisions that could be purchased, such as oranges, limes, and lemons, known to guard against scurvy, and other produce such as bananas, plantains, pineapples, pumpkins, malagueta pepper, beans, sweet potatoes, rice, and millet (figure 5.1). Sources of protein were richly varied as well, with goats and fowls, the main domesticated animals, often being supplemented by wild game—bush cow, several species of antelope, and wild boar. From the sea and the many rivers and streams came a rich bounty of fish and shellfish.[68]

It is therefore not surprising that agents at Bence Island and York Island hired local men as hunters and fishermen to provide themselves and their employees with supplies of fresh meats and seafood. The York Island accounts hold records of almost a dozen such suppliers, two of whom worked for the RAC for over ten years. These two men probably came from communities of Temne and Bullom speakers in the vicinity of the forts, even though they were regularly included in the company's lists of "mulatto" employees.[69] Since European surnames were common among the "mulattos," the single names by which they were known—Bonna and Simon—suggest they were not of Euro-African ancestry.

Surviving records of Bonna's career with the company start in early 1685, when he was listed among the employees of the RAC fort at York Island. From that time until May 1693, he held the position of hunter, alongside "mulattos" such as James Darby and John Billings. His salary rate was not

FIGURE 5.1 Schematic drawing of plants and trees, Guinea Coast, seventeenth c. *Left to right:* millet, pineapple (foreground), banana tree, maize, palm wine tree, fig tree, rice. The National Archives of the UK, Jean Barbot, Part II (1682), ADM 7/830B.

specified, but his yearly withdrawals of goods—six occasions in 1687 and five occasions in 1688—came to totals of just over 9B in value. Unfortunately, it is not possible to assess when and what kinds of game he supplied to the company or what his movements may have been, but it appears that he never delivered any tusks of ivory to the company, which suggests he was not a hunter of elephant. His selections of overseas goods ranged across the spectrum of company inventories, including currencies such as cowries, beads, and bar iron, which he might have used as payments for hunting equipment—the nets and traps for small game hunting or arrows and spear blades for taking down antelope. He regularly chose metalwares, which were useful in salt production, and textiles that could serve as currency or be turned into finished items of dress. On at least two occasions he took out ready-made European-style clothing in the form of tailored men's shirts and trousers. And at least once he selected castile soap, an olive-oil based product of Spain, perhaps intended as a special exotic gift.[70]

Bonna changed careers sometime after 1690, for by May 1693 he was being listed in company records as a fisherman. He appeared in that capacity throughout the various accounts of him, which end in November 1698. There are only two entries showing him making salary withdrawals during this period, and they were greater in value than his earlier ones. He selected coral and red woolen cloth—major prestige items—in August 1694, and in June 1695 he withdrew six dozen knives, 6 cwt. of cowries, and a thousand crystal beads, all to a total of 18B. Records of his account end three years later in 1697, listing a debt to the company of 98B.[71] Overall, his account shows quite clearly that while working for the RAC as a hunter and then as a fisherman, Bonna also became accustomed to participating in the Guinea trade.

Simon, another longtime local employee hired at York Island, started out as a fisherman from at least 1684 and remained in that position until he closed his account in December 1698. As was the case with hunters, fishermen occupied respected places in their societies because of their expertise. The seafood they provided was crucially important in African communities, especially when there was a season of severe hunger when food stores ran out in the weeks before the harvesting of new crops. Traveling by canoe, setting their nets and traps in narrow creeks, on reefs along the seashore, and in small bays and inlets, and then paddling their rounds again to collect their harvests, men like Simon made many varieties of fish available on a regular basis.[72] In addition, and even more so than for hunters, fishermen could also parlay their geographical mobility into valuable social capital and commercial success. Traversing the seascape and waterways in their small craft gave them familiarity with widely scattered towns and villages and put them in a good position to provide valuable messenger services and to be purveyors of news and gossip. At the same time, they could also engage in trade.

Simon was more active than Bonna in drawing out payments on his salary. He was referred to as "Simon Fisherman" in the account books and listed with the "mulattos" in the company's nominal rolls as "Simon, a black fisherman" (see transcription 5.4). During his first several years of employment with the company, he made withdrawals of goods that ranged widely in value, totaling 9B in 1684, 34B in 1685, and then just 3B in 1686. In the 1690s, when there are records of his salary rates, the values of his withdrawals of goods never reached the full amount due. But this apparent restraint does not mean that Simon was unconcerned with profiting from his position. His selections of goods show consistent choices of cotton textiles, both locally made and imports from India, during the 1680s, and items of European-style menswear, mainly shirts but also trousers and shoes. It is possible that some of these textiles were for himself and his family, for bridewealth payments on behalf of a brother, son, or nephew, for example, or for the initiation of a sister, daughter, or niece into the Sande society, an important educational and judicial society of and for women in the region. It is equally possible that he exchanged local cotton cloths for fishing nets or other equipment or perhaps for labor in setting stakes for his traps. A very large withdrawal in December 1685, valued at over 26B, was unusual in its large size and in its composition, mostly metalwares of various kinds— brass and pewter basins, kettles, and pewter pots. If salt makers needed more kettles and brass basins for boiling saltwater down in their workshops and had surplus salt to offer in exchange, some of these items could offer Simon entry into the lucrative kola markets. Pewter vessels and containers were suitable for use in serving, sharing, or offering food or drink, especially on public or ceremonial occasions.[73]

Some of the impacts of the onset of war with France in 1689 can be discerned in the account of "Simon Fisherman." War prompted the RAC to reorganize their forts, and the new system lasted through the 1690s. Considering Bence Island to be indefensible, they ordered their agents to suspend operations there and leave only a skeletal staff of armed soldiers to guard it. A contingent of company employees sailed up north to help defend James Island on the Gambia, while the rest went down to York Island and vicinity, which brought York Island more directly into the circuits of Atlantic trade. Simon responded, adding cowries to his selections of beads, which allowed him more flexibility in making small change payments for labor and services, and he took out longer lengths of red woolen yardage so that he presumably could deal more widely and effectively in the prestige markets where they were so much in demand. Supplies of gunpowder, tobacco, and English brandy, and an elegant striped suit that alone cost him more than two months' salary, together signal that Simon had established a recognizably important position for himself in the Guinea trade. In December 1698, as the war ended, he closed his account with the RAC, taking out the full 145B balance due on his salary. His final assortment was made up of items that were certain to strengthen his position with a wide range of possible trading partners: over twenty dozen knives, 50 cwt. brass basins, and ten shotguns.[74] His timing was prescient. With the news about the company's defeat in Parliament five months earlier and the opening up of England's African trade to private merchants, he must have realized that the RAC monopoly was on the wane. Simon was preparing himself for a new stage in his career.

The unusually long period of apprenticeship with the RAC of a man called Black Harry provides yet another perspective on the company's varied local hires and the kinds of work that they did.[75] It is not clear how old he was or what position he held in September 1683, the first direct mention of him in the surviving company records. At that time, he could have been around twelve or thirteen if he had been the "black boy" apprentice carpenter of Edmund Pierce, the recently deceased factor at Bence Island. When he began to be listed in the company's nominal rolls a year later, he was mate to Glanvill Lamboy, a ship-carpenter at York Island. It is unlikely that he was on salary, but he did take out goods in small amounts in the mid-1680s, usually textiles or brass basins. He was listed as "mate" until July 1690, when Lamboy joined the group of RAC men who were dispatched north to Gambia to defend the fort on James Island. Harry chose to stay behind and continued to work for the RAC until December 1706, a total of anywhere between twenty-three and twenty-eight years.[76]

Despite the patchy records for him, Harry serves as a useful example for taking up the company's dependence on shipbuilding and repair work on the Upper Guinea Coast. Repairing wooden vessels in warm tropical waters was continually necessary, and the RAC tried to keep their forts stocked with equipment and supplies for doing so. However, the related question of naval construction was mentioned only very rarely in the company records, mostly in correspondence to London from York Island in Sherbro. In March 1686, agent Platt wrote that a man named William Coan, apparently neither an RAC employee nor a separate trader, was preparing to build his own vessel. Another brief reference to what must have been ongoing activity by independent builders came in January 1692, when agent Gibson wrote to London complaining that he had been expecting them to send a carpenter (having lost the services of Lamboy) and that as a result he was unable to finish the vessels he had under construction.[77] There was probably much more of this activity going on in northern Guinea, but it is understandable that references to shipbuilding, presumably in cooperation with private traders, would have been left out of the records. The Sierra Leone estuary, where there were innumerable sheltered bays and inlets for establishing makeshift shipyards, had long been a choice site for hauling company vessels ashore for repairs. Forests along the shores of Port Loko Creek and the Rokelle River offered shipwrights a wealth of raw materials for building, fitting, and repairing coasting and perhaps even maritime vessels. Builders there found trees known to provide suitable timber for making masts and planking boards as well as special vines whose fibers produced high-quality ropes for rigging. Oakum, used for caulking seams of boat hulls, was made locally by processing the bark of another species of tree.[78] These valuable resources were surely among the reasons why this part of the Guinea Coast was attractive to so many "interlopers" and other private traders whose movements went largely unrecorded.

After the departure of Lamboy, Black Harry appeared as a ship carpenter based at Sherbro. There are no records of him taking out goods from the RAC stores during this period. He joined the crew of the ship *Experiment,* captained by Robert Chilper, for an Atlantic crossing that delivered eighty-six captives to Antigua in August 1693. The ship then spent some time in Barbados, where Chilper reportedly cheated the company by selling a number of captives he had kept on board for himself. The *Experiment* then set out on its return voyage to Sherbro in October. Harry remained as a crew member on board the *Experiment* into 1694 and was listed as a carpenter up until May 1696. His whereabouts from 1697 onward are unknown because of major gaps in the records. What records there are do not mention him, though he could have been still at sea crewing, either on coasting or transatlantic voyages. The final mention of him comes at the end of January 1707. Captain Thomas Ashby, writing to the RAC from Lisbon, provided an account of the deaths of eight of his crewmen on the *Dorothy* and closed it with a terse addendum: "Black Harry ran away at Cacheu."[79] Harry had indeed been working at sea, at least on this particular voyage, and apparently had seen and done enough with the company. Having witnessed firsthand the transport and sale of captives across the Atlantic, and having spent perhaps as many as twenty-seven years working for the RAC, Black Harry appears to have come to a decision to jump ship while the *Dorothy* lay anchored at Cacheu. Perhaps the outbreak of another European war in the north Atlantic forced him to question more seriously the prospects of life onboard ship. What can be said for certain is that his skills and long experience in ship carpentry were sure to have found a ready market in Cacheu's busy and well-defended harbor.[80]

Conclusion: A Creole Workforce

The RAC employed a varied mix of people on the Upper Guinea Coast, men of European, Euro-African, and African ancestries. London officials were not able to control this faraway workforce or even to know exactly who all of them were. High mortality rates of Europeans in the tropics—along with the company's inability to satisfy the staffing, equipping, and provisioning needs of their forts—meant that agents on the spot had no option but to make up for their deficits as best they could. A major irony of these RAC operations in northern Guinea during this time was that their own inadequacies led them to treat as embezzlement and fraud their employees' successes in trying to meet company expectations. Cleeve, Booker, Quinn, and Corker were skilled and effective traders, not only for themselves but also for the company.

Their personal lives were no less diverse. Company men from England who survived and lived out their lives on the Guinea Coast sometimes married, had families, and created new Anglo-African ancestral lines surviving to the present. Less well known than the marriages of Portuguese and Luso-African men to local women, these English men married in spite of RAC prohibitions and thus usually kept these relationships secret. Company men on the spot, however, not only tolerated such relationships but in some cases actively encouraged them. Thus we see these Anglo-African marriages in the RAC records only as African or Euro-African wives adopting their husbands' surnames, as did the senhoras Betty Bull and Betty Blow. We also see some of their descendants, as male children appear as traders or employees with their fathers' English surnames, such as Thomas Corker Jr., or the Rogers brothers—Zachary Jr., Simon, and Samuel—or Zachary Cumberbatch. Perhaps pointedly distinguished as "mulattos," these Anglo-African descendants of RAC employees were viewed by company officials in London with deep suspicion—precisely because of their cultural ambiguity, uncertain loyalties, and commercial expertise and success, and above all because of their shrewd efforts to remain independent.

Seemingly invisible to RAC officers in London were their employees engaged on the spot as steady provisioners for the forts. It is evident that a variety of local people were providers of foodstuffs to the forts and outstations, even though records of them are sporadic and incomplete. Provisioners who were on salary, and thus entered regularly into the account books, were men with the specialized skills of cattle herding, such as Mamadu, who worked for the James Island fort, or with the skills of hunting wild game or fishing, such as Bonna and Simon, who worked at York Island. The fresh protein they provided must have done much to restore the health and bolster the morale of their fellow RAC employees. And these salaried provisioners, in choosing to work for the company, could use their positions to gain access to overseas goods, which they then circulated in a variety of ways by making social investments, hiring laborers, or even entering into the import-export business to make money as traders.

CONCLUSION
_____

Anglo-African Relations

EARLY MODERN trade on the Guinea Coast joined Afro-Eurasia and the Americas together into a truly global network. Africa's roles in this trade varied from supplying intermediate goods to Europe to providing markets for European exports and reexports to selling captive people and their labor to American planters running businesses in commercial agriculture. This book has examined one important sector of this global network, the Anglo-African trade of the Royal African Company in the late seventeenth century. More precisely, it focuses on the Upper Guinea Coast, a vast zone of Euro-African trade and intercommunication that had been created in the fifteenth century, long before the arrival of the RAC. This particular segment of the Guinea Coast stretched southward from Portudale on the Petite Côte all the way to Cape Mount, a distance of over seven hundred miles. To place its scale in perspective, a comparable stretch of coastline in the United States would be the Atlantic seaboard between New York City and Savanna, Georgia. Upper Guinea was also home to richly diverse populations marked by centuries of economic, social, and cultural interaction.

A goal of this book has been to portray the human dimensions of the Guinea trade, especially how people organized and carried out the African side of it at this particular place and time. The coastal zone of Upper Guinea is historically significant for its being situated at the frontier of the western Sudan region of West Africa.[1] Trading and currencies traversed this frontier in both directions. Trade was not confined to the company's forts, and the forts themselves were not self-enclosed enclaves of Europeans. Europeans, Euro-Africans, and Africans visited, lived, and worked at the forts and at the company's many outposts on an ongoing basis, their numbers fluctuating and changing in composition over time. People came and went by sea, sailing on maritime merchant ships to and from far-off ports in Europe, the Americas, or the Caribbean or Atlantic isles, or on coasting vessels and small craft to and from towns and islands along the Guinea Coast. Others came from the western Sudan and from far-off places in interior regions of West Africa, traveling overland to arrive at entrepôts on the waterways that carried people down to the coast. Those travelers who were free could make the return journey. In other words, the RAC forts and depots and their surroundings were sites of intense social and cultural mixing and exchange, generating at the same time a vibrant creole culture in this newly created Atlantic Africa.

The unusually rich details inscribed in the RAC records during their monopoly period made it possible to write a social history of Anglo-African trading activity. Central to the book was my discovery of and deep interest in the experiences of a wide variety of individual people residing in West Africa who, either by choice or by force, participated in this trade. It was indeed a horrific trade in captives, but it was also a trade in much else. Tracing the lives of named individual free people exposes more sharply and more fully the remarkable social world of the Guinea trade, some of its economic significance and repercussions, and especially its cross-cultural dynamics. Africans and Euro-Africans who chose to participate in coastal commerce did so for all sorts of reasons. It offered them undeniable economic opportunities for earning incomes and amassing personal and family wealth, even though at certain times it posed serious risks and even great dangers. Competition in the import-export sector was especially fierce, sometimes involving the seizing of vessels, cargoes, and people, which might then set off costly or deadly reprisals. Some people managed to generate and sustain careers that lasted over decades, whereas others appear to have been more cautious, setting limits to the degree of their involvement, or were simply less successful. What comes across most surprisingly from the RAC records is the variety of individuals across the social spectrum who took part in the African side of the Guinea trade and the diverse fortunes that they made or lost.

This book deepens and sharpens our historical view of women in early modern Atlantic Africa and the ways they participated in the Guinea trade. It is well known that among the eighteenth- and nineteenth-century merchants in Euro-African communities, there were many prominent women whose success and wealth was publicly recognized by the title senhora or signare. Examples presented here provide invaluable new information about earlier female merchants in the seventeenth century, sometimes with special details about their careers and how long they lasted. They also suggest that Anglo-African marriages may have been more common than previously thought. Less well known but perhaps as numerous were the successful female merchants farther down the coast, especially in and around the Sierra Leone estuary. One important example from the RAC records is Senhora Isabella Gunn, a woman whose trading career lasted for at least seventeen years. And she was not an isolated case. There were other prosperous women traders in the vicinity of Sierra Leone during the late seventeenth century, many of them rice dealers, who owned their own shipping vessels and skillfully managed them and their crews as they made deliveries of provisions in the import-export sector.

Equally important is the widely ranging evidence about slavery, which brings into focus many rare and rich details about individual slaves and the trade in captives. RAC forts on the Upper Guinea Coast in the late seventeenth century witnessed the intersection of a seemingly paternalistic and kin-based (though no less brutal) slave system with a newly forming Atlantic system based on commercial plantations worked by slave gangs. Captives who were recorded most carefully and relatively consistently in the company records are those who were intended to be shipped across the Atlantic and sold as slaves. At the same time, however, their conditions and status could vary. Even so-called sale slaves might be singled out, reclassified in the account books, and treated very differently as grometos or "company slaves." Other captives who were personal household slaves of high-level RAC employees were deliberately kept out of the company accounts. Sometimes called by new names and treated more like servants, they might, on occasion, be given their freedom, though release was strictly at the discretion of their master.

Even so, as studies in comparative slavery have shown, such variability and fluidity in captive/slave conditions did not result in significant structural differences within the institution of slavery itself. Any of these captives or grometos or personal household slaves could have been sold at any time. And unrecorded for the most part was the inherent violence of captivity. Threats of punishment in retaliation for some real or imagined infraction hovered over captives, grometos, and even favored personal slaves, who were forced to witness beatings or executions meted out on one or more of their numbers as an example. Captives' deaths were sometimes recorded but only rarely were the supposed or actual causes. Nevertheless, the records there are of instances of deaths, thefts, runaways, and insurrections provide rare though incomplete glimpses of the lives and acts of people as they refused to accept unfree status. These stories of the enslaved individuals in the anonymous millions of the captives forced onto ships destined for the Americas and slavery are an especially important and poignant contribution this book makes to African, Atlantic, and world history.

An unexpected finding was detailed evidence of how varied and complicated the individual careers of RAC traders from England were. Those who managed to survive their first year on the Upper Guinea Coast and then chose to remain for four or five years or more adapted to local society and creole cultural practices in many different ways. They conducted their work and daily lives in Crioulo, Portuguese, and English while keeping the company records strictly in English. Encouraged by the company's contradictory policies, many of them engaged in trading on their own accounts, and some amassed sizeable personal estates. It was not uncommon for RAC men to live out the rest of their lives on the Guinea Coast, and some of them married local women and founded Anglo-African families, choices that sometimes put them at odds with company officials in London. Others caused ongoing consternation in London by trading independently, dealing with the company and other private traders at will. Desertions from the RAC only added to the numbers of "interlopers" on the Upper Guinea Coast.

Acting on their own, agents at the RAC forts took the initiative of hiring local people on salary, a practice that turned the company workforce itself into a much more complex and multicultural social milieu. Evidence of the diverse individual backgrounds of these local hires and what their jobs were was another unexpected finding that came out of my searches in the RAC archive. Of primary importance were the men skilled in herding, fishing, or hunting who supplied fresh protein to the forts and outposts—beef cattle in the case of James Island and fish and wild game in the case of Bence Island. Their regular deliveries made them available to perform other tasks for the company as needed and also to pass on valuable local news and information. In short, RAC agents found that they could rely on these local people for essential support much more than they could on the promises of their distant supervisors in London.

Viewing movements of people and goods, we see how human fates and fortunes in the Guinea trade varied widely. Profits came to people who never set foot on the Guinea Coast. Death came prematurely to captives forced to the coast from their homes in faraway communities and also to men newly arriving from Europe. People who lived longer lives were able to build families and successful careers or master new skills and knowledge in homes, fields, and workshops on the mainland or by working on waterways or at sea. European wars in the north Atlantic sparked waves of violence that could reach as far as the Upper Guinea Coast. Times of relative peace presented opportunities for feasting and celebration.

All through this book are vivid examples of how English men acted and behaved in this tropical social world inhabited by people of color. Terms such as "negro," "blacks," "whites," and "mulatto" were used, but they did not yet carry the fixed and ideologically charged classifications of "race" that later came to denote intrinsic superiority and inferiority.[2] Many people in this place and time exercised remarkable social and cultural fluidity, their movings and mixings thus creating one of the world's many distinctive creole cultures. They seem for the most part unencumbered by prejudice or chauvinistic presumptions. To provide a contrast, some indication of later changes in the social and political climate of the Upper Guinea Coast can be discerned in a description written by a British naval officer in 1848. Having declared her slave trade illegal forty years earlier, Britain now had Royal Navy ships engaged in an anti-slavery blockade off Sierra Leone and was beginning to envision an informal empire in West Africa. A map accompanying the officer's account displays an oddly worded notation about an area adjacent to Sherbro Island that, it reads, "belongs to a number of independent kings, the Caulkers, Clevelands and others named after English factors who formerly worked there."[3] "Named after" is a curiously awkward formulation. Why would they be "named after" English factors? And who did this "naming"? The author of this comment was either unable or unwilling to imagine or to state outright that these powerful Caulkers, Clevelands, and other prominent families of the coast were, in fact, the descendants of English men of the RAC. Over a century and a half earlier, such men as Thomas Corker Sr. and Jr., founders of the Caulkers, had worked, lived, and married in the Upper Guinea Coast. They founded the Anglo-African families brought out of the recesses of company files in London and onto the pages of this book.

Suggested Further Readings, by Chapter and Topic

Introduction: Atlantic Lives

Atlantic History—For a very useful general overview of Britain's early colonial history from a Euro-American perspective (bringing together Britain, British mainland America, and the British Caribbean), see David Armitage and Michael Braddock, eds., *The British Atlantic World, 1500–1800* (Palgrave Macmillan, 2nd ed., 2009). And for a clearly written and generously illustrated introduction to Atlantic world history, one that includes and integrates the four continents of Europe, Africa, North America, and South America, see Douglas Edgerton, Alison Games, Jane Landers, Kris Lane and Donald Wright, *The Atlantic World* (Harlan Davidson, 2007).

Industrial Revolution—An important starting point in trying to understand this topic is to acknowledge it as far too complex to be describable or comprehensible. It was a momentous set of events and processes in world history that first took place in Britain, roughly between 1760 and 1830, and eventually resulting in Europe, or "the West," being divided from "the rest" by sustained and accelerating economic growth. For an important and influential collection of writings by scholars of economic history in the 1980s, see Joel Mokyr, ed., *The Economics of the Industrial Revolution* (Rowman and Allanheld, 1985). And for an overview of the many debates and controversies it sparked, see Joel Mokyr, ed., *The British Industrial Revolution: An Economic Perspective* (Westview Press, 1999). A major work that examines the effects of industrialization on European consumption is Jan de Vries, *The Industrious Revolution: Consumer Behavior and the Household Economy, 1650 to the Present* (Cambridge University Press, 2008). Another major work, one that seeks to challenge the commonly held view that industrialization was necessarily a particularly "European" or "Western" phenomenon, is Kenneth Pomeranz, *The Great Divergence: Europe, China, and the Making of the Modern World Economy* (Princeton University Press, 2000).

And written in a similar vein and in very accessible prose is Prasannan Parthasarathi's *Why Europe Grew Rich and Asia Did Not: Global Economic Divergence, 1600–1850* (Cambridge University Press, 2011).

Pseudoscientific Ideologies of Race—See suggested reading under Conclusion.

Chapter 1: Buyers and Sellers in Cross-Cultural Trade

Islam in African History—For a general introductory overview, see Nehemia Levtzion, "Islam in Africa to 1800: Merchants, Chiefs, and Saints," in John Esposito, ed., *The Oxford History of Islam* (Oxford University Press, 1999). Ralph Austen's *Trans-Saharan Africa in World History* (Oxford University Press, 2010) provides readers with an appreciation of the importance of travel and trade across the Sahara Desert and its role in African history over centuries. An especially reader-friendly introduction to and survey of Islam in Africa, one that provides vividly rendered case studies of its local and regional histories, is David Robinson's *Muslim Societies in African History* (Cambridge University Press, 2004).

Cotton Currencies in African History—The precolonial history of West Africa's manufacturing sector, especially the production of cotton and cotton currencies since at least the tenth century CE, remains understudied and therefore underappreciated. An early breakthrough overview was Marion Johnson's "Cloth as Money: The Cloth Strip Currencies of Africa" in *Textile History* 11 (1980): 193–202. For my recent study of cotton textiles being both imported and exported in West Africa during the Guinea trade, see "'Guinea Cloth': Production and Consumption of Cotton Textiles in West Africa before and during the Atlantic Slave Trade," in Giorgio Riello and Prasannan Parthasarathi, eds., *The Spinning World: A Global History of Cotton Textiles, 1200–1850* (Oxford University Press, 2009). And for cotton cloth and currencies produced on the Upper Guinea Coast, showing their lower prices relative to overseas imports, see my article "The Importance of Mande Textiles in the African Side of the Atlantic Trade, ca. 1680–1710," in *Mande Studies* 11 (2009, publ. 2011): 1–21. My book *Cloth in West African History* (AltaMira Press, 2006) surveys the importance of textile manufacture in West Africa from the ninth century CE onward.

Chapter 2: "Artificers" and Merchants

Mixed Euro-African or "Creole" Culture—"Creole" culture here is not to be confused with the linguistic meanings of "creole" and how creole languages are created out of pidgins. The literature on the extremely complex history of creole culture in northern Guinea is extensive, and I list here only some of the most important milestones in the English language. Peter Mark's book *"Portuguese" Style and Luso-African Identity: Precolonial Senegambia, Sixteenth-Nineteenth Centuries* (Indiana University Press, 2002) is a masterwork of archival retrieval and meticulous analysis of Euro-African "mixing" in terms of ethnicity (identity) and cultural practices (architecture and manners), copiously illustrated with photographs, maps, drawings, and paintings. George Brooks took up the theme of Eurafricans as a distinct and important social group in his impressive synthesis *Eurafricans in Western Africa: Commerce, Social Status, Gender, and Religious Observance from the Sixteenth to the Eighteenth Century* (Ohio University Press, 2003). And for a recent carefully focused study of the early formative period of Luso-African creole culture in the north Atlantic, see Toby Green, *The Rise of the Trans-Atlantic Slave Trade in Western Africa, 1300–1589* (Cambridge University Press, 2012). Essential reading on this topic from an American perspective is Ira Berlin's "From Creole to African: Atlantic Creoles and the Origins of African-American Society in Mainland North America," *The William and Mary Quarterly* 3rd ser., 53, no. 2 (April 1996): 251–88.

"Landlord" and "Stranger" Relations—This topic is an especially significant one for understanding how African peoples allowed foreigners, including Europeans, into their societies, as well as how they managed and regulated them. An early study by anthropologist Vernon Dorjahn and historian Christopher Fyfe describes it as a relationship between a landlord and his tenant, visiting traveler, or foreign resident: "Landlord and Stranger: Change in Tenancy Relations in Sierra Leone," *Journal of African History* 3 (1962): 391 97. Bruce Mouser's "Landlords-Strangers: A Process of Accommodation and Assimilation," *International Journal of African Historical Studies* 8 (1975): 425–40, focuses on the Pongo and Nunez Rivers north of Sierra Leone and argues that the purpose of the relationship was not so much to control foreigners but to accommodate and assimilate them into the landlord's society in stages over time. George Brooks considers what he calls landlord-stranger reciprocities as an important social practice shared across western Africa and uses it as a central theme in his *Landlords and Strangers: Ecology, Society, and Trade in Western Africa, 1000–1630* (Westview Press, 1993). David Robinson shows specific examples of these kinds of relations, calling them "paths of accommodation," in his study of confrontations and negotiations between Muslim leaders and

French colonizers: *Paths of Accommodation: Muslim Societies and French Colonial Authorities in Senegal and Mauretania, 1880–1920* (Ohio University Press, 2000).

England's Black History—Online on The National Archives (UK) website is a very good general introduction, *Black Presence: Asian and Black History in Britain, 1500–1850*, www.nationalarchives.gov.uk/pathways/blackhistory /index.htm. For a landmark early historical study, see James Walvin, *Black and White: The Negro and English Society, 1555–1945* (Penguin Press, 1973). Another early work, Folarin Shyllon's *Black People in Britain 1555–1833* (Oxford University Press, 1977), includes useful references to ads for runaways and opens up questions and issues having to do with the unclear legal status of "slaves" in England. A more recent book by Imtiaz Habib, *Black Lives in the English Archives, 1500–1677* (Ashgate, 2008), is important especially for the author's painstaking retrieval of archival records from this early period. Kathleen Chater's *Untold Histories: Black People in England and Wales during the Period of the British Slave Trade, c. 1660–1807* (Manchester University Press, 2009) is a remarkable achievement, drawn from her database of over forty-five hundred archival references to black people for this time period. She does a masterful job of grappling with the problems and ambiguities of what their unfree or semifree status might have been as servants or apprentices rather than as legally defined slaves.

Chapter 3: West Africans Profiting in Atlantic Trade

African Contributions to American Cultures—A groundbreaking and essential study (though still underappreciated) is the book by Lorenzo Dow Turner, *Africanisms in the Gullah Dialect,* especially the most recent edition (University of South Carolina Press, 2002). His pioneering work in the 1930s with speakers of Gullah Creole yielded a treasure trove of identifiable influences from many African languages. For an overview of debates about the degree to which African slaves could or did influence American culture, see my chapter "The Conundrum of Culture in Atlantic History" in José Curto and Renée Soulodre-La France, eds., *Africa and the Americas: Interconnections during the Slave Trade* (Africa World Press, 2005): 259–78. The volume edited by Toyin Falola and Matt Childs, *The Yoruba Diaspora in the Atlantic World* (Indiana University Press, 2004), is highly recommended reading on this important topic.

Senhoras / Women Traders—A very good starting place for this topic is the volume edited by Claire Robertson and Martin Klein, *Women and*

Slavery in Africa (University of Wisconsin Press, 1983), especially the chapters by MacCormack, Brooks, and Mouser, which provide examples of prominent women traders of the eighteenth and nineteenth centuries. See also the overview by George Brooks, "The Signares of Saint Louis and Gorée: Women Entrepreneurs in Eighteenth-Century Senegal," in Nancy Hafkin and Edna Bay, eds., *Women in Africa: Studies in Social and Economic Change* (Stanford University Press, 1976). In George Brooks's *Eurafricans in Western Africa,* chapter 5, he makes special reference to five senhoras of the seventeenth century: the well-known Senhora Bibiana Vaz of Cacheu, La Belinguère, and three other senhoras who lived and worked in Senegambia during the second half of the seventeenth century. For an excellent new study focusing on signares in St. Louis, Senegal, from the late eighteenth to early twentieth centuries, see Hilary Jones, *The Métis of Senegal: Urban Life and Politics in French West Africa* (Indiana University Press, 2013).

Muslim Clerics in West African History—For a general English-language introduction to the early history of Islam in West Africa and the role of itinerant Muslim clerics, see Nehemia Levtzion and Randall Pouwels, eds., *The History of Islam in Africa* (Ohio University Press, 2000), chapters 3 and 6. For a major study of clerics in Africa's western Sahel and their relations with French colonials during the early decades of colonial rule, see David Robinson, *Paths of Accommodation.* And for an introduction to Amadu Bamba Mbacke, a prominent Muslim cleric who became a major historical figure and founder of a Sufi brotherhood in colonial Senegal, see Cheikh Anta Babou, *Fighting the Greater Jihad: Amadu Bamba and the Founding of the Muridiyya of Senegal, 1853–1913* (Ohio University Press, 2007).

Rice Production on the Upper Guinea Coast—For the best introduction to the history of rice production in this region, see Judith A. Carney, *Black Rice: The African Origins of Rice Cultivation in the Americas* (Harvard University Press, 2001). Another important study, one that analyzes rice production within the historical context of the Atlantic trade in slaves, is Walter Hawthorne's *Planting Rice and Harvesting Slaves: Transformations along the Guinea-Bissau Coast, 1400–1900* (Heinemann Press, 2003). And for an exhaustively researched, clearly written, and compelling study using evidence from historical linguistics, see Edda L. Fields-Black, *Deep Roots: Rice Farmers in West Africa and the African Diaspora* (Indiana University Press, 2008).

Chapter 4: Company Property

The Atlantic Slave Trade—This topic has generated an enormous literature, especially since the publication of Philip Curtin's *The Atlantic Slave Trade: A Census* (University of Wisconsin Press, 1969). I highlight here four major studies by historians of Africa, each book distinctly different from the others in approach and framework, in order to convey the variety, value, and importance of Africanist perspectives on the Atlantic slave trade. Robert Harms's *The Diligent: A Voyage through the Worlds of the Slave Trade* (Basic Books, 2002) takes readers through the voyage of one ship in the early 1730s, from its investors to the fitting and loading of the ship, and from its travels and stops along the Guinea coast to its Atlantic crossing with human cargo to Martinique and return to Brittany. Joseph Miller's monumental *Way of Death: Merchant Capitalism and the Angolan Slave Trade 1730–1830* (University of Wisconsin Press, 1988) succeeds eloquently in the seemingly impossible task of analyzing and portraying the social and economic workings and effects of Atlantic trade and Portuguese colonization in the crucially important Lusophone sector that connected Angola and Brazil. John Thornton's *Africa and Africans in the Making of the Atlantic World, 1400–1800* (Cambridge University Press, 2nd ed., 1998) has been an invaluable gift to historians of the Americas whose special training made it difficult for them to connect African and American history. And Paul Lovejoy's *Transformations in Slavery: A History of Slavery in Africa* (Cambridge University Press, 3rd ed., 2012) presents readers with a history of slavery in Africa, an introduction to comparative slavery, and an invaluable study of the effects of the Atlantic slave trade on Africa.

Demography and Gender—An important and exceedingly readable book that is both a history of the effects of slavery on men and women in Africa and an introduction to demography and demographic analysis is Patrick Manning's *Slavery and African Life: Occidental, Oriental, and African Slave Trades* (Cambridge University Press, 1990). And for a tour de force in cross-cultural analysis of gender and demography in world history, see Amartya Sen, "More than 100 Million Women Are Missing," *New York Review of Books*, December 6, 1990, 61–66.

Oral Traditions in African History—The essential introduction to oral traditions, what they are and are not, and how with critical analysis and understanding they can be valuable sources for historians, is Jan Vansina's *Oral Tradition as History* (University of Wisconsin Press, 1985). Readers will find a rich selection of historians' case studies from across Africa in Joseph Miller, ed., *The African Past Speaks: Essays on Oral Tradition and History* (Archon Press, 1980). And for discussion and interpretation of major regional genres of African oral traditions, see Stephen Belcher, *Epic Traditions of Africa* (Indiana University Press, 1999).

Chapter 5: Free Agents and Local Hires

Senhoras/Women Traders—See the suggested readings under chapter 3.

Mixed Euro-African or "Creole" Culture—See the suggested readings under chapter 2.

Conclusion: Anglo-African Relations

Pseudoscientific Ideologies of Race—For a useful analysis of the historical development of fixed categorizations about Africans as part of the history of race ideologies, see Philip Curtin, *The Image of Africa: British Ideas and Action, 1780–1850* (University of Wisconsin Press, 1964), especially volume 1, chapter 2, "The Africans' 'Place in Nature.'" The most comprehensive, reliable, and accessible book to expose and refute these ideologies is Stephen Jay Gould's *The Mismeasure of Man* (Norton and Company, rev. ed., 1996). A very informative collection of readings on this topic from a variety of perspectives is the volume edited by Les Back and John Solomos, *Theories of Race and Racism: A Reader* (Routledge, 2nd ed., 2009).

Notes

Introduction: Atlantic Lives

1. P69/JS1/A/002/MS07894, Item 002. St. James Duke's Place, Register of Marriages, 1692–1700. LMA.

2. T 70/831, 832. TNA.

3. PROB 18/24/11, 12 March 1696. TNA. This case study expands on a brief archival abstract written in 1798. A typescript of it appears as Appendix B, An English-African Marriage in the Gambia, 1693, in Donald R. Wright, "Niumi: The History of a Western Mandinka State through the Eighteenth Century," unpublished PhD diss., Indiana University, 1976.

4. PROB 11/427/15, 13 May 1693. TNA. £25 per annum is significantly higher than the range of annual maintenance amounts cited from seventeenth-century English probate records, which was between £1 and £12 for girls, £1 and £10 for boys, and £10–£15 each for parents. Amy Louise Erickson, *Women and Property in Early Modern England* (London: Routledge, 1993), 50, 190.

5. PROB 18/24/11, 12 March 1696. TNA.

6. T 70/11, Heath at James Island to London, 7 March 1694. TNA.

7. The birth was in November of 1694, and the christening was on 5 December. P93/DUN/259, St. Dunstan and All Saints, Stepney, Register of Baptisms, April 1682–98. LMA.

8. PROB 5/737, 23 July 1696. TNA.

9. C 7/152/36 Part I, 7 January 1695/6. TNA.

10. PROB 18/24/11, 12 March 1696. C 7/152/36, Pt. II, 30 April 1697. TNA.

11. C 6/428/30, May 1697. TNA.

12. PROB 18/24/11, 12 March 1696. TNA.

13. See Erickson, *Women and Property*. For introductory reading on Atlantic history, see the Suggested Further Readings section.

14. PROB 18/24/11, 12 March 1696. TNA.

15. John Kennedy, *A History of the Parish of Leyton, Essex* (Leyton, 1894), 117.

16. T 70, Treasury Series. TNA.

17. Robin Law, ed. *The English in West Africa, 1681–1683* (Oxford: Oxford University Press, 1997); *The English in West Africa, 1685–1688* (Oxford: Oxford University Press, 2001); and *The English in West Africa, 1691–1699* (Oxford: Oxford University Press, 2006). The letters in these volumes are from RAC letter-books in the Rawlinson Collection, held in the Bodleian Library, Oxford University.

18. An especially compelling recent contribution to this topic is Stephen Behrendt, Antera Duke, A. J. H. Latham, and David Northrup, *The Diary of Antera*

Duke, an Eighteenth-Century African Slave Trader (Oxford: Oxford University Press, 2010).

19. With respect to the time period of this book, major changes that came *later* and so *not* in evidence here are the Industrial Revolution and the rise of pseudo-scientific racist ideologies. For readings on these topics, see the Suggested Further Readings section.

20. See Colleen Kriger, "'Our Indico Designe': Planting and Processing Indigo for Export, Upper Guinea Coast, 1684–1702," and Robin Law, "'There's Nothing Grows in the West Indies but Will Grow Here': Dutch and English Projects of Plantation Agriculture on the Gold Coast, 1650s–1780s," in *Commercial Agriculture, the Slave Trade and Slavery in Atlantic Africa*, ed. Robin Law, Suzanne Schwarz, and Silke Strickrodt, 98–115, 158–79 (Woodbridge, Suffolk: James Currey Press, 2013).

21. See the indispensable foundational work by A. G. Hopkins, *An Economic History of West Africa* (New York: Columbia University Press, 1973).

22. Useful online resources are The Historical Thinking Project at historybenchmarks.ca and the Stanford History Education Group at sheg.stanford.edu.

Chapter 1: Buyers and Sellers in Cross-Cultural Trade

1. Future archaeological research may very well turn up more evidence for trans-Saharan trade before the Arab-Islamic conquest of North Africa. Such evidence so far is relatively sparse. See Sonja Magnavita, "Initial Encounters: Seeking Traces of Ancient Trade Connections between Western Africa and the Wider World," *Afriques* 4 (2013). http://afriques.revues.org/1145.

2. For readings on Islam in African history, see the Suggested Further Readings section.

3. Philip Curtin, *Economic Change in Precolonial Africa: Senegambia in the Era of the Slave Trade* (Madison: University of Wisconsin Press, 1975), 68–91.

4. Timothy Insoll and Thurstan Shaw, "Gao and Igbo-Ukwu: Beads, Interregional Trade, and Beyond," *African Archaeological Review* 14, no. 1 (1997): 9–23; Thurstan Shaw, *Igbo-Ukwu: An Account of Archaeological Discoveries in Eastern Nigeria* (Evanston, IL: Northwestern University Press, 1970).

5. Carnelian is a special variety of agate or patterned quartz. A. J. Arkell, "Cambay and the Bead Trade," *Antiquity* 10, no. 39 (1936): 292–305; Insoll and Shaw, "Gao and Igbo-Ukwu."

6. George Brooks, *Landlords and Strangers: Ecology, Society, and Trade in Western Africa, 1000–1630* (Boulder, CO: Westview Press, 1993), 52–53; Curtin, *Economic Change*, 275–77, 282–86.

7. Len Pole, "Recent Developments in Iron-Working Research in West Africa," in *West African Archaeology: New Developments, New Perspectives*, ed. Philip Allsworth-Jones (Oxford: British Archaeological Reports, 2010), 53–65; Roderick J. McIntosh, *Ancient Middle Niger: Urbanism and the Self-Organizing Landscape* (Cambridge: Cambridge University Press, 2005), 151–52.

8. The Konyan highlands are usually shown on topographical maps as the Guinean dorsal.

9. George Brooks, *Landlords and Strangers,* 50–53. Archaeological research on iron production in rainforest regions is relatively thin, in part because of the difficulties of surveying in areas of dense vegetation and relatively low population. See, for example, Susan L. White, "Iron Production and Iron trade in Northern and Central Liberia: History of a Major Indigenous Technology," unpublished paper, Liberian Studies Conference, Madison, Wisconsin (April 1974), 1–19.

10. André Álvares de Almada, *Brief Treatise on the Rivers of Guinea,* trans. and ed. P. E. H. Hair, typescript, Department of History, University of Liverpool (July 1984), chapter 6, 53.

11. Roland Portères, "La monnaie de fer dans l'Ouest-Africain au XX siècle," *Recherches africaines* 4 (1960): 3–13; Gordon C. Thomasson, "'Primitive' Kpelle Steelmaking: A High Technology Indigenous Knowledge System for Liberia's Future?" *Liberian Studies Journal* 12, no, 2 (1987): 152.

12. Nehemia Levtzion and J. F. P. Hopkins, transl. and eds., *Corpus of Early Arabic Sources for West African History* (Cambridge: Cambridge University Press, 1981), 77–87.

13. Ibid., 107–11.

14. Hopkins, *Economic History,* 46–48, 67–68; Timothy Garrard, *Akan Weights and the Gold Trade* (London: Longman, 1980), 213–25.

15. Almada, *Brief Treatise,* chapter 5, 47–49.

16. Jan Hogendorn and Marion Johnson, *The Shell Money of the Slave Trade* (Cambridge: Cambridge University Press, 1986), 16; Ghislaine Lydon, *On Trans-Saharan Trails: Islamic Law, Trade Networks, and Cross-Cultural Exchange in Nineteenth Century Western Africa* (Cambridge: Cambridge University Press, 2009), 74–75.

17. Levtzion and Hopkins, *Corpus,* 267–69.

18. Ibid., 281, 300.

19. Hopkins, *Economic History,* 70; Marion Johnson, "The Cowrie Currencies of West Africa, Part I," *Journal of African History* 11, no. 1 (1970): 37–46.

20. Colleen Kriger, "Mapping the History of Cotton Textile Production in Precolonial West Africa," *African Economic History* 33 (2005), 90–92; idem, *Cloth in West African History* (Lanham, MD: AltaMira Press, 2006). Clothing was made from other fibers, such as raphia, bast, and some varieties of wool, as well as bark cloth, animal pelts, and cured or tanned hides.

21. Kriger, "Mapping," 92–100.

22. See Rita Bolland, *Tellem Textiles: Archaeological Finds from Burial Caves in Mali's Bandiagara Cliff* (Amsterdam: Tropenmuseum, 1991).

23. Levtzion and Hopkins, *Corpus,* 78, 260, 265; Kriger, "Mapping."

24. For readings on cotton currencies in African history, see the Suggested Further Readings section.

25. Levtzion and Hopkins, *Corpus,* 78, 260, 265; Yedida Kalfon Stillman, *Arab Dress: A Short History* (Leiden: Brill, 2000), 7, 11. A cubit is an ancient measure, fingertip to elbow, or 17 to 22 inches.

26. Almada, *Brief Treatise*, chapter 11, 111; Curtin, *Economic Change*, 214; Colleen E. Kriger, "'Guinea Cloth': Production and Consumption of Cotton Textiles in West Africa before and during the Atlantic Slave Trade," in *The Spinning World: A Global History of Cotton Textiles, 1200–1850*, ed. Giorgio Riello and Prasannan Parthasarathi (Oxford: Oxford University Press, 2009), 105–26; idem, "The Importance of Mande Textiles in the African Side of the Atlantic Trade, ca. 1680–1710," *Journal of Mande Studies* 11 (2009): 1–21.

27. Marion Johnson, "The Ounce in Eighteenth-Century West African Trade," *Journal of African History* 7, no. 2 (1966): 197–214.

28. P. E. H. Hair, "Sources on Early Sierra Leone: (2) Andrade (1582), Ruiters (1623), Carvalho (1632[5])," *Africana Research Bulletin* 5/1 (1974): 51–52. Eight reals equaled the Spanish silver dollar, which in the western Sudan was considered equal in weight to the North African trade ounce. Garrard, *Akan Weights*, 218. Salt, accumulating regularly by tidal depositing, was freely available on these islands in endless supply. See T. Bentley Duncan, *Atlantic Islands: Madeira, the Azores, and the Cape Verdes in Seventeenth Century Commerce and Navigation* (Chicago: University of Chicago Press, 1972), 161, 184–85.

29. Thora Stone, "The Journey of Cornelius Hodges in Senegambia, 1689–90," *English Historical Review* 39, no. 153 (January 1924): 89–95; Curtin, *Economic Change*, 212, 276–77.

30. Francisco de Lemos Coelho, *Description of the Coast of Guinea (1684)*, trans. P. E. H. Hair, typescript, Department of History, University of Liverpool (October 1985), chapter 2, 25–26.

31. Coelho, *Description*, chapter 2, 27–28.

32. Toby Green, *The Rise of the Trans-Atlantic Slave Trade in Western Africa, 1300–1589* (Cambridge: Cambridge University Press, 2012), 116–18; Brooks, *Landlords*, 155.

33. John Gray, *A History of The Gambia* (1940; reprint, New York: Barnes and Noble, 1966), 16–20; Almada, *Brief Treatise*, chapter 3, 28, chapter 6, 58; Brooks, *Landlords*, 324.

34. Richard Jobson, *The Discovery of River Gambra (1623)*, ed. D. P. Gamble and P. E. H. Hair (London: The Hakluyt Society, 1999), 160–61.

35. T. Bentley Duncan, *Atlantic Islands*, 216–18.

36. Jobson, *Discovery*, 160–61.

37. Coelho, *Description*, chapter 1, pp. 6, 12–13.

38. Ibid., chapter 7, pp. 7–8.

39. Ibid., chapter 9, pp. 23–24.

40. P. E. H. Hair, Adam Jones, and Robin Law, trans. and eds., *Barbot on Guinea: The Writings of Jean Barbot on West Africa 1678–1712*, 2 vols. (London: The Hakluyt Society, 1992), 1:102.

41. Ibid., 278n1.

42. Ibid., 265–71.

Chapter 2: "Artificers" and Merchants

1. Seventeenth-century RAC reexports of French brandy and exports of English spirits were overshadowed by goods in the textiles, metalwares, and beads

categories. K. G. Davies, *The Royal African Company* (1957; reprint, New York: Octagon Books, 1975), 173, 178, and appendix 1, 350–57.

2. Ibid., 176–77.

3. Ibid., 353–54.

4. K. N. Chaudhuri, "The Structure of the Indian Textile Industry in the Seventeenth and Eighteenth Centuries," in *Technology and European Overseas Enterprise*, ed. Michael Adas (Aldershot, UK: Variorum, 1996), 367–74; Ian C. Wendt, "Four Centuries of Decline? Understanding the Changing Structure of the South Indian Textile Industry," in *How India Clothed the World: The World of South Asian Textiles, 1500–1850*, ed. Giorgio Riello and Tirthankar Roy (Leiden: Brill, 2009), 205–12.

5. Sletias came to London by way of Hamburg, and the RAC purchased the bulk of its supplies of them from London importers. Davies, *Royal African Company*, 172. The region is now part of southwest Poland. Also traded on the Upper Guinea Coast were Roan, Polonia, and Shock linens. T 70/648, 649, 650, 651, 653; 829, 830, 831. TNA. Shock was the name given in Bohemia and Silesia to 60-ell pieces. Adam Jones, *Brandenburg Sources for West African History, 1680–1700* (Stuttgart: Franz Steiner, 1985), 318.

6. For the preparation of flax for spinning, see John Horner, *The Linen Trade of Europe before the Spinning Wheel* (Belfast: McCaw, Stevenson, and Orr, 1920), 374–83.

7. Maxine Berg, Pat Hudson, and Michael Sonenscher, "Manufacture in Town and Country before the Factory," in *Manufacture in Town and Country Before the Factory*, ed. Maxine Berg, Pat Hudson, and Michael Sonenscher (Cambridge: Cambridge University Press, 1983), 24–25; Jürgen Schlumbohm, "Seasonal Fluctuations and Social Division of Labour: Rural Linen Production in the Osnabrück and Bielefeld Regions and the Urban Woolen Industry in the Niederlausitz (c.1770–c.1850)," in Berg, Hudson, and Sonenscher, *Manufacture*, 106–7; Herbert Kisch, "The Textile Industries in Silesia and the Rhineland: A Comparative Study in Industrialization," in *The Textile Industries*, ed. D. T. Jenkins (Oxford: Blackwell Publishers, 1994), 352–55.

8. Davies, *Royal African Company*, 176–77; Florence Montgomery, *Textiles in America, 1650–1870* (New York: W. W. Norton, 2007).

9. W. B. Stephens, *Seventeenth-Century Exeter: A Study of Industrial and Commercial Development, 1625–1688* (Exeter: University of Exeter, 1958); W. G. Hoskins, *Industry, Trade, and People in Exeter, 1688–1800* (Manchester: Manchester University Press, 1935), 30–39, 53.

10. Davies, *Royal African Company*, 176–77, 234–35; David Jeremy, "British and American Yarn Count Systems: An Historical Analysis," *Business History Review* 45, no. 3 (1971), 344–45.

11. Davies, *Royal African Company*, 45, 170–72, 351. Other sources show a range of weights for "voyage" iron, between seventy and eighty-five bars per ton. Lengths of a single bar ranged from ten to thirteeen feet. Chris Evans and Göran Rydén, *Baltic Iron in the Atlantic World in the 18th Century* (Leiden: Brill, 2007), 165–66; Walter Rodney, *A History of the Upper Guinea Coast, 1545–1800* (Oxford: Clarendon Press, 1970), 194.

204 NOTES TO PAGES 43-51

12. Göran Rydén and Maria Ågren, *Ironmaking in Sweden and Russia: A Survey of the Social Organization of Iron Production before 1900* (Uppsala: Uppsala University Department of History, 1993), 16–18, 32.

13. Ibid., 18, 25–30; Karl-Gustaf Hildebrand, *Swedish Iron in the 17th and 18th c.* (Stockholm: Jernkontorets, 1992); Anders Florén, et al., "The Social Organization of Work at Mines, Furnaces, and Forges," in *Ironmaking Societies: Early Industrial Development in Sweden and Russia, 1600–1900*, ed. Maria Ågren (Oxford: Berghahn Books, 1998), 61–140.

14. T 70/13, Amsterdam to RAC, 8 Jan. 1703/4; T 70/361. TNA. Davies, *Royal African Company*, 170–72, 178, 219, 351; H. Cotterell, *Old Pewter; Its Makers and Marks* (London: B. T. Batsford, 1929), 1–5; "The Case of the Pewterers of England, as to the Exportation of Pewter," Petition to the House of Commons (1690?[1711]), 816.m.13. (87.), British Library. I established the date of 1711 for this document's printing based on Charles Welch, *History of the Worshipful Company of Pewterers of the City of London*, 2 vols. (London: Blades, 1902), 2:170.

15. Davies, *Royal African Company*, 173–77; John S. Cooper, *For Commonwealth and Crown: English Gunmakers of the Seventeenth Century* (Gillingham: Wilson Hunt, 1993), 91; Howard L. Blackmore, *A Dictionary of London Gunmakers, 1350–1850* (Oxford: Phaidon Christies's, 1986), 17–18.

16. John Adams, *Sketches Taken during Ten Voyages to Africa, between the Years 1786 and 1800* (1822; reprint, New York: Johnson Reprint, 1970), 261.

17. T 70/361, 19 August 1682 and 23 August 1683; T 70/546, 15 Dec. 1684; T 70/1434, October 1704. TNA.

18. Eric Williams, *Capitalism and Slavery* (Chapel Hill: University of North Carolina Press, 1944), 81.

19. See a discussion of the myth in Curtin, *Economic Change*, 309–11.

20. Davies, *Royal African Company*, 172–77, 357; Hogendorn and Johnson, *Shell Money*; and T 70 Series, TNA.

21. T 70/130, 17 February 1703. TNA.

22. Curtin, *Economic Change*, 70.

23. Bence Island is the usual spelling in the RAC records of this period. Other spellings, especially in the eighteenth century, are Bance and Bunce.

24. T 70/20, Bence Island, Edmond Pierce to London, 5 August 1679. TNA.

25. It was customary for RAC agents to hold a sale of the personal property of an employee who died. Purchases would be credited to his account, but his unsold property was not usually accounted for. His relatives in England presumably would be entitled to claim the net owed him in pounds sterling. However, there were often irregularities and gaps in the accounting records, which caused problems and disputes between officials in London and the families of their deceased employees.

26. T 70/546, Nov. 1685, Jan. 1686, June 1686, Aug. 1686. TNA.

27. T 70/546, Dec. 1683, March 1684, Oct. 1684; T 70/11, 15 Dec. 1684. TNA. These back-and-forth voyages between the Guinea Coast and London are not included in the Trans-Atlantic Slave Trade database, even though some of them brought

captives to England. See *Voyages: The Trans-Atlantic Slave Trade Database* (2009), http://www.slavevoyages.org.

28. T 70/360, 361; 546, 547; 587, 588, 589. TNA.

29. C. Kriger, "'Our Indico Designe,'" in Law, Schwarz, and Strickrodt, *Commercial Agriculture*. The gum that was occasionally exported from Sierra Leone and Sherbro was for treating the wooden hulls of trading vessels, not the kind of gum made from the resin of acacia trees and exported from Senegal for use in European textile manufacture.

30. English sources anglicize the Portuguese toponym Vintang as Bintang.

31. Juffure is known to people today as the hometown of Kunta Kinte, putative ancestor of Alex Haley as recounted in his family history, *Roots* (Garden City, NY, 1976). See Donald R. Wright, "The Effect of Alex Haley's *Roots* on How Gambians Remember the Atlantic Slave Trade," *History in Africa* 38 (2011): 295–318.

32. Gray, *Gambia*, 11. T 70/546; T 70/1441. TNA.

33. T 70/360, 361; 587, 588, 589. T 70/1441, 1442. TNA. The name Tassily for this RAC post comes from anglicizing the French name—Trois-îles—for its island location. See Anonymous, "Relations des îles et environs des rivières de Bresalme, Gambie, Zamenée, S. Domingue, Gève, et autres, etc.," in Jacques-Joseph Le Maire et al., *Les voyages du sieur Le Maire aux îles Canaries, Cap-Verd, Sénégal, et Gambie* (Paris: Collombat, 1695); and the map of Cacheo River in John Barbot, "A Description of the Coasts of North and South Guinea," in Awnsham and John Churchill, *A Collection of Voyages and Travels* (London: John Walthoe, 1732), vol. 5, plate 4. Coelho referred to this island as "Ilhetas." See Coelho, chapter 5, p. 3. Most maps show it as "Jeta," "Jata," or "Jatts."

34. For introductory readings on Euro-African or creole culture, see the suggested Further Readings section.

35. Richard S. Dunn, *Sugar and Slaves: The Rise of the Planter Class in the English West Indies, 1624–1713* (Chapel Hill: University of North Carolina Press, 1972); Russell Menard, *Sweet Negotiations: Sugar, Slavery, and Plantation Agriculture in Early Barbados* (Charlottesville: University of Virginia Press, 2006).

36. Davies, *Royal African Company*, 60, 346–49.

37. For introductory readings on "landlord" and "stranger" relations, see the Suggested Further Readings section.

38. Wright, "Niumi," 135–37.

39. Curtin, *Economic Change*, 66–72, 282–83; Donald Wright, *The World and a Very Small Place in Africa: A History of Globalization in Niumi, The Gambia*, 2nd ed. (Armonk, NY: M. E. Sharpe, 2004), 78; Donald Wright, "Darbo Jula: The Role of a Mandinka Jula Clan in the Long-Distance Trade of the Gambia River and its Hinterland," *African Economic History* 3 (1977): 35–36.

40. Coelho in Jobson, *Discovery*, 291, 306–7.

41. There are important exceptions, of course, but usually from the nineteenth century, such as the rich collection of slave narratives collected by Koelle in Freetown, Sierra Leone. The five major ways people became captives were the following: being taken prisoner in war; being kidnapped; being sold by relatives or superiors;

being sold to settle debts; or being found guilty in a judicial proceeding. See P. E. H. Hair, "The Enslavement of Koelle's Informants," *Journal of African History* 6, no. 2 (1965): 193–201.

42. Davies, *Royal African Company*, 363. Estimates of mortality—from point of captives' origins to arrival on the coast, during captivity while held on the coast, and during the middle passage itself—were not considered. Much to his credit, however, he included in his count those captives who went to ships' captains on their commissions and part-payment of freight.

43. From *Voyages: The Trans-Atlantic Slave Trade Database*.

44. See David Eltis's discussion of the variability of estimates of the unrecorded interloper trade in "The British Trans-Atlantic Slave Trade before 1714," in *The Lesser Antilles in the Age of European Expansion*, ed. Robert Paquette and Stanley Engerman (Gainesville: University Press of Florida, 1996), 182–205.

45. Curtin noted that the meaning of the term "Bambara" in this context was ambiguous since it was not stated if the captives themselves were ethnically Bambara or if they were captives of Bambara. Curtin, *Economic Change*, 178–79. Wright adds Mandinka to the list of probable identities of slaves coming from the interior. Wright, "Darbo Jula," 33.

46. Curtin, *Economic Change*, 284–85.

47. *Voyages: The Trans-Atlantic Slave Trade Database*, s.v. query "voyages between 1650 and 1700; originating in England; principal place of slave purchase Senegambia and Sierra Leone" (accessed 3 November 2012). Of the sixty-one total voyages, the place of slave landing was given for fifty-seven.

48. T 70/14, 12 February, 23 March, and 9 April 1704, Dalby Thomas at Cape Coast Castle to London. TNA.

49. For readings on England's early black history, see the Suggested Further Readings section.

50. Davies, *Royal African Company*, 180–83, 360.

51. Curtin, *Economic Change*, 171–73, 224; Rodney, *History*, 156–57.

52. Curtin, *Economic Change*, 223; Rodney, *History*, 158. For an early mention of beeswax (Valentim Fernandes, ca. 1508), see Jobson, *Discovery*, 270.

53. Like their Juula counterparts who would put slaves to work temporarily in agriculture, processing, or manufacture, before selling them. Curtin, *Economic Change*, 170–71.

54. Davies refers to it generically as redwood. Davies, *Royal African Company*, 181. Its botanical name is *Baphia nitida*. J. M. Dalziel, *The Useful Plants of West Tropical Africa* (London: Crown Agents, 1937), 232–33; D. Cardon and P. C. M. Jansen, "*Baphia nitida* Lodd," in P. C. M. Jansen and D. Cardon, eds., *PROTA, Plant Resources of Tropical Africa* (Wageningen, Netherlands, 2005), http://database.prota .org/search.htm (accessed 19 November 2012).

55. Christopher Fyfe, *Sierra Leone Inheritance* (London: Oxford University Press, 1964), 59–62; Rodney, *History*, 159–60, 193.

56. Curtin, *Economic Change*, 218–21; Nize Isabel de Moraes, "Le Commerce des Peaux à la Petite Côte au XVIIe siècle (Sénégambie)," *Notes africaines* 136 (October

1972): 113; Hair, Jones, and Law, *Barbot on Guinea*, 103, 113n13, based on Dapper; Jobson, *Discovery*, 294, 309, from Coelho in the mid-seventeenth century.

57. See for example Barbara E. Frank, "Soninke *Garankéw* and Bamana-Malinke *Jeliw*: Mande Leatherworkers, Identity, and the Diaspora," in *Status and Identity in West Africa: Nyamakalaw of Mande,* ed. David C. Conrad and Barbara E. Frank (Bloomington: Indiana University Press, 1995), 133–50.

58. Hair, Jones, and Law, *Barbot on Guinea*, 102–3; Oswald Durand, "Les industries locales au Fouta," *Bulletin du Comité d'études historiques et scientifiques de l'Afrique occidentale française* 15 (1932): 61–62. The divisions of labor in the twentieth century show interesting variations. In Mande communities where leatherworkers were men, they recruited help in tanning from family labor, that is, their wives and children. Some men claimed that in the past their fathers had used slave labor for tanning. In Moorish and Tuareg herding communities, both tanning and leatherworking were done by women. Barbara E. Frank, *Mande Potters and Leather-Workers: Art and Heritage in West Africa* (Washington, DC: Smithsonian Institution Press, 1998), 103, 165n2.

59. De Moraes, "Le commerce des peaux," *Notes africaines* 134 (April 1972): 37–45 and 136 (October 1972): 111–16; Davies, *Royal African Company,* 219; Curtin, *Economic Change,* Supplement, 66–67.

Chapter 3: West Africans Profiting in Atlantic Trade

1. Jan S. Hogendorn and Henry A. Gemery, "The 'Hidden Half' of the Anglo-African Trade in the Eighteenth Century: The Significance of Marion Johnson's Research," in *West African Economic and Social History: Studies in Memory of Marion Johnson,* ed. David Henige and T. C. McCaskie (Madison: University of Wisconsin African Studies Program, 1990), 81–91.

2. T 70/10, Gambia, Thurloe to London, 28 May 1678. TNA.

3. T 70/165, Book of Orders and Instruction, 15 November 1700, 27 July 1702, 9 September 1704. TNA. To simplify the text, I will be using the English word "king" throughout these chapters as a generic term for ruler. *Palavra,* Portuguese for "word," is here used to mean a dispute or discussion. This usage is sometimes anglicized as *palaver.* Law, *The English in West Africa,* 3:xvi. The trade language on the coast was Crioulo, a Portuguese-based creole.

4. For Mandinka terminology for landlord-stranger relations—*jati* (landlord or host), *suruga* and *samalan* (dependent or independent stranger)—see Donald Wright, "Niumi," 135–37. See also an alternative translation from French as "host-guest" in C. Giesing and V. Vydrine, *Ta:rikh Mandinka de Bijini (Guinea-Bissau)* (Leiden: Brill, 2007), xvi.

5. T 70/10, Gambia, Thurloe to London, 23 April 1678. TNA.

6. RAC records refer to the Fogny kingdom as Foni. T 70/830, 831, 832. TNA.

7. T 70/830, 831, 832; 546, 547. TNA.

8. "Alcade" [Portuguese *alcaide-mor*]: governor of a town or fortress. Malyn Newitt, *The Portuguese in West Africa, 1415–1670: A Documentary History* (Cambridge: Cambridge University Press, 2010), 231.

9. T 70/546. TNA. RAC records show anglicized spellings: Barrow; Sangrigo; Cumbo; Foni; Jorunko; Barsallia; Berefet; Bintan; Jellifree; Secca; and Banyan. For salaries and conversion from pounds sterling to Bars, see Davies, *Royal African Company*, 252–53, 238.

10. *Bur* (ruler) Saalum, anglicized as Barsally or Barsallia. T 70/829, 832, 833; 546, 547. TNA.

11. T 70/360, 361. Bence Island Journals. TNA. Anglicized spellings are Tassily, Samoes, Logoes, Scasseras River, Nunes, and Punga. Trois-îles was also known as Três Ilhetas in Portuguese and as Djeta in Crioulo. André Donelha, *An Account of Sierra Leone and the Rivers of Guinea of Cape Verde (1625)* (Lisbon: Junta de Investigações Científicas do Ultramar, 1977), 318–19.

12. See Barbot's description of his visit with John Thomas in Hair, Jones, and Law, *Barbot on Guinea*, 1:184, 186–89.

13. T 70/360, 10 January 1678/9 and 10 November 1680. TNA.

14. T 70/360, 30 December 1680. TNA. Maria Kecskési, *African Masterpieces and Selected Works from Munich: The Staatliches Museum für Völkerkunde* (New York: The Center for African Art, 1987), 44–46. For a description of royal investiture in Guinala on the Rio Grande and involving the ceremonial sounding of ivory trumpets, see Donelha, *An Account of Sierra Leone*, 177–79. And for issues of dating and provenance of Luso-African ivories, see Peter Mark, "'Bini, Vidi, Vici'—On the Misuse of 'Style' in the Analyses of Sixteenth Century Luso-African Ivories," *History in Africa* 42 (2015): 323–34.

15. T 70/361, 18 March 1683. TNA.

16. *Baphia nitida,* called *kam* in the West Atlantic language of Temne and *bundoi* and *mbundona* in the Mande languages of Mende and Loko, respectively. Dalziel, *Useful Plants*, 232–33.

17. Zachary Rogers account, T 70/828; 829. Gambia Ledgers, 1665–66. TNA. The Company of Royal Adventurers Trading to Africa (1660–75) and for northern Guinea, Company of Gambia Adventurers (1669–75). Davies, *Royal African Company*, 30, 99–101.

18. T 70/10 Zachary Rogers, Sherbro to London, 5 August 1678; T 70/20 Zachary Rogers, Sherbro to London, 29 September 1679. TNA.

19. T 70/1 Captain William Goose, Sherbro to London, 6 March 1681. TNA.

20. Ibid.

21. Matthew Skinner was listed as "mulatto" in RAC records. T 70/1442. TNA.

22. T 70/ 587; 880, 881, 882. T 70/21, Sherbro, Corker to London, 21 June 1697. TNA.

23. T 70/587; 361. Sherbro and Bence Island journals. TNA. This is perhaps one of the earliest recorded instances of a "cry" in precolonial Sierra Leone. For the remarkable history of a Mende funeral dirge carried across the Atlantic and passed down over generations by women in a Gullah family, see the film "The Language You Cry In," directed by Alvaro Toepke and Angel Serrano (San Francisco: California Newsreel, 1998). For further reading on African contributions to American cultures, see Suggested Further Readings section.

24. T 70/587. Sherbro Journal. TNA.

25. T 70/16, Sherbro, Platt to London, 24 November 1681. TNA.

26. T 70/587. Salary figures for the 1680s are sparse, but they show Henry Ballard, who became a factor at Sierra Leone, as drawing a yearly salary of £50, which when converted into Bars would be 166B. Platt used the usual rate of 6s to a Bar in his accounting of the king's charges due for freeing up the wood. T 70/361. TNA. See also Davies, *Royal African Company,* 238.

27. T 70/16, Sherbro, Platt to London, 24 November 1681. TNA.

28. See Fyfe, *Sierra Leone Inheritance,* 59–62. For brass pans in the making of sea salt in the vicinity of Sherbro, see Adam Jones and P. E. H. Hair, "Sources on Early Sierra Leone: (11) Brun (1624)," *Africana Research Bulletin* 7, no. 3 (1977): 55; John Matthews, *A Voyage to the River Sierra-Leone, on the Coast of Africa* (London, 1788), 37. For La Courbe's brief description of small-scale sea salt production by solar evaporation, see Prosper Cultru, ed., *Premier Voyage de Sieur de la Courbe fait á la Coste d'Afrique en 1685* (Paris, 1913), 192.

29. T 70/877, 878, 879; 881, 882. Sherbro Ledgers. TNA.

30. T 70/588. TNA.

31. T 70/11, Sherbro, Gibson to London, 24 January 1691/2. TNA.

32. T 70/11, Sherbro, Corker to London, 31 July 1698. TNA.

33. T 70/51, London, RAC to King of Sherbro, 11 July 1699. TNA.

34. Peter Mark, *'Portuguese' Style and Luso-African Identity: Precolonial Senegambia, Sixteenth–Nineteenth Centuries* (Bloomington: Indiana University Press, 2002), 15–16; Walter Hawthorne, *Planting Rice and Harvesting Slaves: Transformations along the Guinea-Bissau Coast, 1400–1900* (Portsmouth, NH: Heinemann, 2003), 58–59; T. Green, *Rise of the Trans-Atlantic Slave Trade,* 12–13.

35. Davies, *Royal African Company,* 110–11. The policy was designed to prevent moral hazard, and the RAC hoped that having higher salary rates would make up for the prohibition on private trading. Their hopes were mistaken. Experienced agents and factors regularly wrote letters requesting raises or commissions on sales or permission to trade on their own account as well as for the company, and it was not uncommon for them to quit the company to engage in private trade.

36. T 70/10 Gambia to London, 15 March 1678. TNA.

37. T 70/20 Gambia to London, 22 March 1678. TNA.

38. T 70/10 Gambia to London, 28 May 1678. TNA.

39. T 70/10 Gambia to London (Cleeve), 24 August 1680; T 70/17 Gambia to London (Booker), 19 August 1689. TNA. Geregia is called Sangrigo in the RAC records.

40. T 70/546; 831, 832; 1441. TNA.

41. T 70/50, London to Gambia, 30 August 1687. TNA.

42. T 70/828, 830. TNA.

43. T 70/830. TNA. A ream of paper consisted of twenty quires, each quire either 24 or 25 sheets, for a total of 480 or 500 sheets.

44. T 70/831. TNA.

45. T 70/832. TNA.

46. T 70/832; 546. TNA.

47. Also known as the Nine Years' War or the War of the Grand Alliance (1689–97), with England, the Netherlands, and Austria allied together against France.

48. T 70/833; 547. TNA.

49. For readings on senhoras and other women traders, see Suggested Further Readings section.

50. T 70/546; 1441. TNA.

51. Silva's name is anglicized in the records as Anthony Silver. T 70/830, 831, 832; 546. TNA. In his description of his visit to Geregia in 1686, La Courbe mentioned that Luso-African merchants sent their slaves to Bagnun villages to purchase wax, which they brought back for processing and molding into cakes. Cultru, *Premier Voyage*, 205.

52. For analysis and description of the social and cultural complexity of trading towns such as Geregia, see Mark, *'Portuguese' Style*, especially 81–96.

53. Upriver prices for male captives ranged between 16 and 25B, depending on the seller; the price on the coast was usually 30B. T 70/832, 834; 546. TNA.

54. Siddiqui's name was anglicized in the records as "Ciddiquy." A 1687 accounting of RAC slaves or grometos at outposts lists one slave lent or entrusted to Siddiqui at Combo. T 70/830, 831, 832. TNA. He is not to be confused with "Sidisongo," a Muslim cleric whom La Courbe met in Albreda in 1686 and who claimed to be working for both the English and French companies. Cultru, *Premier Voyage*, 200.

55. Sidi was referred to as "Cassang, or Seddy the bicherine at Alberdach," which suggests that he was originally from the upriver port of Cação, or Cassan, but currently living at Albreda. T 70/828, 829. TNA. "Bicherine" (also bexerins, bixerim) is from Arabic, *el-Mubecherin*, an itinerant preacher. Newitt, *The Portuguese in West Africa*, 231. Such Muslim holy men were also known as "marabout," from Arabic *murabitun*. Mervyn Hiskett, *The Course of Islam in Africa* (Edinburgh: Edinburgh University Press, 1994), 11. Portuguese sources derogatorily ridiculed their selling of amulets and religious relics as superstitions, e.g., Donelha, *An Account of Sierra Leone*, 151, 161, 303. For a more respectful approach to the Islamic amulets made by Muslim clerics, see René Bravmann, *African Islam* (Washington, DC: Smithsonian Institution Press, 1983), especially chapter 2; and Labelle Prussin, *Hatumere: Islamic Design in West Africa* (Berkeley: University of California Press, 1986), esp. 146–47, 228.

56. Muslim clerics were identified as such either by the term "bicherine" or by one of the Mandinka terms for marabout, *mori* or *fode*, anglicized as "more" and "fuddy." Maurice Delafosse, *La langue mandingue et ses dialectes*, 2 vols. (Paris: Geuthner, 1955), 2:215, 512–13. For readings on Muslim clerics in West African history, see the Suggested Further Readings section.

57. T 70/830, 831. TNA. Locally made cotton cloths were known generically in Mandinka as *fani* or *fanu*, whereas imported European cottons were called *bagui/bagi*. Delafosse, *La langue mandingue*, 2:181; Anonymous, *Dictionnaire français-malinké et malinké-français* (Conakry, 1906); Etienne Peroz, *Dictionnaire français-mandingue* (Paris, 1891). The Mandinka term for bridewealth is *furu-fe*. Delafosse,

2:232. Wright's informants recalled times past when a woman's family would require fifty or more of the local cottons in bridewealth transactions. Wright, "Niumi," 131.

58. Commercial canoes (*kulu* or *kunu* in Mandinka), observed in the Gambia trading sphere in the 1680s, were large dugout canoes that could carry fifty or sixty men and loads of up to ten tons. They were usually paddled but could also be fitted with sails. François de Paris, *Voyage to the Coast of Africa (1682 and 1683)*, trans. and ed. Aimery Caron (Madison, WI: African Studies Program, 2001), 30–31; Cultru, *Premier Voyage*, 193. Siddiqui's loads of overseas goods were usually about two tons, suggesting a large-sized canoe with planks elevating the sides to hold his heavier loads. Prices indicate a range in vessel sizes: fishing canoes were valued at 3B; a "great canoe" purchased at Bence Island cost 12B. A 22-foot-long pinnace that came in to James Island from London was valued at 36B. T 70/546; 361; 52. TNA.

59. T 70/830; 546. Bento Sanchy was spelled variously as "Vinty Santia" or "Benty Sanchia." T 70/830; 832. TNA.

60. Cultru, *Premier Voyage*, 191. For Maliki law and commercial practice in nineteenth-century trans-Saharan trade, see Ghislaine Lydon, *On Trans-Saharan Trails*, esp. 274–339.

61. T 70/546; 831. TNA.

62. T 70/11; 21; 588, 589; 648, 649; 651, 652, 653; 828; 881. TNA.

63. T 70/360. TNA.

64. For a map of the Sierra Leone estuary, see chapter 2, figure 2.3.

65. T 70/360. TNA. For a description of Tombo at the time of his residence in northern Guinea (ca. 1640–63), see Coelho, *Descriptions*, chapter 9, pp. 33–34.

66. T 70/163; 361; 648, 649. TNA.

67. T 70/649, 650, 651, 652, 653. TNA.

68. T 70/11; 50. TNA.

69. T 70/588, 589; 881. TNA.

70. Rice was grown along the Upper Guinea Coast from the Gambia River southward to today's Liberia. For readings on rice production in this region, see the Suggested Further Readings section.

71. Jones and Hair, "Sources on Early Sierra Leone," 60; Coelho, *Descriptions*, chapter 9, pp. 22, 24, 26.

72. Cultru, *Premier Voyage*, 196–98.

73. Léonce Crétois, *Dictionnaire sereer-français*, 6 vols. (Dakar, 1972–77), 3:604–5; Arame Fal, Rosine Santos, and J. L. Doneux, *Dictionnaire wolof-français* (Paris, 1990), 123; Jean Diouf, *Dictionnaire wolof-français et français-wolof* (Paris: Karthala, 2003), 204. In Sereer, *be* is the equivalent of *boo e*, which intensifies an expression or renders it superlative. Hence *be linger* might mean greatest or most successful or powerful holder of the title. Crétois, *Dictionnaire sereer-français*, 1:138. For reference to past holders of the title and their political roles, see James Searing, *West African Slavery and Atlantic Commerce: The Senegal River Valley, 1700–1860* (Cambridge: Cambridge University Press, 1993), 16, 21, 22, 43, 74, 149; Boubacar Barry, *Senegambia and the Atlantic Slave Trade* (Cambridge: Cambridge University Press, 1998; translation of 1988 French ed.), 181, 191.

74. T 70/ 546; 831, 832. TNA. Subsequent ledgers show no account for her. *Be linger* was anglicized as "Billingary" in the RAC records.

75. Senhora Bibiana Vaz of Cacheu is relatively well known in the historical literature. But other seventeenth-century women documented in the RAC records and discussed here in this book are, to my knowledge, entering the historical literature for the first time. Women who traded in the RAC's Gambia sphere were Senhora Maria, Senhora Domingo, Senhora Cumbo, and the senhoras Isabel Diaz, Betty Bull, Betty Blow, and Betty Thurle, the latter three wives or daughters of former RAC employees. Women who traded in the RAC's Sierra Leone sphere were the senhoras Francisca Lopez and Francisca Fernandez of Tombo, the senhoras Isabella Gunn and Bibiana Veira, and Senhora Maria Lopez of Nunez. T 70/647, 648, 649, 650, 651, 652, 653; 832, 834; 881. TNA.

76. T 70/ 11, Corker to London, 7 and 9 October 1695. T 70/649; 881. TNA.

77. T 70/589; 649; 653; 881. TNA. The second *John* voyage is #9717 in *Voyages: The Trans-Atlantic Slave Trade Database* (accessed 3 June 2015). It erroneously identifies the place of slave purchase as Sherbro because the database does not include the coasting voyage to the northern rivers.

78. T 70/11, Corker to London, 7 and 9 October 1695. TNA. Davies, *Royal African Company,* 260, 272.

79. T 70/589; T 70/11, Corker to London, 17 May 1696. Richard Bridgman and his brother William were hired by the RAC to help them establish indigo plantations and processing at Sierra Leone. Both of them were listed as "mulattos" in company records. T 70/50, London to Gibson at Sherbro, 24 October 1691; T 70/11, Gibson to London, April 1692; T 70/1442. TNA.

80. T 70/589. William was listed as a seaman at York Island. T 70/1442, 1443. TNA.

81. T 70/882. T 70/21, Corker to London, 21 June 1697. TNA.

82. PROB 11/452/118. TNA. £230 in today's currency would be about £27,110. Measuring Worth, www.measuringworth.com.

83. T 70/590. TNA.

Chapter 4: Company Property

1. For important introductory readings on the Atlantic slave trade, see the Suggested Further Readings section.

2. For a very informative account of 179 liberated slaves in Freetown, Sierra Leone, in the mid-nineteenth century, including how they became slaves, see Hair, "Enslavement of Koelle's Informants."

3. See descriptions of punishments in David Buisseret, ed., *Jamaica in 1687: The Taylor Manuscript at the National Library of Jamaica* (Kingston: University of West Indies Press, 2008), 269–70, 277–78. For English slave codes, see Edward B. Rugemer, "The Development of Mastery and Race in the Comprehensive Slave Codes of the Greater Caribbean during the Seventeenth Century," *William and Mary Quarterly,* 3rd ser., 70, no. 3 (2013): 429–58. For an English translation of the 1685 French Code Noir, see http://chnm.gmu.edu/revolution/d/335/ (accessed 5 December 2016).

4. François Froger, *Relation d'un voyage fait en 1695, 1696, et 1697* (Paris, 1700), 148–50.

5. See the essential classic in comparative slavery, Orlando Patterson, *Slavery and Social Death: A Comparative Study* (Cambridge, MA: Harvard University Press, 1982), especially 1–14.

6. Drawing on data from two slaving voyages of an early seventeenth-century Portuguese private trader who operated in and around Cacheu and Bissau, Newson and Minchin suggest that for that time and place, slaves coming from Upper Guinea were drawn from coastal areas less than sixty-two miles inland. Linda Newson and Susie Minchin, *From Capture to Sale: The Portuguese Slave Trade to Spanish South America in the Early Seventeenth Century* (Leiden: Brill, 2007), 73. However, considering the Upper Guinea Coast more broadly as a region stretching from Cape Verde to Cape Mount, records from the second half of the seventeenth century show a more complex pattern, with overland caravans from distant interior regions also supplying coastal traders on a regular basis at major entrepôts.

7. For a description of gang slave labor on sugar cane plantations in the seventeenth-century English Caribbean, see Dunn, *Sugar and Slaves,* 198–201.

8. Kriger, "Importance of Mande Textiles," 4–5, 15.

9. T 70/128. Minutes of Committee of Goods, 26 July 1692; T 70/829, 830, 831, 832; T 70/547. TNA. Imported wool cards were used to separate the cleaned cotton fibers; in other parts of West Africa, this work was done with a spinning bow.

10. Bagnun peoples were sometimes referred to as Bainunk. Mark, *"Portuguese Style,"* 6, 82–87, 199. Their name is rendered as Banyun in English. See David Dalby, "Provisional Identification of Languages in the Polyglotta Africana," *Sierra Leone Language Review* 3 (1964): 83–90; and Philip D. Curtin and Jan Vansina, "Sources of the Nineteenth Century Atlantic Slave Trade," *Journal of African History* 5, no. 2 (1964): 185–208.

11. Cultru, *Premier voyage,* 201–2. In a later narrative, published as "Second voyage de Brüe . . . en 1698," in C. A. Walckenaer, *Histoire générale des voyages* (Paris, 1826), vol. 3, a portion of La Courbe's description is blended with information about another Luso-African woman. The latter apparently was married to the English captain Cornelius Hodges, called "Agis" in the French account. The description of her is anachronistic since Hodges died in 1692.

12. Kriger, "Importance of Mande Textiles," 10, 12, 15. Early British "cottons" of the eighteenth century were actually fustians, that is, cloth of mixed fiber, with linen used as warps. See John Styles, "East Meets West: Everyday Fashion in Eighteenth-Century London," *Interwoven Globe Symposium,* Metropolitan Museum of Art, New York City, 4 October 2013. www.metmuseum.org/metmedia/video/lectures/interwoven-globe-symposium-6 (accessed 6 December 2016).

13. Curtin, *Economic Change,* 271–72; Delafosse, *La langue mandingue,* vol. 2, 661.

14. Records of these two upriver voyages are in T 70/834. TNA.

15. The records show an anglicized form "sillatee" for the Mandinka *silatigui.*

16. The order was for "young, lusty, and most males." T 70/14 Weaver to London 10 June 1704. TNA.

17. The senhoras with English surnames were Betty Bull, Betty Blow, and Betty Thurle. The first two were probably wives of Benjamin Bull and William Blow, former RAC employees at James Island. Betty Thurle was either the elderly widow of Thomas Thurloe or his daughter. Thurloe, former RAC agent at James Island, died 4 April 1680. T 70/831, 832, 833. For Thurloe's death, T 70/1 Horde at James Island to London, 22 June 1680. TNA. For the *Bumi* title, see Martin Klein, *Islam and Imperialism in Senegal: Sine-Saloum, 1847–1914* (Stanford, CA: Stanford University Press, 1968), 261. *Bumi* was anglicized in the RAC records as "Boomy."

18. Prices at James Island averaged 30B per adult in the 1680s, 25B thereafter. At Bence Island and Sherbro, prices were on average about 20 to 22B per adult.

19. T 70/834. TNA.

20. T 70/16 Steede in Barbados to London, 19 March 1683. TNA.

21. T 70/360, 361; 547; 647. TNA.

22. T 70/20 Pierce at Sierra Leone to London, 5 August 1679. TNA. Francis Moore, *Travels into the Inland Parts of Africa,* 2nd ed. (London, 1738), 34.

23. T 70/589. TNA.

24. T 70/20 Pierce at Sierra Leone to London 5 August 1679; T 70/11 Booker at James Island to London, 25 April 1693. TNA.

25. Froger, *Relation d'un Voyage,* image facing page 32.

26. A. W. Lawrence, *Trade Castles and Forts of West Africa* (London: J. Cape, 1963), 250–61, figs. 64, 65.

27. T 70/831 November 1688, two male slaves with brickmakers at Brefet; T 70/11 Heath at James Island to London, December 1693; T 70/1442 12 December 1693, vessels *Swan* and *Charles* gone fetching stones. TNA.

28. An analysis of forty-eight ships (of varying tonnage) from the 1790s shows the average space allotment for slaves was 5.6 square feet. Charles Garland and Herbert S. Klein, "The Allotment of Space for Slaves aboard Eighteenth-Century British Slave Ships," *William and Mary Quarterly* 42, no. 2 (1985): 239–40, 244–47.

29. T 70/831; 1441, 1442; T 70/1 Kastell at James Island to London, 2 March 1681. TNA.

30. T 70/15 Horde at James Island to London, 22 June 1680; T 70/11 Booker at James Island to London, 23 April 1693. TNA.

31. T 70/545, 546, 547; 831. TNA.

32. T 70/360, 361. TNA.

33. T 70/360; 546; 589. TNA.

34. Herbert S. Klein, Stanley L. Engerman, Robin Haines, and Ralph Shlomowitz, "Transoceanic Mortality: The Slave Trade in Comparative Perspective," *William and Mary Quarterly* 58, no. 1 (2001): 93–118; Philip Curtin, *The Image of Africa: British Ideas and Action, 1780–1850* (Madison: University of Wisconsin Press, 1964), 361.

35. Women tended to have slightly lower death rates than men on the middle passage. See Klein et al., "Transoceanic Mortality," 102. For readings on demography and gender, see the Suggested Further Readings section.

36. High mortality among Europeans arriving in the colony of Sierra Leone in the 1820s gave it the reputation of a "white man's grave," terminology that came to be applied to tropical Africa more generally. Mortality rates of Europeans in Sierra

Leone between 1821 and 1826 were 44.5 percent for civilians and 56.5 percent for military and civilians. Curtin, *Image of Africa*, 179, 484.

37. Average numbers of RAC men were estimated based on figures recorded eight times over six years between 1688 and 1694. The range was 62–86. T 70/1442. For captives, the estimates came from figures in account books: the lower end of the range of captive men's population numbers was 100, the higher end was 200; for women, estimated at a three-to-one male-to-female ratio, the lower end of the population number is 25, with the higher end at 50. T 70/546, 547. TNA.

38. K. G. Davies, "The Living and the Dead: White Mortality in West Africa, 1684-1732," in *Race and Slavery in the Western Hemisphere: Quantitative Studies*, ed. Stanley Engerman, Eugene Genovese, and Alan Adamson (Princeton, NJ: Princeton University Press, 1975), 92.

39. T 70/545; 360. TNA.

40. T 70/546. TNA.

41. T 70/360, 361; 322; 332; 589; 1; 11; 14; 52; 84. TNA.

42. Barbot's description of the middle passage ought not to be taken as representative of shipboard conditions in general since he made only two voyages himself and his account seems to minimize the threat of slave revolts at sea. Hair, Jones, and Law, *Barbot on Guinea*, 2:774–75.

43. Stephen Behrendt, "Ecology, Seasonality, and the Transatlantic Slave Trade," in *Soundings in Atlantic History: Latent Structures and Intellectual Currents, 1500–1830*, ed. Bernard Bailyn and Patricia Denault (Cambridge, MA: Harvard University Press, 2009), 472n63; daily rations for employees of the French Compagnie des Indes ca. 1750 were two pounds of millet per person per day. Searing, *West African Slavery*, 85.

44. T 70/16 Kastell at James Island to London, 24 January 1682. TNA.

45. T 70/1441; 546. TNA.

46. T 70/1441; 546; T 70/11 Cleeve at James Island to London, 30 November 1685. TNA. An error in the accounting records has this insurrection taking place on the *Sarah*, whereas the RAC letters note the ship as the *John and Sarah*, which was indeed a vessel in service at James Island.

47. T 70/1441; 830, 831. TNA.

48. T 70/831. TNA.

49. T 70/1441, 1442; 832. TNA.

50. T 70/17 Booker at Gambia to London 17 June 1691. TNA.

51. T 70/11 Case at Bence Island to London 24 March 1687; T 70/360, 361; 546; 587; 1441, 1442. TNA.

52. T 70/11 Booker at James Island to London 20 July 1691; 10 December 1691; 25 January 1691/2. TNA.

53. Gray, *Gambia*, 111–12; T 70/946 25 February 1693; T 70/547. TNA.

54. T 70/11 Booker at James Island to London 14 March 1693, 23 April 1693; T 70/946 23 April 1693; T 70/547. TNA.

55. T 70/547; T 70/11 Booker to London, 25 April 1693. TNA. Accounts suggest at least twenty-two deaths among the captives.

56. T 70/1433 Factor at Barbados, May 1693. TNA.

57. T 70/834. At Jour, 16 May 1704, purchase of a "ballafue and drum to divert the Negroes at sea." TNA. *Balafon,* from *bala* and *fo* (to play), is a term used by early European observers to refer to the musical instrument. The drum was probably a *jembe,* which was often played alongside the *bala.* Eric Charry, *Mande Music: Traditional and Modern Music of the Maninka and Mandinka of Western Africa* (Chicago: University of Chicago Press, 2000), 133 45. On general instructions to "divert" slaves, see T 70/51, 6 July 1699. TNA.

58. T 70/13 Tozer at Gambia River to London 2 May 1704; T 70/1434 John Tozer of the *Postillion,* 10 June 1704. TNA.

59. Cultru, *Premier Voyage,* 195–96.

60. David Conrad, transl. and ed., *Sunjata: A West African Epic of the Mande Peoples* (Indianapolis: Hackett, 2004), xiv, xviii, 198, 200; Charry, *Mande Music,* 42. For readings on oral traditions in African history, see the Suggested Further Readings section.

61. Charry considers the *bala* to be one of the most potent symbols of Mande identity. Charry, *Mande Music,* 152.

62. T 70/14 Weaver at James Island to London, 10 June 1704. TNA.

63. On ransoming, see Sylviane Diouf, "The Last Resort: Redeeming Family and Friends," in S. Diouf, ed., *Fighting the Slave Trade: West African Strategies* (Athens: Ohio University Press, 2003): 81–100.

64. Coelho, *Descriptions,* chapter 3, p. 4 and chapter 4, p. 5.

65. T 70/546. TNA.

66. T 70/360, 361. TNA.

67. T 70/587, 588, 589. TNA.

68. Coelho, *Descriptions,* chapter 7, p. 10 and chapter 9, p. 18; Jean Boulègue, *Les Luso-Africains de Sénégambie* (Lisbon, 1989), 15; Duncan, *Atlantic Islands,* 212. RAC company slaves on the Gold Coast were called "castle slaves." See Rebecca Shumway, "Castle Slaves of the Eighteenth-Century Gold Coast (Ghana)," *Slavery and Abolition* 35, no. 1 (2014): 84–98.

69. T 70/546. TNA.

70. T 70/14 Bence Island to London, 26 January 1703. TNA.

71. T 70/544, 546, 547; 360, 361; 587, 588. T 70/16 Pierce at Bence Island to London, 21 February 1682. For the death of Leads, see T 70/832, f. 89. TNA.

72. See Judith A. Carney, *Black Rice: The African Origins of Rice Cultivation in the Americas* (Cambridge, MA: Harvard University Press, 2001), esp. 122–36.

73. Gambia and Combo, Balanta and Biafada, respectively.

74. T 70/360, 361; 546; 831. TNA.

75. T 70/1433 Jamaica to London, July 1689. TNA.

76. T 70/546; 832; 1441. TNA.

77. T 70/ 361; 587. TNA.

78. T 70/546. TNA.

79. T 70/1 Pierce at Bence Island to London 9 August 1670. TNA.

80. T 70/360, 361; 587, 589; T 70/163 13 Sept. 1692. TNA.

81. T 70/51 London to Gambia, 24 February 1702; T 70/15 London to Sierra Leone, 4 August 1702; T 70/1463 Cape Coast Castle Memorandum Book (1703–4). TNA.

Chapter 5: Free Agents and Local Hires

1. Davies, *Royal African Company,* 347–48.

2. T 70/17 Booker to London 17 June 1691. TNA.

3. Davies, *Royal African Company,* 252–53.

4. The iron bar was revalued on the Upper Guinea Coast at about two-thirds the prime cost of one bar in England. Davies, *Royal African Company,* 238.

5. T 70/546; 832; 1441, 1442. TNA. £11:13:1 at 20s to the £ comes to 233s and 1p. Converted to Bars at 6s per B, the local value is 38B, 5s, and 1p, or 38B:5:1.

6. T 70/832; 1441. TNA.

7. T 70/827, 829, 830, 831, 832, 833. TNA.

8. T 70/546; 832; 1441, 1442. TNA.

9. Whether this is the same "Billingary," or *be linger,* discussed in chapter 3 cannot be determined.

10. PROB 11/427/15, 13 May 1693. TNA.

11. T 70/1428, 24 July 1688; PROB 11/420/298, 1688; PROB 18/29/19, 1707. TNA.

12. PROB 5/737, 23 July 1696; PROB 18/29/19, 1707. TNA

13. Currency conversion from Measuring Worth, www.measuringworth.com .uk/compare/ (accessed 16 September 2015). It is important to point out that before the mid-eighteenth century, cash values of land and moveable goods were relatively close, which is in striking contrast to the sharply divergent values of them in our own times. See Erickson, *Women and Property,* 64–67.

14. C 6/524/181, 9 November 1697. TNA.

15. C 6/428/30, May 1697. TNA.

16. C 6/336/36, May 1703; PROB 32/47/97, February 1703/4. TNA.

17. Measuring Worth, www.measuringworth.com/uk/compare/ (accessed 5 September 2015).

18. T 70/1 22 June 1680, Horde at James Island to London; 2 March 1681 Kastell at James Island to London. TNA.

19. The name was usually spelled in the account books as "Franciscoe Lopus" and was anglicized in the RAC London correspondence as "Francis Lopus."

20. T 70/546. TNA.

21. T 70/11 Cleeve at James Island to London, 31 May 1684, 4 October 1684, 15 December 1684, 9 March 1685; T 70/50 London to Cleeve at James Island, 30 August 1687. TNA.

22. T 70/50 London to Booker at James Island, 7 January 1690; T 70/17 Booker at James Island to London, 17 June 1691. TNA.

23. Davies, *Royal African Company,* 69, 377, 379. See Davies's list of forty-one separate traders based in London, 372–73. Currency conversion from Measuring Worth, www.measuringworth.com/uk/compare/ (accessed 3 January 2016).

24. T 70/10 Cleeve at James Island to London, 24 August 1680; T 70/546; 831, 832; 1441. TNA. Cleeve referred to the specific Bur Saalum outpost as "Mangego"; RAC account books refer to Geregia as "Sangrigoe."

25. T 70/546; 1441, 1442. T 70/11 Booker at James Island to London, 12 February 1689; T 70/17 Booker at James Island to London, 19 August 1689. TNA.

26. Gray, *Gambia*, 97; George Brooks, *Eurafricans in Western Africa: Commerce, Social Status, Gender, and Religious Observance from the Sixteenth to the Eighteenth Century* (Athens: Ohio University Press, 2003), 154.

27. Cultru, *Premier Voyage*, 189–99. T 70/1441, 24 June 1686. TNA.

28. Cultru, *Premier Voyage*, 200–205.

29. Gray, *Gambia*, 98. T 70/83 20 January 1691, 27 February 1691. T 70/1428. TNA. For a brief description of what London's debtor's prisons were like, see M. Roth, *Prisons and Prison Systems: A Global Encyclopedia* (Westport, CT: Greenwood, 2006), 105–6. A view of the Wood Street Compter, published in 1793, can be seen in Walter Thornbury, "Cheapside: Northern Tributaries, Wood Street," in *Old and New London*, vol. 1 (London, 1878), 364–74. Online at www.british-history.ac.uk /old-new-london/vol1/pp364-374 (accessed 10 December 2014).

30. T 70/589. TNA.

31. T 70/589; 882; 1442, 1443. TNA.

32. For his letter of appointment as agent, see Fyfe, *Sierra Leone Inheritance*, 62–65.

33. T 70/11 Corker at York Island to London, 9 October 1695; T 70/21 Corker at York Island to London, 21 June 1697; T 70/50 London to Corker, 28 January 1697; T 70/1443 22 October 1697. TNA.

34. T 70/50 London to Corker, 21 December 1697; London to Corker, 14 January 1698. TNA.

35. Davies, *Royal African Company*, 132–35. T 70/11 Corker at Sherbro to London, 31 July 1698. TNA.

36. The 1698 act of Parliament opened up England's Africa trade to separate traders who were to pay a 10% duty on their English exports to support the RAC's forts. The RAC monopoly ended in 1712 when the 1698 act expired. Davies, *Royal African Company*, 46.

37. T 70/51 London to Corker and Bowman at York Island, 12 July 1698; 6 September 1698; 13 September 1698; 25 October 1698; London to Corker at Gambia, 16 September 1698; 25 October 1698. T 70/589; 1443. TNA. Corker's son Thomas would have been probably about six or seven at this time. Benjamin and Lawrence Corker, who accompanied Corker on a trading voyage north to Gambia in October of 1697, could have been either his sons or nephews. They were not included in the lists of RAC employees. T 70/1443 Voyage to Gambia in *Sherbro* and *Exchange*. TNA.

38. T 70/51 London to Corker and Pindar at James Island, 3 October 1699. T 70/1434 Gershaw Report, 28 November 1699. TNA.

39. Davies, *Royal African Company*, 386. T 70/548, 10 May 1699. TNA.

40. T 70/51 London to Pindar at James Island, 13 February 1700. TNA.

41. T 70/51 Declaration James Island, 20 February 1700; London to Sherbro, 16 April 1700. T 70/50 London to Corker at James Island, 20 February 1700. T 70/591;

1445. TNA. Gray, *Gambia*, 131; Fyfe, *Sierra Leone Inheritance*, 62. There is confusion in the historical literature between the lives and chronologies of Thomas Corker Sr. and Jr.

42. T 70/11 Booker to London, 25 April 1690, 25 January 1692, 25 April 1693; T 70/17 Booker to London 17 June 1691. T 70/831. TNA.

43. T 70/546; 832. TNA. John Bull and James Bull served on the RAC Court of Assistants in London. Davies, *Royal African Company*, 379.

44. For readings on Senhoras/Women Traders, see the Suggested Further Readings section.

45. T 70/546; 832, 833, 834; 1441; T 70/51 London to James Island, 3 October 1699. TNA.

46. T 70/831, 832; 1441. TNA.

47. T 70/832, 834; 1441, 1442, 1443, 1445. TNA.

48. T 70/828, 829. TNA. For an oral tradition see James Roques and M. Luseni, "The Origin of the Kpakas or Rogers," *Sierra Leone Studies* Old Series (December 1929): 59–62.

49. T 70/652, 653; 1441, 1442. TNA.

50. The "Marry" factory was probably at Gallinas, on the Moa River. Gallinas was the main location associated with the Rogers descent group.

51. T 70/589, 590; 881; 1442, 1443; 611. TNA.

52. Adam Jones, "White Roots: Written and Oral Testimony on the 'first' Mr. Rogers," *History in Africa* 10 (1983): 151–62.

53. T 70/360; 587, 588, 589; 880; 1441. TNA.

54. For readings on Mixed Euro-African or "Creole" culture, see the Suggested Further Readings section.

55. T 70/587, 588, 589; 880; 1441, 1442. TNA.

56. T 70/11 Corker at Sherbro to London, 17 May 1696; T 70/21 Corker at Sherbro to London, 21 June 1697. TNA.

57. T 70/588; 1441, 1442. TNA.

58. T 70/589, 590; 1442. TNA.

59. For an overview of these problems as experienced by the Royal Navy, see N. A. M. Rodger, *The Command of the Ocean: A Naval History of Britain, 1649–1815* (New York: W. W. Norton, 2005), 192–94.

60. T 70/611 1698–99. TNA. Matthews, *A Voyage to the River Sierra-Leone*, 53–54; Duncan, *Atlantic Islands*, 161; Toby Green, "The Emergence of a Mixed Society in Cape Verde in the Seventeenth Century," in *Brokers of Change: Atlantic Commerce and Cultures in Pre-Colonial Western Africa*, ed. T. Green (Oxford: Oxford University Press, 2012), 217–36.

61. T 70/831, 832. TNA. He is referred to in the RAC records as "More Mamadue" but is no longer mentioned after 1688. *Mori* is a Mandinka word for a learned Muslim or Muslim teacher. Delafosse, *La langue mandingue*, 2:512–13.

62. Curtin, *Economic Change*, 218–19.

63. There was usually only one cow for every ten head of cattle. Moore, *Travels*, 16–17.

64. Moore, *Travels*, 22–25. Fulbe in the vicinity of the lower Gambia were known as Fula by speakers of Mandinka. Moore's narrative renders Fula as "Pholey."

65. T 70/832. TNA. Moore, *Travels*, 32, 47.

66. T 70/831, 832. TNA.

67. For the remarkable story of a Muslim Fulbe man who was robbed and sold into slavery, shipped to America, later freed and hired by the RAC to lead a trading expedition in Senegambia, see "Ayuba Suleiman Diallo of Bondu," in *Africa Remembered: Narratives by West Africans from the Era of the Slave Trade*, ed. Philip Curtin (Madison: University of Wisconsin Press, 1967), 17–59.

68. Manuel Álvares, *Ethiopia Minor and a Geographical Account of the Province of Sierra Leone (c. 1615)*, trans. P. E. H. Hair, typescript, Department of History, University of Liverpool (September 1990), part 2, chapter 1, pp. 5, 8, 17; Donelha, *Account of Sierra Leone*, 89–95, 353; Hair, Jones, and Law, *Barbot on Guinea*, 2:184, 187–88, 214–15. European sources made erroneous references to lions and mistakenly called antelope "deer."

69. Both Bonna and Simon were sometimes referred to as "black" in the company records. Bonna was probably a Temne or Bullom name. A century later, a young boy named Bonna was forced onto a slave ship anchored at Sherbro in 1817; he and his fellow slaves were rescued and later liberated in an international court in Freetown, Sierra Leone. See the African Names Database, www.slavevoyages.org (accessed 21 May 2015).

70. T 70/880; 1441. TNA. For hunting equipment, see Álvares, *Ethiopia Minor*, part 2, chapter 2, p. 5.

71. T 70/589; 881, 882; 1442, 1443. TNA.

72. Álvares, *Ethiopia Minor*, part 2, chapter 2, pp. 4–5; Hair, Jones, and Law, *Barbot on Guinea*, vol. 2, 217–18; Jones, *Brandenburg Sources*, 26.

73. T 70/587; 878, 880. TNA. An early seventeenth-century description of the Sande society referred to it as the "society of Menas," the term "menas" supposedly designating the young female initiates. Álvares, *Ethiopia Minor*, part 2, chapter 7, pp. 2–4. For an overview of its importance and influence on the positions of women in the region, see Carol MacCormack, "Slaves, Slave Owners, and Slave Dealers: Sherbro Coast and Hinterland," in *Women and Slavery in Africa*, ed. Claire Robertson and Martin Klein (Madison: University of Wisconsin Press, 1983), 271–94.

74. T 70/588, 589, 590; 881; 1442. TNA.

75. An indenture for "Harry the Black" as carpenter's apprentice was entered into the RAC security book on 18 February 1680. T 70/1428. TNA.

76. T 70/1 Pierce at Bence Island to London, 24 December 1678. T 70/878; 1441, 1442, 1445. TNA. His RAC account refers to him as "Black Harry," but he was misnamed several times as "Black Henry." Pierce suggested that his "poor black boy" was not his own biological child. After Pierce's death sometime in 1681, his widow and little son and daughter by her were seen still living on Bence Island in 1682 by a visiting merchant from Brandenburg. Jones, *Brandenburg Sources*, 27.

77. T 70/11, 11 March 1685, Platt at Sherbro to London; 24 January 1692, Gibson at Sherbro to London. TNA.

78. CO 700/SierraLeone3. TNA. Álvares, *Ethiopia Minor*, part 2, chapter 1, pp. 6–7, 18; Hair, Jones, and Law, *Barbot on Guinea*, 1:189, 218.

79. T 70/323; 946; 1433, 1442, 1445. TNA. *Voyages: The Trans-Atlantic Slave Trade Database* does not include Ashby's 1706 voyage of the *Dorothy*. It took place in between his voyages of 1705 and 1707–8, which are listed in the database as #24106 and #9750, respectively. Another voyage, #24105, is a duplication of voyage #24106 (accessed 20 May 2015).

80. The War of the Spanish Succession lasted from 1701 to 1713. Coelho gives a brief summary of major sites for ship repair in northern Guinea: Cassan on the Gambia River; a town of runaway black shipwrights and blacksmiths on the Casamance River; Cacheu; and Bissau. Coelho, chapter 2, p. 15; chapter 3, p. 4; chapter 5, p. 11.

Conclusion: Anglo-African Relations

1. Paul E. Lovejoy, "The Upper Guinea Coast and the Trans-Atlantic Slave Trade Database," *African Economic History* 38 (2010): 16, 27n22.

2. For a useful discussion of English attitudes toward Africans in pre-1650 primary sources, see P. E. H. Hair, "Attitudes to Africans in English Primary Sources on Guinea up to 1650," *History in Africa* 26 (1999): 43–68. For introductions to the development of pseudoscientific race ideologies, see the Suggested Further Readings section.

3. Frederick Forbes, *Six Months' Service in the African Blockade* (1849; reprint, London: Dawsons, 1969), frontispiece map; Curtin, *Image of Africa*, 457–78.

Works Cited

Archival Sources

London Metropolitan Archives, London, UK (LMA)
  Parish Registers:
    St. James, Duke's Place, City of London
    St. Dunstan and All Saints, Stepney
The British Library, London, UK
  Petitions to the House of Commons
  "The Case of the Pewterers of England, as to the Exportation of Pewter" (1690? [1711])
The National Archives, Kew, UK (TNA)
  Court of Chancery, Litigation: Chancery Equity Suits after 1558 (C 6 and 7)
  Prerogative Court of Canterbury: Wills and Probate (PROB 5, 11, 18, 32, 36)
  Treasury Records, T 70 series

Published Contemporary Sources and Documents

Adams, John. *Sketches Taken during Ten Voyages to Africa, between the Years 1786 and 1800.* New York: Johnson Reprint, 1970. Reprint of 1822 edition.

Almada, André Álvares de. *Brief Treatise on the Rivers of Guinea.* Translated and edited by P. E. H. Hair. Typescript. Department of History, University of Liverpool, July 1984.

Álvares, Manuel. *Ethiopia Minor and a Geographical Account of the Province of Sierra Leone (c. 1615).* Translated by P. E. H. Hair. Typescript. Department of History, University of Liverpool, September 1990.

Anonymous. "Relations des îles et environs des rivières de Bresalme, Gambie, Zamenée, S. Domingue, Gève, et autres, etc." In *Les voyages du sieur Le Maire aux îles Canaries, Cap-Verd, Sénégal, et Gambie,* edited by Jacques-Joseph le Maire et al., 181–205. Paris: Collombat, 1695.

Barbot, John. "A Description of the Coasts of North and South Guinea." In *A Collection of Voyages and Travels,* vol. 5, edited by Awnsham Churchill and John Churchill. London: John Walthoe, 1732.

Behrendt, Stephen, Antera Duke, A. J. H. Latham, and David Northrup. *The Diary of Antera Duke, an Eighteenth-Century African Slave Trader.* Oxford: Oxford University Press, 2010.

Buisseret, David, ed. *Jamaica in 1687. The Taylor Manuscript at the National Library of Jamaica.* Kingston: University of West Indies Press, 2008.

Cultru, Prosper, ed. *Premier voyage de Sieur de la Courbe fait á la Coste d'Afrique en 1685*. Paris: E. Champion, 1913.

Donelha, André. *An Account of Sierra Leone and the Rivers of Guinea of Cape Verde (1625)*. Translated and edited by A. Teixeira da Mota and P. E. H. Hair. Lisbon: Junta de Investigações Científicas do Ultramar, 1977.

Forbes, Frederick. *Six Months' Service in the African Blockade*. London: Dawsons of Pall Mall, 1969. Reprint of 1849 edition.

Froger, François. *Relation d'un voyage fait en 1695, 1696, et 1697*. Paris: N. le Gras, 1700. Second edition.

Fyfe, Christopher. *Sierra Leone Inheritance*. London: Oxford University Press, 1964.

Hair, P. E. H. "Sources on Early Sierra Leone: (2) Andrade (1582), Ruiters (1623), Carvalho (1632[5])." *Africana Research Bulletin* 5, no. 1 (1974): 47–56.

Hair, P. E. H., Adam Jones, and Robin Law, trans. and eds. *Barbot on Guinea: The Writings of Jean Barbot on West Africa 1678–1712*. 2 vols. London: The Hakluyt Society, 1992.

Jobson, Richard. *The Discovery of River Gambra (1623)*. Edited by D. P. Gamble and P. E. H. Hair. London: The Hakluyt Society, 1999.

Jones, Adam, trans. *Brandenburg Sources for West African History, 1680–1700*. Stuttgart: Franz Steiner, 1985.

Jones, Adam, and P. E. H. Hair. "Sources on Early Sierra Leone: (11) Brun (1624)." *Africana Research Bulletin* 7, no. 3 (1977): 52–64.

Kennedy, John. *A History of the Parish of Leyton, Essex*. Leyton, UK: Phelps Brothers, 1894.

Law, Robin, ed. *The English in West Africa, 1681–83*. Oxford: Oxford University Press, 1997.

———, ed. *The English in West Africa, 1685–1688*. Oxford: Oxford University Press, 2001.

———, ed. *The English in West Africa, 1691–1699*. Oxford: Oxford University Press, 2006.

Lemos Coelho, Francisco de. *Description of the Coast of Guinea (1684)*. Translated by P. E. H. Hair. Typescript. Department of History, University of Liverpool, October 1985.

Levtzion, Nehemia, and J. F. P. Hopkins, trans. and eds. *Corpus of Early Arabic Sources for West African History*. Cambridge: Cambridge University Press, 1981.

Matthews, John. *A Voyage to the River Sierra-Leone, on the Coast of Africa*. London: B. White and Son, 1788.

Moore, Francis. *Travels into the Inland Parts of Africa*. London: Henry and Cave, 1738. Second edition.

Newitt, Malyn. *The Portuguese in West Africa, 1415–1670: A Documentary History*. Cambridge: Cambridge University Press, 2010.

Paris, François de. *Voyage to the Coast of Africa (1682 and 1683)*. Translated and edited by Aimery Caron. Madison, WI: African Studies Program, 2001.

Walckenaer, C. A. "Second voyage de Brüe sur le Sénégal, jusqu'au royaume de Galam . . . en 1698." In *Histoire générale des voyages*, by C. A. Walckenaer, vol. 3, book 4, chapter 10. Paris: Chez Lefèvre, 1826.

Secondary Sources

Anonymous. *Dictionnaire français-malinké et malinké-français*. Conakry: Mission des PP du Saint-Espirit, 1906.

Arkell, A. J. "Cambay and the Bead Trade." *Antiquity* 10, no. 39 (1936): 292–305.

Barry, Boubacar. *Senegambia and the Atlantic Slave Trade*. Cambridge: Cambridge University Press, 1998. Translation of 1988 French edition.

Behrendt, Stephen. "Ecology, Seasonality, and the Transatlantic Slave Trade." In *Soundings in Atlantic History: Latent Structures and Intellectual Currents, 1500–1830*, edited by Bernard Bailyn and Patricia Denault, 44–85, 461–85. Cambridge, MA: Harvard University Press, 2009.

Berg, Maxine, Pat Hudson, and Michael Sonenscher. "Manufacture in Town and Country before the Factory." In *Manufacture in Town and Country before the Factory*, edited by Maxine Berg et al., 1–32. Cambridge: Cambridge University Press, 1983.

Blackmore, Howard L. *A Dictionary of London Gunmakers, 1350–1850*. Oxford: Phaidon Christies's, 1986.

Bolland, Rita. *Tellem Textiles: Archaeological Finds from Burial Caves in Mali's Bandiagara Cliff*. Amsterdam: Tropenmuseum, 1991.

Bravmann, René. *African Islam*. Washington, DC: Smithsonian Institution Press, 1983.

Brooks, George. *Landlords and Strangers: Ecology, Society, and Trade in Western Africa, 1000–1630*. Boulder, CO: Westview Press, 1993.

———. *Eurafricans in Western Africa: Commerce, Social Status, Gender, and Religious Observance from the Sixteenth to the Eighteenth Century*. Athens: Ohio University Press, 2003.

Carney, Judith A. *Black Rice: The African Origins of Rice Cultivation in the Americas*. Cambridge, MA: Harvard University Press, 2001.

Charry, Eric. *Mande Music: Traditional and Modern Music of the Maninka and Mandinka of Western Africa*. Chicago: University of Chicago Press, 2000.

Chaudhuri, K. N. "The Structure of the Indian Textile Industry in the Seventeenth and Eighteenth Centuries." In *Technology and European Overseas Enterprise*, edited by Michael Adas, 343–98. Aldershot, UK: Variorum, 1996.

Conrad, David, trans. and ed. *Sunjata: A West African Epic of the Mande Peoples*. Indianapolis: Hackett, 2004.

Cooper, John S. *For Commonwealth and Crown: English Gunmakers of the Seventeenth Century*. Gillingham: Wilson Hunt, 1993.

Cotterell, Howard H. *Old Pewter: Its Makers and Marks*. London: B. T. Batsford, 1929.

Crétois, Léonce. *Dictionnaire sereer-français*. 6 vols. Dakar: Centre de Linguistique, 1972–77.

Curtin, Philip. *The Image of Africa: British Ideas and Action, 1780–1850*. Madison: University of Wisconsin Press, 1964.

———. *Africa Remembered: Narratives by West Africans from the Era of the Slave Trade*. Madison: University of Wisconsin Press, 1967.

———. *Economic Change in Precolonial Africa: Senegambia in the Era of the Slave Trade.* Madison: University of Wisconsin Press, 1975.

Curtin, Philip, and Jan Vansina. "Sources of the Nineteenth Century Atlantic Slave Trade." *Journal of African History* 5, no. 2 (1964): 185–208.

Dalby, David. "Provisional Identification of Languages in the Polyglotta Africana." *Sierra Leone Language Review* 3 (1964): 83–90.

Dalziel, J. M. *The Useful Plants of West Tropical Africa.* London: Crown Agents, 1937.

Davies, K. G. *The Royal African Company.* New York: Octagon Books, 1975. Reprint of 1957 edition.

———. "The Living and the Dead: White Mortality in West Africa, 1684–1732." In *Race and Slavery in the Western Hemisphere: Quantitative Studies,* edited by Stanley Engerman, Eugene Genovese, and Alan Adamson, 83–98. Princeton, NJ: Princeton University Press, 1975.

Delafosse, Maurice. *La langue mandingue et ses dialectes.* 2 vols. Paris: Geuthner, 1955.

Diouf, Jean. *Dictionnaire wolof-français et français-wolof.* Paris: Karthala, 2003.

Diouf, Sylviane. "The Last Resort: Redeeming Family and Friends." In *Fighting the Slave Trade: West African Strategies,* edited by S. Diouf, 81–100. Athens: Ohio University Press, 2003.

Duncan, T. Bentley. *Atlantic Islands: Madeira, the Azores, and the Cape Verdes in Seventeenth Century Commerce and Navigation.* Chicago: University of Chicago Press, 1972.

Dunn, Richard S. *Sugar and Slaves: The Rise of the Planter Class in the English West Indies, 1624–1713.* Chapel Hill: University of North Carolina Press, 1972.

Durand, Oswald. "Les industries locales au Fouta." *Bulletin du Comité d'études historiques et scientifiques de l'Afrique occidentale française* 15 (1932): 42–71.

Eltis, David. "The British Transatlantic Slave Trade before 1714." In *The Lesser Antilles in the Age of European Expansion,* edited by Robert Paquette and Stanley Engerman, 182–205 Gainesville: University Press of Florida, 1996.

Erickson, Amy Louise. *Women and Property in Early Modern England.* London: Routledge, 1993.

Evans, Chris, and Göran Rydén. *Baltic Iron in the Atlantic World in the 18th Century.* Leiden: Brill, 2007.

Fal, Arame, Rosine Santos, and J. L. Doneux. *Dictionnaire wolof-français.* Paris: Karthala, 1990.

Florén, Anders, et al. "The Social Organization of Work at Mines, Furnaces, and Forges." In *Ironmaking Societies: Early Industrial Development in Sweden and Russia, 1600-1900,* edited by Maria Ågren, 61–140. Oxford: Berghahn Books, 1998.

Frank, Barbara E. "Soninke *Garankéw* and Bamana-Malinke *Jeliw*: Mande Leatherworkers, Identity, and the Diaspora." In *Status and Identity in West Africa: Nyamakalaw of Mande,* edited by David C. Conrad and Barbara E. Frank, 133–50. Bloomington: Indiana University Press, 1995.

——. *Mande Potters and Leather-Workers: Art and Heritage in West Africa*. Washington, DC: Smithsonian Institution Press, 1998.

Garland, Charles, and Herbert S. Klein. "The Allotment of Space for Slaves aboard Eighteenth-Century British Slave Ships." *William and Mary Quarterly* 42, no. 2 (1985): 238–48.

Garrard, Timothy. *Akan Weights and the Gold Trade*. London: Longman, 1980.

Giesing, C., and V. Vydrine. *Ta:rikh Mandinka de Bijini (Guinea-Bissau)*. Leiden: Brill, 2007.

Gray, John. *A History of The Gambia*. New York: Barnes and Noble, 1966. Reprint of 1940 edition.

Green, Toby. *The Rise of the Trans-Atlantic Slave Trade in Western Africa, 1300–1589*. Cambridge: Cambridge University Press, 2012.

——. "The Emergence of a Mixed Society in Cape Verde in the Seventeenth Century." In *Brokers of Change: Atlantic Commerce and Cultures in Precolonial Western Africa*, edited by Toby Green, 217–36. Oxford: Oxford University Press, 2012.

Hair, P. E. H. "The Enslavement of Koelle's Informants." *Journal of African History* 6, no. 2 (1965): 193–201.

——. "Attitudes to Africans in English Primary Sources on Guinea up to 1650." *History in Africa* 26 (1999): 43–68.

Hawthorne, Walter. *Planting Rice and Harvesting Slaves: Transformations along the Guinea-Bissau Coast, 1400–1900*. Portsmouth, NH: Heinemann, 2003.

Hildebrand, Karl-Gustaf. *Swedish Iron in the 17th and 18th Centuries: Export Industry before the Industrialization*. Stockholm: Jernkontorets, 1992.

Hiskett, Mervyn. *The Course of Islam in Africa*. Edinburgh: Edinburgh University Press, 1994.

Hogendorn, Jan, and Marion Johnson. *The Shell Money of the Slave Trade*. Cambridge: Cambridge University Press, 1986.

Hogendorn, Jan S., and Henry A. Gemery. "The 'Hidden Half' of the Anglo-African Trade in the Eighteenth Century: The Significance of Marion Johnson's Research." In *West African Economic and Social History: Studies in Memory of Marion Johnson*, edited by David Henige and T. C. McCaskie, 81–91. Madison: University of Wisconsin African Studies Program, 1990.

Hopkins, A. G. *An Economic History of West Africa*. New York: Columbia University Press, 1973.

Horner, John. *The Linen Trade of Europe before the Spinning Wheel*. Belfast: McCaw, Stevenson, and Orr, 1920.

Hoskins, W. G. *Industry, Trade, and People in Exeter, 1688–1800*. Manchester: Manchester University Press, 1935.

Insoll, Timothy, and Thurstan Shaw. "Gao and Igbo-Ukwu: Beads, Interregional Trade, and Beyond." *African Archaeological Review* 14, no. 1 (1997): 9–23.

Jeremy, David. "British and American Yarn Count Systems: An Historical Analysis." *Business History Review* 45, no. 3 (1971): 336–68.

Johnson, Marion. "The Ounce in Eighteenth-Century West African Trade." *Journal of African History* 7, no. 2 (1966): 197–214.

———. "The Cowrie Currencies of West Africa, Part I." *Journal of African History* 11, no. 1 (1970): 17–49.

Jones, Adam. "White Roots: Written and Oral Testimony on the 'First' Mr. Rogers." *History in Africa* 10 (1983): 151–62.

Kecskési, Maria. *African Masterpieces and Selected Works from Munich: The Staatliches Museum für Völkerkunde.* New York: The Center for African Art, 1987.

Kisch, Herbert. "The Textile Industries in Silesia and the Rhineland: A Comparative Study in Industrialization." In *The Textile Industries,* edited by D. T. Jenkins, 351–74. Oxford: Blackwell Publishers, 1994.

Klein, Herbert S., Stanley L. Engerman, Robin Haines, and Ralph Shlomowitz. "Transoceanic Mortality: The Slave Trade in Comparative Perspective." *William and Mary Quarterly* 58, no. 1 (2001): 93–118.

Klein, Martin. *Islam and Imperialism in Senegal: Sine-Saloum, 1847–1914.* Stanford, CA: Stanford University Press, 1968.

Kriger, Colleen E. *Cloth in West African History.* Landham, MD: AltaMira Press, 2006.

———. "'Guinea Cloth': Production and Consumption of Cotton Textiles in West Africa before and during the Atlantic Slave Trade." In *The Spinning World: A Global History of Cotton Textiles, 1200–1850,* edited by Giorgio Riello and Prasannan Parthasarathi, 105–26. Oxford: Oxford University Press, 2009.

———. "The Importance of Mande Textiles in the African Side of the Atlantic Trade, ca. 1680–1710." *Journal of Mande Studies* 11 (2009): 1–21.

———. "Mapping the History of Cotton Textile Production in Precolonial West Africa." *African Economic History* 33 (2005): 87–116.

———. "'Our Indico Designe': Planting and Processing Indigo for Export, Upper Guinea Coast, 1684–1702." In *Commercial Agriculture, the Slave Trade and Slavery in Atlantic Africa,* edited by Robin Law, Suzanne Schwarz, and Silke Strickrodt, 98–115. Woodbridge, Suffolk: James Currey Press, 2013.

Law, Robin. "'There's Nothing Grows in the West Indies but Will Grow Here': Dutch and English Projects of Plantation Agriculture on the Gold Coast, 1650s–1780s." In *Commercial Agriculture, the Slave Trade and Slavery in Atlantic Africa,* edited by Robin Law, Suzanne Schwarz, and Silke Strickrodt, 158–79. Woodbridge, Suffolk: James Currey Press, 2013.

Lawrence, A. W. *Trade Castles and Forts of West Africa.* London: J. Cape, 1963.

Lovejoy, Paul E. "The Upper Guinea Coast and the Trans-Atlantic Slave Trade Database." *African Economic History* 38 (2010): 1–27.

Lydon, Ghislaine. *On Trans-Saharan Trails: Islamic Law, Trade Networks, and Cross-Cultural Exchange in Nineteenth Century Western Africa.* Cambridge: Cambridge University Press, 2009.

MacCormack, Carol. "Slaves, Slave Owners, and Slave Dealers: Sherbro Coast and Hinterland." In *Women and Slavery in Africa,* edited by Claire Robertson and Martin Klein, 271–94. Madison: University of Wisconsin Press, 1983.

McIntosh, Roderick J. *Ancient Middle Niger: Urbanism and the Self-Organizing Landscape.* Cambridge: Cambridge University Press, 2005.

Mark, Peter. *"Portuguese" Style and Luso-African Identity: Precolonial Senegambia, Sixteenth-Nineteenth Centuries.* Bloomington: Indiana University Press, 2002.

———. "'Bini, Vidi, Vici'—On the Misuse of 'Style' in the Analyses of Sixteenth Century Luso-African Ivories." *History in Africa* 42 (2015): 323–34.

Menard, Russell R. *Sweet Negotiations: Sugar, Slavery, and Plantation Agriculture in Early Barbados.* Charlottesville: University of Virginia Press, 2006.

Montgomery, Florence. *Textiles in America, 1650–1870.* New York: W. W. Norton, 2007.

Moraes, Nize Isabel de. "Le commerce des peaux à la Petite Côte au XVIIe siècle (Sénégambie)." *Notes africaines* 134 (April 1972): 37–56 and 136 (October 1972): 111–16.

Newson, Linda, and Susie Minchin. *From Capture to Sale: The Portuguese Slave Trade to Spanish South America in the Early Seventeenth Century.* Leiden: Brill, 2007.

Patterson, Orlando. *Slavery and Social Death: A Comparative Study.* Cambridge, MA: Harvard University Press, 1982.

Peroz, Etienne. *Dictionnaire français-mandingue.* Paris: J. D. Maillard, 1891.

Pole, Len. "Recent Developments in Iron-Working Research in West Africa." In *West African Archaeology: New Developments, New Perspectives,* edited by Philip Allsworth-Jones, 53–65. Oxford: British Archaeological Reports, 2010.

Portères, Roland. "La monnaie de fer dans l'Ouest-Africain au XX siècle." *Recherches africaines* 4 (1960): 3–13.

Prussin, Labelle. *Hatumere: Islamic Design in West Africa.* Berkeley: University of California Press, 1986.

Rodger, N. A. M. *The Command of the Ocean: A Naval History of Britain, 1649–1815.* New York: W. W. Norton, 2005.

Rodney, Walter. *A History of the Upper Guinea Coast, 1545–1800.* Oxford: Clarendon Press, 1970.

Roques, James, and M. Luseni. "The Origin of the Kpakas or Rogers." *Sierra Leone Studies* Old Series (December 1929): 59–62.

Roth, Mitchel. *Prisons and Prison Systems: A Global Encyclopedia.* Westport, CT: Greenwood, 2006.

Rugemer, Edward B. "The Development of Mastery and Race in the Comprehensive Slave Codes of the Greater Caribbean during the Seventeenth Century." *William and Mary Quarterly* 70, no. 3 (2013): 429–58.

Rydén, Göran, and Maria Ågren. *Ironmaking in Sweden and Russia: A Survey of the Social Organization of Iron Production before 1900.* Uppsala: Uppsala University Department of History, 1993.

Schlumbohm, Jürgen. "Seasonal Fluctuations and Social Division of Labour: Rural Linen Production in the Osnabrück and Bielefeld Regions and the Urban Woollen Industry in the Niederlausitz (c.1770–c.1850)." In *Manufacture in Town and Country before the Factory,* edited by Maxine Berg et al., 92–123. Cambridge: Cambridge University Press, 1983.

Searing, James. *West African Slavery and Atlantic Commerce: The Senegal River Valley, 1700–1860.* Cambridge: Cambridge University Press, 1993.

Shaw, Thurstan. *Igbo-Ukwu: An Account of Archaeological Discoveries in Eastern Nigeria.* Evanston, IL: Northwestern University Press, 1970.

Shumway, Rebecca. "Castle Slaves of the Eighteenth-Century Gold Coast (Ghana)." *Slavery and Abolition* 35, no. 1 (2014): 84–98.

Stephens, W. B. *Seventeenth-Century Exeter: A Study of Industrial and Commercial Development, 1625–1688.* Exeter: University of Exeter, 1958.

Stillman, Yedida Kalfon. *Arab Dress: A Short History.* Leiden: Brill, 2000.

Stone, Thora. "The Journey of Cornelius Hodges in Senegambia, 1689–90." *English Historical Review* 39, no. 153 (January 1924): 89–95.

Thomasson, Gordon C. "'Primitive' Kpelle Steelmaking: A High Technology Indigenous Knowledge System for Liberia's Future?" *Liberian Studies Journal* 12, no. 2 (1987): 149–64.

Welch, Charles. *History of the Worshipful Company of Pewterers of the City of London.* 2 vols. London: Blades, 1902.

Wendt, Ian C. "Four Centuries of Decline? Understanding the Changing Structure of the South Indian Textile Industry." In *How India Clothed the World: The World of South Asian Textiles, 1500–1850,* edited by Giorgio Riello and Tirthankar Roy, 193–215. Leiden: Brill, 2009.

White, Susan L. "Iron Production and Iron Trade in Northern and Central Liberia: History of a Major Indigenous Technology." Paper presented at the Liberian Studies Conference, Madison, Wisconsin, April 1974.

Williams, Eric. *Capitalism and Slavery.* Chapel Hill: University of North Carolina Press, 1944.

Wright, Donald R. "Niumi: The History of a Western Mandinka State through the Eighteenth Century." PhD diss., Indiana University, 1976.

———. "Darbo Jula: The Role of a Mandinka Jula Clan in the Long-Distance Trade of the Gambia River and its Hinterland." *African Economic History* 3 (1977): 33–45.

———. *The World and a Very Small Place in Africa: A History of Globalization in Niumi, The Gambia.* 2nd ed. Armonk, NY: M. E. Sharpe, 2004.

———. "The Effect of Alex Haley's *Roots* on How Gambians Remember the Atlantic Slave Trade." *History in Africa* 38 (2011): 295–318.

Online Sources

African Names Database. http://www.slavevoyages.org.

Code Noir. English translation from the French. http://chmn.gmu.edu/revolution/d/335/.

Historical Thinking Project. historybenchmarks.ca.

Jansen, P. C. M., and D. Cardon, eds. *PROTA, Plant Resources of Tropical Africa.* Wageningen, the Netherlands, 2005. http://database.prota.org/search.htm.

Magnavita, Sonja. "Initial Encounters: Seeking Traces of Ancient Trade Connections between Western Africa and the Wider World." *Afriques* [online] 4 (2013). http://afriques.revues.org/1145.

Measuring Worth—Relative Worth Comparators and Data Sets. https://www
.measuringworth.com/.

Stanford History Education Group. https://sheg.stanford.edu.

Styles, John. "East Meets West: Everyday Fashion in Eighteenth-Century London."
Presentation given at the Interwoven Globe Symposium, Metropolitan Museum
of Art, New York City, October 4, 2013. www.metmuseum.org/metmedia/video
/lectures/interwoven-globe-symposium-6.

Thornbury, Walter. "Cheapside: Northern Tributaries, Wood Street." In *Old and
New London,* vol. 1 (London, 1878): 364–74, online at www.british-history.ac.uk
/old-new-london/vol1/pp364-374.

Voyages: The Trans-Atlantic Slave Trade Database. 2009. http://www.slavevoyages.org.

Film

Toepke, Alvaro, and Angel Serrano, directors. *The Language You Cry In.* San Francisco: California Newsreel, 1998.

Index

alcohol, 31, 34, 73
Almada, André Álvares de, observations
    written by, 15, 18, 22, 28–29
ancient Ghana, 16–17
Anglo-African men: Bridgman, Richard,
    80, 102, 161; Corker, Thomas, Jr., 164;
    Cumberbatch, John, sons of, 172–75;
    Rogers, Zachary, sons of, 170–72;
    Skinner, James and Thomas, 76, 159;
    Skinner, Matthew, 76, 80, 159, 161, 173
Arabic, sources written in, 10–11, 16–22
arbitrage trading: coastal, by ship,
    25–26; definition of, 25; overland, by
    caravan, 26–28; slaves in, 108–9
archaeological sites, West African: ancient
    Benin, 11; Gao, 11; Igbo-Ukwu, 10–11;
    Jenne-jeno, 14; Ma'den Ijafen, 11, 19;
    Sanga, 20–21
artisans, European, 37, 39–46, 64, 146, 160
artisans, South Asian, 39
artisans, West African: carpenters, 182;
    ironworkers, 14–16, 30; leather-
    workers, 62–63, 207n58; tailors,
    173; textile producers, 20–23; use of
    captive labor, 109–12
assortment bargaining: definition of,
    23–24; descriptions of, 24–28
Atlantic trade: crossings of Atlantic, 125,
    132; multicultural social networks
    in, 4; opening up of, 5–6, 37; slave
    preferences in, 109; on Upper Guinea
    Coast, 48, 51–52, 54, 57–59

Baltic trade, 37, 42, 44, 48, 63
Barbot, Jean, observations written by, 32–34
Benin Kingdom, 11, 47

bilad al-sudan, Land of the Black People,
    9, 17
Billingary, RAC account of a *linger,* 99–
    100, 102, 149. *See also* La Belinguère
Black Harry, RAC employee, 182–83
Blow, William, RAC employee, 128, 129,
    169–70
Bonna, RAC employee, 178–80
Booker, Hope, child/house slave of John
    Booker, 2, 87, 149, 169
Booker, John, RAC employee, 1, 2, 87,
    129–31, 157, 167; estate of, 149–52
brandy: as customs payment, 73, 76,
    78; as gift, 34, 137; as payment for
    curing sale slaves, 120; as payment of
    salary, 156; as reward for returning
    runaways, 135; in slave ships'
    provisions, 124; in trade assortments,
    91, 100
bridewealth, 90, 174, 177, 181
Bridgman, Richard, RAC employee, 80,
    102–4, 212n79; will of, 103–4
Bull, Benjamin, RAC employee, 167–69

Cacheu, port of: in Luso-African arbitrage
    trade, 25; as major market for bar
    iron, 15; overland route to, 158; RAC
    contracts with merchants of, 154–55;
    RAC trade with, 80–88; as source of
    beeswax exports, 54, 61; as source of
    captives, 108
Cape Verde Islands: in Luso-African
    arbitrage trade, 25–26; map of,
    49; and Portuguese crown, 28–29;
    producers of "high cloth," 50, 98;
    uncertain source of provisions, 175

53, 83, 156–58; Jemasar, 128, 156, 168; Jogery, 71, 128; Juffure, 53, 62, 70, 71, 119–20; Kittam, 54, 72, 172, 174; Loko, 54, 72; Mangegar, 53, 128–29, 156; Saalum, 127, 153, 156; Samo, 54; Tankular, 53, 127–28; Tassily, 54, 72, 108, 138; Vintang, 53, 71
RAC prohibitions: on cohabiting with women, 146, 167; on employee trading, 81, 145–48, 152, 209n35
RAC provisioners, salaried, 176–80, 188
RAC salaries, Upper Guinea Coast, 70, 79, 145–49
RAC seizure of St. Louis and Gorée, 129–31
ransoming, 70, 88, 134, 140, 148
rice, West African. *See* provisions trade, West African rice
Rogers, Samuel, RAC employee, son of Zachary, Sr., 170–72
Rogers, Simon, RAC employee, son of Zachary, Sr., 170–72
Rogers, Zachary, Jr., RAC employee, son of Zachary, Sr., 170–72
Rogers, Zachary, Sr., RAC employee, 74–79, 170; funeral of, 76–77
Rogers, Zachary, Sr., wife of, 75, 78–79
Royal African Company (RAC): archives, 4–5; formation, 55–56; major exports and re-exports, 37–38; policies, 144–48; violations of company policies, 153–58, 162–65

Saharan Berbers, 9, 17
Sande, society for women, 181, 220n73
seasonal labor, West Africa: in agriculture, 90, 110; in cattle herding, 62; in cotton textile manufacture, 110; in cutting and transporting camwood, 61; in ironworking, 16
Senegal River, 22, 26, 29, 62, 129
senhoras: in Gambia trade, 87, 92, 115–16, 168–70, 212n75; in Sierra Leone trade, 94–98, 100–101, 102–4, 212n75
senhors: in Gambia trade, 115; in Sierra Leone/Sherbro trade, 173, 174
separate traders, 141, 156, 161, 163
Serra-Lioa, 25–26
Sherbro. *See* RAC forts, Upper Guinea Coast, York Island
ship-based trade, 52–55, 72

ship-based trade, regular destinations of: Barrakunda, 108, 113, 128; Cape Mount, 55, 74, 173; Jour, 113–14; Nunez River, 54–55, 72, 108; Petite Côte, 54, 62–63, 71, 108, 130; Pongo River, 54–55, 72, 108; Saalum, 71, 108, 113–14, 127–28; Samo, 54, 72, 108; Tassily (Trois-îles), 54, 72, 108
shipbuilding, Upper Guinea Coast, 182–83
Siddiqui, RAC supplier, 89–94, 100
Sierra Leone. *See* RAC forts, Upper Guinea Coast, Bence Island
Silva, António, RAC supplier, 88–89
slave codes, 107
slave labor in West Africa: agriculture, 90; cotton textile manufacture, 110, 112; headloading in caravans, 113; processing beeswax for export, 61, 89
slavery, 2, 4, 106–8, 187–88; chattel, 107–9, 187; plantation, 106, 109, 187
slaves, categories of: child slaves, 2, 87, 104, 138–39, 149; company slaves (grometos), 106, 108, 137–42, 154; house slaves, 2, 118, 187; sale slaves, 108, 117–36, 187. *See also* captives
slaves, preferences for: in Atlantic markets, 27, 109; in Muslim markets, 109
slaves and namelessness, 108, 134
slaves and punishment, 107–8, 117, 126, 138, 187
slave shackles, 116–17, 131–32, 137
slave trades from Africa, pre-Atlantic, 6
slave trade to Americas, 6, 52, 58–59, 123–25
slave trade to England, 51–52, 59, 69, 123
Sunjata Epic, 133–34. *See also* Mali Empire

tailored clothing, European: in customs payments, 73–74; worn by company slaves, 102, 140–41
tailored clothing, West African: early Islamic, 17, 20–21; in camwood trade, 74; made by Fulbe artisans, 177; made in Cape Mount, 74, 140; worn by Sestos king and courtiers, 33
Timbuktu, city of, 9, 11
trans-Saharan trade: early history of, 9–22; intersection with east-west trade, 26–27, 48; slave preferences in, 109
tropical foodways, 178

tropical products: Afro-Asian, 6, 37, 38,
    50–52; American, 56, 106, 109

Valentine, RAC employee, 147–48
Vaz, Jane, RAC supplier, 86–87, 88
Vaz, Peter, RAC supplier, 84–86, 88
Virginia, 52, 59, 134

War of the League of Augsborg (1689–97),
    87, 101, 129, 160, 181
West African exports, Upper Guinea
    Coast: beeswax, 52, 59–61, 82–84, 156;
    camwood, 52, 61, 74–78; captives, 52,
    58–59, 88–89; gold, 59, 67, 151; hides,
    52, 62–63, 83, 88–89, 156; ivory, 52,
    59–60, 82–83. *See also* captives
West African language/ethnic groups:
    Bagnun, 112; Bamanakan, 131; Bambara,
    58, 131; Bullom, 178; Fulbe, 62,
    176; Mande languages, 62, 133–34;
    Mandinka, 56, 99, 112, 126; Maninka,
    132; Sereer, 99–100; Tanda, 58, 64;
    Temne, 73, 78; Wolof, 99–100, 131
White, John, RAC employee, 148–49